The Management of Catering Operatio

The Management of Catering Operations

PAUL MERRICKS, BSc (Hons)

Acting Head, Hotel and Catering School
Middlesex Polytechnic

PETER JONES, BA (Hons), Cert. Ed., MHCIMA

Head, Department of Service Sector Management,
Brighton Polytechnic

CASSELL

Cassell Educational Limited
Villiers House, 41/47 Strand, London WC2N 5JE
England

First published 1986 by Holt, Rinehart and Winston

Reprinted 1991

British Library Cataloguing in Publication Data
Merricks, Paul
   The Management of catering operations. –
   1. Food service management
   I. Title   II. Jones, Peter, 1951 Apr 3 –

   647'95'068   TX911.3.M27

ISBN 0-304-32550-3

Typeset by Oxford Print Associates Ltd, Oxford
Printed and bound in Great Britain by Mackays of Chatham Ltd.

Contents

Preface

This book begins by enquiring into why catering businesses are so different from each other and it examines what managers have to do in particular types of business in order to be successful.

From an analysis of the main variables that affect the nature of the catering business, the book proceeds to identify what the authors regard as the key issues in successful catering management which are referred to as 'key result areas'. These include increasing sales volume, improving profitability, quality management, developing subordinates, protecting assets, increasing productivity and controlling costs. These too are analysed to identify how performance can be improved by applying knowledge and techniques drawn from disciplines such as operations management, marketing, finance, behavioural sciences and so on. Finally different types of organisation are compared and contrasted and the extent to which they are appropriate for their own specific environment assessed.

Each of the key result areas will be relevant to all catering operations, but will be of varying degrees of importance from one sector to another. For instance, in hospital catering reducing costs is likely to be much more significant than increasing sales volume. Initially, then, it is important to evaluate the relative significance of each issue in its application to different catering operations. This is followed within each chapter by the range of options that are available to management to deal with each of the issues. The authors do not prescribe specific solutions but advocate a problem-solving approach that demands a selection of the most appropriate approach for the circumstances of a particular catering operation. In other words, the focus of the book is not on how to do things right but on how to do the right things. All too often junior managers concentrate on carrying out tasks in a technically correct way, even if these do not achieve the essential results for that business.

Throughout the book case examples have been used to illustrate points under discussion. Whilst it is obviously the aim of the authors to ensure that these examples provide an accurate portrayal of the industry it has been neither their intention nor their policy to relate actual cases except those of their own experience. Other than those bearing the name of either author no case example is a factual report and any resemblance they may bear to specific cases is purely coincidental.

Acknowledgements

The authors would like to thank the following people for their help and advice in the writing of this book:

Cliff Goodwin of Brighton Polytechnic, Clive Finch of the Middlesex Business School, Simon Lake of Holt, Rinehart and Winston, Paul Lock of the Middlesex Business School, Andrew Lockwood from the University of Surrey, Roy Westbrook from the London Business School and Steve Young of Brighton Polytechnic.

ERRATUM

*The following paragraph and references have been omitted from
the end of the Introduction*

All too often, the management style of catering managers is 'management by crisis'.
We have already identified some of the reasons for this – having to perform operative
tasks, working with the short time horizons or under a high level of stress with
unpredictable demand and so on. But catering managers do not fail because they do
not have the tools to do the job. A student who leaves a catering college, or a trainee
manager who has worked in the industry for two or three years carries around with
him or her a most impressive tool kit. The major problem lies in being sure which
tools are needed. We hope that, faced with problems, this book will help them to
select and use in the right way the best tools for the job.

REFERENCES

1. Nevett, W., 'Operations management perspectives and the hospitality industry', *International Journal of Hospitality Management* vol. 4 no. 4, 1985.
2. Adam, E.E. and Ebert, R.J., *Production and Operations Management: Concepts, Models and Behaviour*, Prentice Hall, 1982.
3. Hales, C.P. and Nightingale, M., *Managerial Work Roles in Organisations in the Hotel and Catering Industry* Corpus of Knowledge Update 2 HCIMA Report, June 1984.
4. Humble, J., *Management by Objectives*, Gower Press, 1979.
5. Euromonitor, *The Catering Industry*, 1985.
6. Nevett, W. *op. cit.*

Introduction

This book is about what managers do in order to improve their operation's performance and why they use certain approaches to achieve these ends. It was almost complete when we read an article by Nevett[1] that expressed exactly our own thoughts about what students and managers in the catering industry need to know. He quoted Adam and Ebert[2] who stated that there was a 'large gap between what [managers] must deal with operationally and what they studied in production/operations texts'.

One approach to catering management is to ask managers themselves what they do, as in the Nightingale study.[3] The major problem with this open-ended approach is to identify all of the extremely wide range of different activities and responsibilities. Moreover, there is some disagreement between levels of management as to what is the most important of these activities and responsibilities. For instance, the director of a family restaurant chain identified the achievement of gross profit as one of the most important targets for their unit managers, whereas the unit managers did not perceive this as a clearly identifiable objective.

Another approach is to examine job profiles and job descriptions for catering management positions since newly appointed managers are given these by their employing organisations in the hope, presumably, that they will meet the criteria laid down. One such job profile, from a multi-national hotel chain's operations manual, describes in some detail what the manager's role is – 'running a progressive, creative and unique food and beverage department' – and what the manager is responsible for – such things as service improvement, pricing, marketing, selection and training of staff, preparing budgets, and so on.

So, both asking managers what they do and looking at what managers are told to do fail to give any indication whatsoever of *how* the manager is to be successful, and perhaps more importantly give no indication of how *performance* will be judged.

This book, as the framework for examining managerial effectiveness, therefore concentrates on what it is that managers actually have to achieve. This is based on the work of John Humble[4] who recommends that there is no point in looking at the inputs to a job on a day-to-day basis because these may or may not result in successful outputs. For instance, the manager may indeed price the menu, prepare budgets, select staff and so on but there is no way of guaranteeing that this will produce the right results. The only way to measure effectiveness is to measure the outputs i.e. the actual results.

One of the great advantages of using outputs as a framework for analysis is that it recognises the unique role of a manager within the UK catering industry. The main features of the industry are its wide geographical spread, the small size of individual units, the low sales turnover per unit, the wide range of markets served, that it is highly labour intensive and the wide range of 'packages' available in it. In our opinion, these features make the catering industry one of the last remaining 'cottage industries' of the twentieth century. Whereas most other major industries in this country are now heavily concentrated, in terms of ownership especially, this has happened more slowly in the catering industry. In some sectors there has been fairly rapid concentration of ownership: in particular, the 'Big Six' brewing companies now control over 60 per cent of all the pubs in this country. But there still remains a very great number of individually owned and operated units, for example, in the 'traditional restaurant' sector out of an estimated 6500 units, the biggest six chains only account for 500 units and 11 per cent of the market.[5]

The impact of these features on the manager is that because units are likely to be independent, then the unit manager has to take responsibility for unit development, product development, marketing, personnel, financial control and day-to-day management. The small unit size and the fluctuations in demand require that management also take on operational roles, for example, that of a cashier, at particular times of the day or week. Indeed in some sectors, such as industrial catering, unit managers are working chefs. This places an additional burden on the managers' time. Not only do they have the normal managerial problems of planning their time, they also have to fit a number of operational duties into their working day. Probably in no other industry today do you find the 'manager' working on the 'shop floor' to the extent that this happens in the catering industry. It is often for this reason that managers themselves fail to recognise the requirements for business survival for which they are responsible.

Nevett[6] also stated that 'Management techniques . . . all too often appear to hospitality management students as solutions looking for problems'. This book reverses that approach. Most of the chapters (chapters 3 to 10) actually identify problem areas that a manager may have to tackle – attracting more customers, reducing costs, achieving the best from staff and so on. We recognise that the approach to problem solving will vary from unit to unit, organisation to organisation and sector to sector. We explore the reasons for this in chapter 1, which identifies the external environmental factors that shape the catering industry and the firms competing in it. We explain how firms establish strategies to cope with the environment and how these are translated into organisational goals. Chapter 2 explores in more detail the nature of these goals and the process by which they are made more explicit objectives for each operating unit. The effective unit manager must both understand how such unit targets are set and be capable of translating these into targets understandable to his or her workforce.

Such targets will fall into one or other of the key result areas discussed in chapters 3 to 10. Each of these chapters examines and reviews the range of options available to a unit manager in order to maintain satisfactory performance or to take corrective action. We also identify the characteristics of each option so that the manager can understand why some are more appropriate for his or her unit than some others. We emphasised that this is not a prescriptive text; it does not say 'this is what you should do'. Rather, we hope it illustrates that a manager will have a great many management tools and techniques available to him or her and only some of these may be necessary or relevant to a particular problem.

In the final chapter we relate all that has been discussed to the organisational context in which the manager must operate. We analyse the nature of organisations and how they should 'fit' the business environment in which they operate. In theory, the closer this 'fit' the easier the manager's job will be. We also look at the extent to which both the environment and organisation are dynamic and conclude by examining how the catering manager should go about managing change.

1

Understanding the Environment

OBJECTIVES

Differentiate between manufacturing and service management . . . identify the 'stakeholders' in a typical catering business . . . identify the variables that create the diversity of catering businesses in the United Kingdom . . . examine alternative approaches to collecting information about the environment.

INTRODUCTION

The years 1975 to 1985 have seen major changes in the British catering industry. The most noticeable changes have occurred in the restaurant sector – which has seen the arrival of American restaurant chains such as Ponderosa, Pizza Hut as well as Burger King, and the emergence and growth of new British chains such as Roast Inns, Allied Brewery's Exchange restaurants and Strikes restaurants. Among the major success stories of the last decade Trusthouse Forte and Grand Metropolitan, the pre-1975 giants, have developed and expanded their chains, Berni Inns have been revitalised as the new Host Group and the Granary self-service restaurants have been launched. Other operators have expanded by acquisition – Kennedy Brookes, for example, has taken over Mario and Franco, Wheeler's, Bertorelli and Les Amis restaurants. Some independent operators have taken advantage of franchise opportunities provided by companies as diverse as the Hard Rock Cafe and Mr Big Burger restaurants. As the expansion plans for the companies mentioned above include many hundreds of new units this growth in chain restaurants is bound to continue into the 1990s.[1]

The importance of this change in the restaurant sector cannot be ignored by other sectors of the industry, including those at present in the public sector. Over the next ten years catering must be managed against this backdrop of rapidly expanding, fiercely competitive chains with carefully formulated products and substantial advertising and promotions budgets. The modern manager will need all his or her expertise to succeed in this new climate.

THE CHARACTERISTICS OF SERVICE MANAGEMENT

One of the major distinctions in any economy is that between manufacturing industry and service provision. Nevett[2] has reviewed a selection of positions concerning differences between the two sectors and concludes that 'operations management necessarily involves some consideration of the technology of the industry' and service industry in general has a 'technology' that is essentially different. This difference is most acute in those service industries where contact between consumer and provider is relatively high. Indeed it has been argued that managers of service organisations do not only need to use the conventional techniques and management tools of manufacturing, but have additional problems to face that demand further techniques.[3] This is due primarily to the fact that few service firms *only* provide a service, there is usually a product associated with their provision. This is particularly true in the catering industry, where, arguably, the two main components of the 'meal experience' are the food and beverage product and the service element. This is illustrated in figure 1.1. The nature of the product/service mix results in service industries having certain characteristics that strongly influence the style and nature of service management:

- services are *perishable*. A restaurant seat which is unsold at lunch-time cannot be stored until the evening. This problem is particularly acute because food and beverage businesses are subject to fluctuating demand on an hourly, daily, weekly or seasonal basis.
- services are *intangible*. It is often difficult to pin-point the benefits of visiting a particular type of catering establishment. They may be associated either with the personality of the staff, the image of the establishment, or the attraction of associating with other customers. In these circumstances gaining and promoting a competitive advantage is a major task.
- services are *heterogenous*. The service given to one customer may differ from the service given to a group on the next table. This may be deliberate, perhaps because one table is in a hurry, whilst another is out for a relaxed evening; or it may be because staff favour serving one type of customer over other types. It is therefore more difficult to establish and monitor quality standards for service than for manufactured products.
- services are *contact dependent*. Either the customer has to come to the service outlet, as with most eating establishments, or the service must go to the customer, as with mobile fish and chip vans, for example. This is primarily because the product component of the service provision is usually manufactured very close to the time of its sale. This also means that most service provision has a relatively local market.
- service purchase does not give the consumer *ownership* of whatever it is that has

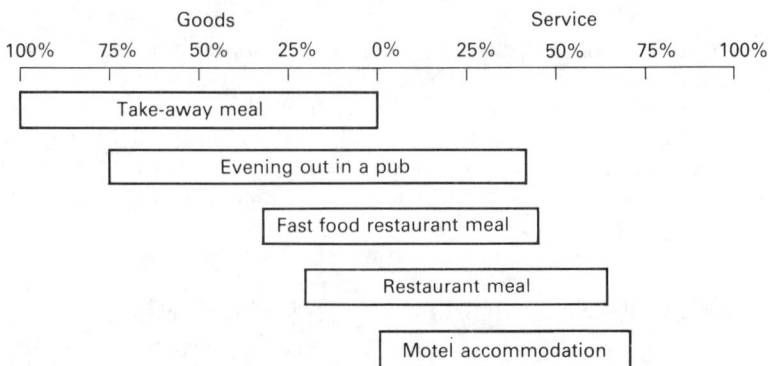

Figure 1.1   *Comparison of goods and service packages in hospitality industry.* Adapted from *Management of Service Operations*, Sasser, Olsen and Wyckoff.

been purchased. All the physical attributes necessary for the provision of the meal remain the property of the caterer. In effect, the customer is hiring these facilities for the time that they are eating there. Thus the relationship between caterer and customer is very different to that between a shopkeeper and his customers.

'STAKEHOLDERS' IN CATERING BUSINESSES

There are six groups which will influence the success of the catering business. They are, so to speak, the 'stakeholders': financial backers; competitors; customers; employees; central and local government and suppliers. Each of these groups will require the management to act and at certain stages of the business they may have a greater or lesser influence. Each will contribute something to the business and each will expect something from it in return.

Financial backers contribute the capital needed to allow the business to develop and grow. In return for this they expect growth in the value of their investment and an adequate rate of return.

In the 1980s it is increasingly rare to find a large organisation that is solely in the business of catering. Most large chain operations are part of a diversified group of companies. One of the pressures behind such diversification is the reduction of risk for the financial backers. In some catering businesses the financial backers have chosen to invest because it is complementary to their main business activity, for instance, British Airways have a catering business to assist in the successful marketing of their airline seats and department stores have restaurants to attract people to shop there. In catering, therefore, financial backers may sometimes expect benefits other than straightforward financial return.

It is easy to overlook the relationship which is often made with *competitors*. Often there are unwritten rules about pricing and in certain market situations – for example in a small seaside town – the caterer who breaks the unwritten rules about price maintenance by undercutting may reduce the profitability of not only his own business but, in the long run, everyone else's. More obvious than the co-operation required between competitors is the necessity for managers to maintain a competitive position. The clearest way of measuring competitive advantage is by market share. Market share gives an indication of what proportion of the potential purchasers prefer one particular product to another. For large catering businesses – for example, the large steak house chains – it is possible to buy market research data to achieve an accurate measurement of market share. This gives management an indication of the success of their product in relation to that of their competitors. For smaller catering businesses it is often much more difficult to acquire useful market share data. They will, therefore, only have a rough idea of how they compare in the market.

Customers' expectations usually relate to value for money. The cash which they contribute to the business is dependent upon the product meeting their personal requirements. Managers are interested in finding a way of assessing how to effectively meet the requirements of consumers. For a restaurant one of the best methods is measuring the repeat-purchase rate. Other factors that indicate an increasing degreee of satisfaction may include a growth in the volume of sales or an increase in the average spend. These three factors can be brought together under the general heading of sales effectiveness.

Employees' expectations of the quality of working life are changing. There is a gradual shift towards, and increased desire for, participation in decision making and better conditions of employment. What managers expect from employees can be assessed through productivity measures – for example, sales per man hour. Catering businesses are labour intensive so that improving productivity becomes a major management objective. If employees' expectations are not met they may exercise sanctions against the business ranging from withdrawal of co-operation to going on strike or resignation. Where poor working relations exist and profitability is affected by sanctions, then employee satisfaction may become more important than productivity in the short term.

Central and local government provide a range of essential business services ranging from sewage to job centres. In return a business must fulfil a number of statutory obligations including paying rates and taxes and meeting health and safety standards, employment standards, and so on. Another vital requirement for managers in the catering industry is compliance with the law. Government may also be concerned with the generation of trade for catering businesses through national and local initiatives to increase tourism.

The last group of people who have influence over a catering business are the *suppliers*. Catering products require the utilisation of a wide variety of commodities, frequently purchased in relatively small quantities. It is the duty of catering managers to maintain an effective supply – the right material, at the right time, in the right quantity, at the right price. The complexity of the management task will depend on the types of suppliers encountered. For example, the unit manager who receives all purchases from a central distribution point may have less cause for concern than a unit manager who buys all commodities fresh from a market.

Case example 1.1   The District Hospital

Consider a typical district general hospital with about 500 beds. What are the particular characteristics of the financial backers, competitors, customers, employees, government bodies, and suppliers which affect catering management in this business?

The financial backer of a hospital catering operation is the Local Health Authority. This body expects the catering operation to be subsidised, but only to a minimum level and certainly not to a level greater than that required by a competitive outside tender. Through the DHSS many operating procedures and standards of performance are closely prescribed and little discretion is left for the unit manager.

Most hospitals have little or no competition, at least for meal provision to their patients. However as a means of minimising their costs they do need to encourage staff to eat on site since as they pay a price for meals there is a possibility for some profit.

The main customers of a hospital caterer are, of course, patients who present no opportunity for additional sales, and sometimes have special dietary requirements. The number of meals to be served is relatively stable and, therefore, easily forecast.

Employees in hospital catering are likely to belong to a union. This is a distinctive feature of the sector and is not found to the same extent in most other sectors.

Hospitals have not been subject to the same legislation concerning health and hygiene as specifically profit-making catering businesses. This is somewhat ironic in view of the very great care needed by hospital caterers to ensure that hygienic practices are enforced. Indeed, following deaths in hospitals due to food poisoning it seems very likely that legislation will be introduced to make hospitals subject to the same health and hygiene regulations as other sectors of the industry.

Suppliers to hospitals are usually nominated suppliers by the Local Health Authority from a list prepared by the DHSS. This has the result that unit managers are not concerned with supplier selection, merely purchasing administration.

This book shows throughout how catering management conducts business affairs to take account of stakeholders' interests and the way in which they represent the broad spectrum of the external environment in which all businesses are conducted. Whilst the stakeholders will have a relatively direct impact on the aims of the business, the environmental context is less direct and indeed is often only mediated through the stakeholders. This is illustrated in figure 1.2.

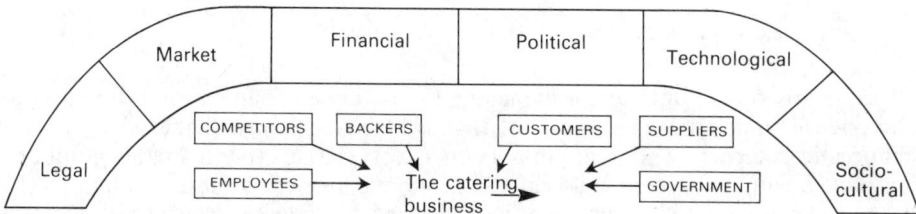

Figure 1.2 *Influence of stakeholders and external environment.*

The starting point must be a fairly detailed look at the environment, since any action by management has to take place in this context. This is most clearly stated by Rogers and Phipps – 'Decisions about output, price and competitive strategy depend upon the environment'.[4]

THE EXTERNAL ENVIRONMENT

For the purpose of discussion in this chapter, it is necessary to explain in more detail each of the six environmental factors already identified. The *market factor* is concerned with some specific characteristics of the catering industry's market environment – namely the relationship between provider and consumer, market conditions, and the level of industry concentration. With regard to the *financial environment*, our major concerns are those financial matters that may affect business objectives or investment decisions – such aspects as interest rates, exchange rates and taxation. The *socio-cultural aspect* is primarily concerned with the consumer and in particular with changes in attitude and life-style. The *political environment* is closely related to economic and legal matters. But quite clearly a caterer who ignored the present political climate towards privatisation of the public sector, would either be ignoring a possible threat if they work in the public sector, or a possible opportunity if they work in the private sector. The *legal environment* is becoming increasingly more complex for business people and for the catering industry. It is, moreover, in the area of employment legislation and of licensing law that major changes may take place in the future. Finally, there is the *impact of technology* and the growing trend towards a technocratic approach amongst members of the catering industry.

None of these factors are isolated one from the other but are interrelated, as figure 1.2 attempts to illustrate. This interrelationship can also be illustrated by analysing the reasons underlying the growth of service industry in comparison with manufacturing industry in the United Kingdom. The extent of this change is illustrated in table 1.1. Trends and changes in the catering industry's environment must also be measured against the overall shift in the balance between these two main sectors of the economy.

During the early 1980s this change has been due to economic factors associated with the world-wide uncompetitiveness of UK manufactured products; political factors,

Table 1.1   *Employees in employment in UK (000).*

	1979	1980	1981	1982	1983
All industries/ services	23 200	23 000	21 900	21 500	21 200
Service industry	13 600	13 700	13 400	13 500	13 500
Hotel & catering	950	980	950	980	970

Source: *Annual Abstract of Statistics* 1985 Edition HMSO.

such as a monetarist approach to managing the national economy; and the impact of technological innovation, similar to that which has caused the shift towards technocratic catering. The result has been a very large growth in the number of unemployed with a consequent social and economic impact on the environment. This has been accompanied by changes in the law, particularly with regard to trade unions and minimum wage levels.

The shift in the balance between manufacturing and service sectors of the economy has resulted in a change in government attitude towards service industries. There is a growing belief that problems of high unemployment, slow economic growth, and low levels of investment can be solved by much greater attention to service industries. In particular, following the Young Report in 1985, tourism is seen as a major factor in stimulating the economy. This report, *Pleasure, Leisure and Jobs – the Business of Tourism*, is likely to result in less bureaucracy, simplified planning procedures, better training, and a more positive attitude towards tourism from local authorities. Quite clearly, food-service managers must relate their business activity to these environmental influences.

Research in the United States of America has sought to find out how food-service chains 'scan the environment for relevant information [and] how they actually perceive their environment'.[5] Although only tentative conclusions can be drawn, it seems that most firms were interested in the activity directly affecting their particular

Table 1.2   *Size and turnover of the UK catering industry (£m ex VAT).*

Description	Year	No. of businesses	Sales of F & B	Turnover [+] Total	Average	F & B	Gross Profit (%)
Hotels	1980	14 280		2 480			
	1981	13 930		2 750			
	1982	13 380	1 430	2 880	0.215	693	51.6
Restaurants	1980	11 500		1 430			
	1981	11 700		1 530			
	1982	11 800	1 570	1 640	0.140	620	60.5
Take-aways	1980	22 700		1 100			
	1981	25 000		1 280			
	1982	26 250	1 360	1 500	0.057	600	56.0
Public houses	1980	40 600		4 860			
	1981	40 150		5 270			
	1982	41 500	5 500	6 000	0.145	2 700	51.2
Contract	1980	1 200		575			
	1981	1 300		650			
	1982	1 300	640	740	0.570	310	51.9

Source: *Statistical Review of the Hotel and Catering Industry* 1984.
+ Includes sales of accommodation, cigarettes, and other goods and services.

market segment followed by overall industry activity. Of much less significance was technological innovation and the overall environment. With regards to customers, competitors and suppliers, the findings are even less conclusive. What is clear is that the firm's perception strongly influences their opinion about the stability and complexity of these three stakeholders, and that those firms which believe their environment is relatively stable and uncomplicated may be facing long-term strategic problems. This is especially true if their focus continues to be on their own segment of the industry, rather than on the overall economic environment.

Before a consideration of the various factors shaping the catering industry's environment is made table 1.2 will provide a useful summary of the current size and scale of the industry.

There are three main dimensions of the *market environment* relevant to the catering industry. One dimension of this is the relationship between *the provider and the consumer*. In most manufacturing industry, employees have little or no contact with customers and so have a simple two-way relationship with management. This is also the case in the catering industry for those staff who work back-of-house. But for staff who do have contact with the customer, from which such staff often derive a great deal of job satisfaction, there is a three-way relationship. Indeed, staff may, on occasions, forget that they are working for their employer and regard themselves as working for the customer. In other sectors this relationship is made even more complex – for instance in contract catering or public sector catering. This is because there are two types of 'customer': the consumer who eats the meal and the client who acts on behalf of the consumer. Thus, most if not all catering within the public sector is undertaken as an ancillary to the main function of the enterprise, for instance education, the health service, and armed forces. The authorities tend to act on behalf of the consumer group as arbiters of what is needed . . . this means the consumers – school children, old people, hospital patients – have little or no say in the standard or provision.[6] Even in the private sector the caterer's client may be differentiated from actual consumers, notably in the industrial catering sector. Young[7] has suggested that this relationship should be called 'mediated demand'.

The second dimension is the degree to which different sectors serve a *captive market*. Two examples of truly captive markets are oil rigs for which industrial caterers provide meals and prisons catered for by the public sector. It is usually the case that in a mixed economy, such as Britain, there are few captive markets except those that are State owned monopolies – British Gas, the National Coal Board and so on. But catering provides a product for which there is, on average, a demand three times a day from every person in the country. Just as the caterer loses out if a seat is not sold at lunch-time, so the consumer cannot easily delay their purchase decision, unless they are prepared to go hungry. There is therefore an unusually large number of sales made to consumers who are captive or semi-captive.

The third dimension to the market structure is the degree of *concentration* of firms in the different sectors. We have called the catering industry the 'last remaining cottage industry' and although there continues to be a very large number of individually owned and operated units, there is a general increase in the level of concentration. This is most clearly seen in the public house sector, where the 'big six' firms manufacture over 70 per cent of the beer sold in the UK and control over 60 per cent of the licensed premises.

Quite clearly a manager working for a public sector organisation serving a captive market has very different problems to a manager in the commercial sector, although the nature of the meal product, the production and service systems may be almost identical.

The *financial environment* focuses on the cost and investment structure of the catering business. An examination of cost structures will enable the catering manager to pin-point much more accurately the nature of his or her business than has thus far been possible. The market factors so far considered are not necessarily related to one specific sector. For instance, Travellers Fare, the catering division of British Rail, is a public sector service – although privatisation of some parts is being discussed – it serves a captive market on trains and a semi-captive market on stations, competing at its main-line stations with the licensed trade, restaurant and fast food sectors of the industry. However, it is much more likely that a business's cost structure will reflect quite closely the operational nature of the enterprise.

In essence there are two types of cost: fixed costs – those costs which arise irrespective of the volume of business transacted; and variable costs – those costs which vary according to the level of transactions. Some catering businesses tend to have a high proportion of fixed costs, such as up-market restaurants, hotels; whilst other businesses have only a low proportion of fixed costs, notable amongst these is contract industrial catering. Businesses that have high fixed costs must be much more market conscious than those with low fixed costs, simply because a fall in demand quickly results in them running at a loss. For the unit catering manager the most significant impact is from legislative and tax reforms such as VAT changes, national insurance increases and so on. Existing capital investment may affect the goals set for the unit, but changes in the tax structure affect the day-to-day running costs of the business.

Socio-cultural changes in attitude and life-style have an even more subtle impact than economic changes. Demographic change is most easily identified, that is to say the changes in the population's age profile, size of family, proportion of males to females, and so on. These inevitably have economic consequences, but their influence on life-style is just as significant. For instance, it is known that young, single people spend significantly more of their income on eating out than married couples. The reasons for this are obvious. Single people probably live at home or in rented accommodation and have only themselves to support, whereas a married couple may have only one income and a mortgage to finance. Thus, the trend towards people marrying at an older age may also be significant. This examples illustrates the two major problems associated with analysing demographic trends. Firstly the changes they initiate are extremely slow in taking effect. Secondly, there are many factors, all of which may be having different effects.

Those catering operations serving non-captive markets will be most quickly affected by changes in life-style, although increasingly sectors such as industrial catering, the health service and schools recognise that they are now competing with the commercial sector. The most significant factor is undoubtedly the trend towards more leisure time. Apart from eating and sleeping, people spend most of their life at leisure. The working week is decreasing from over 40 hours per week to around 37 hours per week, there is an increase in flexitime working so that employees have the opportunity to work four-day weeks, there is significant interest in job-sharing, and the retirement age is gradually being lowered. In addition to having more free time people also have more disposable income to spend in leisure pursuits because of higher wages, two-income families and smaller family units.

With both the opportunity and means of enjoying themselves there have been some significant developments in people's life-style and attitudes. There has been a growth in travel for pleasure with UK residents travelling abroad and foreign visitors coming to Britain (the situation is illustrated in table 1.3). This growth is partly because of changes in life style in which people are placing less significance on the acquisition of material assets and greater emphasis on enjoyment. This is reflected, most certainly

Table 1.3 *Tourism trends 1974–1982.*

Visits to the UK by foreign residents (millions)

	Total	Business	Leisure
1974	8.5	1.8	6.8
1976	10.8	1.9	8.9
1978	12.6	2.3	10.3
1980	12.4	2.6	9.8
1982	11.6	2.4	9.2

Source: *Statistical Review of the Hotel and Catering Industry* 1984.

in America and to some extent in Great Britain, in less emphasis on putting everything into one's job. This change in the work ethic is also reflected in the much greater concern with health and fitness. There is a growing awareness that stress, lack of exercise and the wrong diet can cause ill health and premature death. Not only are people working less hard, but they are using their free time to look after themselves by participating in active recreation and healthy eating. Thus, between 1974 and 1982 there has been an annual growth in consumer spending on sports and recreation of 2.5%. At the same time catering and accommodation showed an annual deline of 0.5%.

The major impact of life-style change is not so much concerned with change in the overall pattern of demand for catering, but much more to do with the nature of this demand. Current attitudes indicate a number of ways in which the catering product should reflect contemporary life-styles. Meal experiences are much more informal than in the past; there is a shift towards 'snack' type meals rather than eating two or more courses; portion sizes are decreasing; the nutritional content is assuming greater significance. In the past dieting has only been associated with the desire to lose weight. In the present climate, diet is now concerned with a much wider range of health factors and consumers are eating much less fat, salt and sugar in their diet. There has also been a significant increase in vegetarianism, mainly among 18 to 25-year old females. Assuming that these people will maintain their dietary habits, it seems likely that they will have a significant impact on the eating habits of the next generation. Finally, increased foreign travel has created a demand for a wide range of ethnic cuisines and dishes. Pizza, moussaka, curries, are now very common items on menus throughout the industry.

Political environmental factors are often ignored in texts concerning catering, although as we shall see there is a very strong interface with the *legal environment*. In the 1980s, however, the most important issues for many caterers are political. As an article about privatisation in the *Catering Times* records – 'What daunts many, is that it [privatisation] is subject to political whims and local politics on a grand scale'.[8] Political whims affect four main areas, although there are many other instances, both now and in the past, where the political climate has had very great influence on the industry. The four main areas are privatisation, licensing law, employment legislation and the food supply industry.

As already indicated, a very large proportion of the catering industry in this country is in the public sector. The current government plans to operate such catering activities as commercial enterprises as quickly as possible. This has meant that, in both the Health Service and Local Education Authorities, catering has now to be put out to tender, so the existing in-house caterers and industrial catering organisations are in competition with each other. Whatever the arguments for and against this privatisation, it is evident that the ethos and goals of catering operators in these sectors will be very different to those of the 1960s and 1970s.

It also seems likely, if Government acts upon the Young Report and listens to the catering lobby, that there will be considerable changes to licensing law in the next few years. The most likely change is with regard to opening hours, which will probably become much less restricted, in line with current Scottish licensing legislation.

Employment legislation touches upon all industry, not just catering. There is no doubt that there has been a significant increase in the amount of legislation concerning employment practices which has resulted in significantly less freedom of action for management. This has meant that labour has become much more of a fixed cost to the employer who in turn makes more use of part-time employees. As the HCITB *Statistical Review* reports, with regard to employment in the industry 'the most marked trend has been towards part-time work'.[9] Legislation also affects minimum wage levels along with trade unions and their involvement in the industry.

Finally, the Government has become very involved with the move towards healthier eating. Following the report *Diet and Cardiovascular Disease* by the Committee on Medical Aspects of Food Policy, the Minister for Health stated in the House of Commons 'we must translate its contents into a form the public can easily understand'. This was done by the Joint Advisory Committee on Nutrition Education who prepared a guide entitled *Eating for a Healthier Heart*. However the DHSS has intervened to modify this guide, in an effort to reduce the impact of the committee's advice on the consumption of butter, milk and meat. Committee members have suggested that the reason for this intervention is that there is already £500 million worth of butter, skimmed milk and beef in storage because of over production in this country and the Government is reluctant to shift demand even further away from these products. It has also been suggested by the Director of the Coronary Prevention Group that 'the food industry makes major contributions to Conservative Party funds and the shires [i.e. the farming lobby] have a lot of influence with ministers'.[10]

Finally, the *technological environment* has always had an impact on the catering industry. If a catering operation is viewed as a system which takes inputs of food, drink, money, plant, machinery and energy and produces outputs of meals, profit, customer satisfaction, payments to suppliers and so on, then any technical innovation that changes the nature of the inputs will have some significance. This systems model is illustrated in figure 1.3.

There are two prevailing tendencies influencing the catering industry. Firstly, there is an increase in the 'technocratic approach'. That is to say that technology is generally replacing labour within the system. Secondly, there is a move towards separating front-of-house activities from those back-of-house. This too is made possible partly by the availability of new technology.

The technocratic approach is to prescribe the specific system in detail, manage the operation according to these specifications and closely monitor performance. This is made possible by both 'hard' technology such as computerised point-of-sale equipment and up-to-date production equipment, or 'soft' technology such as standard recipes, performance appraisal, manuals, and so on. The catering manager today has more information available than ever before concerning the performance of the business. It is debatable, however, that he or she always knows what to do with such data.

The availability of modern food production equipment and new sources of raw materials, often semi- or fully processed, have encouraged the idea of separation. Whilst scale economies are rarely possible front-of-house, as there is little customer appeal in very large eating-out places, it is possible to create them back-of-house, as

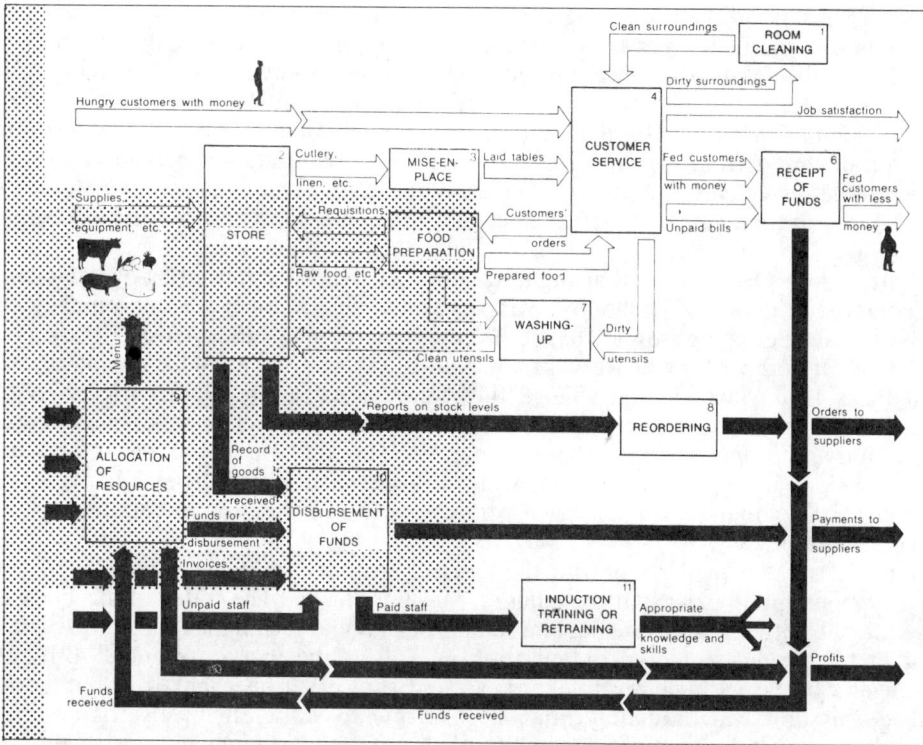

Figure 1.3   *The catering system. Reproduced with permission.*

cook–chill and cook–freeze units have demonstrated. Indeed, the Roux brothers are to open a restaurant where their nouvelle cuisine dishes have been prepared using boil-in-the-bag techniques. This dichotomy in a business practice makes a great deal of sense when premises are sited in locations likely to attract customers. These premises can then be used primarily for serving the customers, since their costs, such as rent and rates, are likely to be high, whilst cheaper premises, perhaps serving several units, are used for preparing the meals. As a number of cook–chill units have demonstrated, savings can also be made with regard to capital investment in plant and equipment in the long run and in labour costs almost immediately.

IMPACT OF THE ENVIRONMENT ON SECTORS OF THE INDUSTRY

Slattery and Olsen[11] suggest that the environment for each sector of the catering industry will depend upon three factors. Firstly, there is the state of *variability* in the environment that is to say the pattern, frequency and scale of change in the environment. Commercial catering businesses exist in a highly variable environment. One research study[12] has shown the restaurant industry to be extremely volatile in comparison with a range of manufacturing industries. Welfare sectors of the industry however, are subject to much less variability, because they are buffered from environmental change by the primary function of their respective sectors, such as education or health care, which also create fairly predictable levels of demand. Secondly, there is the state of environmental *complexity*. This refers to the fact that large organisations, with catering activities across a range of sectors, face a more complex environment than those organisations which operate in only one sector. Equally, multi-national organisations have more complex environments than organisations operating in only one country. Single unit operations have the least complex environment. Finally, the third state is environmental *illiberality*, which refers to the 'degree of threat from external factors which face organisational decision-makers'. This was discussed earlier in the consideration of each of the six environmental factors – the sense of threat many hospital caterers feel from competitive tendering, and so on.

Slattery and Olsen argue that organisations can either be viewed as dynamic and responsive to the rate of variability, complexity and illiberality in the environment, or stable, hence creating some change in the environment themselves. They cite examples of companies with very strong brands, such as McDonald's, Holiday Inns, and Pizza Hut which do not change their operational approach from location to location, or even from country to country. Their approach is one of product-orientation as opposed to market-orientation. The role of the manager and his relationship with the environment will thus be very different in this type of organisation to that of the manager who operates in an entrepreneurial, market-focused unit.

We believe that in the long run the catering industry must be responsive to the environment and in particular to changing consumer tastes. The thrust of this book is operational, rather than strategic, and so approaches and techniques will be discussed that fit the product-oriented organisation as well as the market-oriented. But the manager who is permanently blinkered to and shut-off from changes in the world outside his unit will ultimately find he is unable to work effectively for another organisation, and his organisation will find that its management team is unable to implement such changes as will inevitably come.

HAVING THE RIGHT INFORMATION

If managers are to remain aware of the environment, influence their circumstances and mould their operational activity to fit strategic goals, their greatest need is for information about what is happening around them. For many operators this information is derived in the very *ad hoc*, informal manner that might traditionally be regarded as the natural style of the manager or entrepreneur. Customers are asked if they enjoyed the meal; repeat customers are recognised; articles in the local press about new restaurants opening or about major redundancies in the area are noted; competitors' price increases are examined on the menu display outside their establishments and so on. There is nothing wrong with informal methods such as these, and they have the great advantage of costing very little. Indeed, at a recent conference[13] the informal approach was advocated –

> Our approach to identification of the market sector [is] very simple; all common sense (deductive logic); no research. . . . It's very interesting to note that US high technology product introductions are increasingly being developed precisely on these 'project' lines– with a far higher success level than the old 'remove all risk before we do anything' approach. . . .

The major problem is their lack of sophistication and their failure to provide a totally objective and rigorous evaluation.

In essence there are two major types of information. The first is data itself, and the second is forecasts based on the interpretation of data. (If either of these methods are adopted it must be remembered that the cost of implementing them must at least be covered by the additional benefits derived from having the information.) Data collection can be either desk research or field research.

Desk research

This refers to the collection of information through published material which may be bought through newsagents or bookshops, on subscription, or direct from the publisher, or borrowed from public libraries or from specialist hotel and catering libraries to be found in local catering colleges or the head offices of a variety of associations.

For caterers, just as for many other business people, there is a wide range of published material which may provide invaluable information. Such material includes the following:

(1) General or national sources

The Central Statistics Office each month publishes up-to-date information about a large number of topics such as employment, income-levels, consumer spending and so on. Another source is Business Monitor, a weekly industrial news publication from the Department of Trade and Industry. It produces quarterly figures relating to the tourism market, including a month-by-month analysis of the number of overseas visitors, and their country of origin. It also publishes an annual summary of catering business performance based on VAT returns under the Standard Industrial Classification.

(2) Hotel and catering industry sources

Trade and professional associations publish regular magazines or bulletins that may provide up-to-date market information, and hold conferences which are often followed up by the publication of conference papers. For instance, the HCIMA publishes a monthly journal, *Hospitality*, and sponsors the annual FASE conference. In 1983 the topic was 'Making It Pay'. Further to this the HCITB has recently started to publish other material including their *Statistical Review* and a number of research reports. These tend to concentrate on employment in the industry, rather than business aspects, reflecting, naturally enough, the role of the Training board. Thirdly, the catering press produces many valuable surveys. For instance, in June the *Caterer and Hotelkeeper* usually publishes a survey of catering that looks at the size of units, average spends in different sectors, level of take-away food sales, and so on. Finally, market research organisations and financial analysts such as Euromonitor, Key Note and Jordans also publish regular analyses of the industry or specific sectors of it. For instance, the *Catering Report* by Euromonitor for 1984 looks in detail at all the main catering sectors and makes suggestions as to future developments, likely trends and the future outlook for operators. Some of their material is derived from sources already identified, such as CSO and British Business, but it has the advantage of being well presented and relevant, although by no means cheap.

(3) Regional and local sources

The *County Report* is a detailed analysis of census results from the 1981 census. It provides detailed demographic statistics for a particular locality, incuding total number of residents in the county, house ownership, age, sex, married status and so on. And local magazines and newspapers can be a rich source of information.

Field research

This includes the informal methods previously mentioned, but adds to these consumer surveys and more formal comparative studies. The main advantage of field research over desk research is that it is usually specifically designed to discover information of relevance to a particular locality or operation. Naturally enough, this makes it considerably more expensive. In addition, whilst desk research may conceivably be carried out by a well-informed amateur, field research, particularly when it includes questionnaire design, is very much the province of expert market researchers. The two main types of field research that might be carried out are consumer surveys and comparative studies.

Consumer surveys   are usually in the form of questionnaires and attempt to establish the characteristics of the consumers, their likes and dislikes. Since it is impossible to ask everyone they rely on taking a sample, which immediately introduces an element of statistical analysis in order to establish whether the sample accurately represents the population under investigation. Surveys may be conducted by post, which is relatively cheap but requires that a very large number of surveys be sent out since response rates are usually very low; or in person, which is costly but tends to be more accurate, assuming that the market researcher does not influence the consumers' responses.

Comparative studies   use data and information about other business operations to provide information for the business under review. This may include a performance study of a particular catering operation in one locality to help predict the performance of a new unit in a similar locality; or an analysis of the performance of other operations in similar business spheres within one area to establish local socio-economic trends.

Case example 1.2   Happy Eater Market Research

The Happy Eater chain of restaurants regularly conducts market research surveys for a variety of purposes. An early survey, carried out in 1978, was concerned with identifying their market appeal – in other words what attracted customers to their units and what market segmentation was taking place. The survey was carried out in three separate units during the period 3–9 July. Questionnaires were given to customers, who were requested to complete them. The response rate was high, so that there was a large sample. The results can therefore be regarded as an accurate representation of customer opinion.

   The data collected from each restaurant was aggregated to find the overall attitude towards the chain. In most cases the responses of each unit were closely correlated with each other, showing a consistent pattern with regards to market appeal. The information collected included data on the following:

- Number in group   43 per cent of the sample were couples
- Customer status   Over 60 per cent were eating out for pleasure
- Age of customer   Nearly 60 per cent were over 30

The remainder of the questionnaire was concerned with attitudes to the unit and reasons for stopping. This included questions about whether children had influenced the choice; attitudes to the decor and colour scheme; opinions of level of cleanliness and service; whether there was value for money; whether they had purchased sundry items, such as T-shirts, puzzles, etc. and how the customer had come to hear of the restaurant.

SUMMARY

This chapter began with a review of the competitive nature of the modern catering industry and went on to identify the characteristics of service management that differentiate it from other sectors. This was followed by a breakdown of the nature of catering management emphasising the need to measure output as the most effective way of testing managerial performance.

Six stakeholders were identified that influence not only catering operations but any business. These six – financial backers, competitors, customers, employees, government and suppliers – have roles of relative importance, within each particular sector of catering. These roles vary according to the age, size and location of the business. The emphasis on stakeholders is a means of talking about the environment that lays stress on a distinctive and important feature of the catering industry – *people*. A recurring theme of this book is the impact of people on operational effectiveness. People as consumers – how should we meet their needs? how can we influence their behaviour? how do we cope with their diversity? And people as workers, without whom the operation could not function. In addition to the influence of the stakeholders, there is the environment in which any business must operate. This too, has been divided into six principal components namely market, financial, socio-cultural, political, legal and technological. In addition to the direct impact on a business of changes in these factors, there is the direct influence they bring to bear on the stakeholders, and thence on the catering operation. The variability, complexity and illiberality of the environment for each sector of the industry will vary and so the strategy and structure of particular organisations should fit the circumstances. We shall look at this in chapter 2 when we consider Schaffer's model. Briefly however, there is a tendency for organisations to adopt either a market-oriented, flexible approach, or a product-oriented, strongly branded style. This has major implications for both the unit catering manager and the operational systems.

The chapter concluded with a consideration of the caterer's need for information about both the broad and the local environment and identified means of collecting such data. The next chapter goes on to explain how the caterer uses this information in order to create a strategy or business plan. From this can be established the range and nature of targets set for the manager.

REFERENCES

1. Barker, E., Publicans and profit, *Foodservice Today*, April 1985.
2. Nevett, W., 'Operations Management Perspectives and the Hospitality Industry', *International Journal of Hospitality Management* vol. 4 no. 4, 1985.
3. Sasser, W. E., Olsen, R. P., and Wyckoff, D. D., *Management of Service Operations*, Allyn & Bacon, 1978.
4. Rogers, H. A., and Phipps, D. K., *Economics for the Hotel and Catering Industry*, Barrie & Jenkins Ltd., 1977.
5. de Noble, A., and Olsen, M. D., The relationship between the strategic planning process and the service delivery system, in Pizam, A. et al. (Eds.), *The Practice of Hospitality Management*, AVI Publishing Co. Inc., 1982.
6. Jones, P., *Food Service Operations*, Holt, Rinehart and Winston, 1983.
7. Young, S., Mediated Demand in the Hotel & Catering Industry, Brighton Polytechnic (unpublished), 1985.
8. Sutton, A., 'Going private', *Catering Times*, September 1983.
9. HCITB, *Statistical Review of the Hotel and Catering Industry*, CIU, 1984.
10. *The Sunday Times*, August 4, 1985.
11. Slattery, P., and Olsen, M., 'Hospitality organisations and their environment', *International Journal of Hospitality Management* vol. 3 no. 2 pp. 55–60, 1984.
12. Slattery, P., and Olsen, M., *op. cit.*
13. Milton, J., *Market Identification – An Essential Step Towards Successful Business*, HCIMA, FASE Conference Papers, 1983.

2

Setting Targets
(for the Organisation and the Operating Unit)

OBJECTIVES

Understand strategic planning criteria . . . examine the influence of product life-cycle on the strategy and objectives of organisations . . . analyse the pro-active operational responses to environmental change . . . identify approaches to managing demand and supply . . . set objectives to satisfy business performance criteria.

INTRODUCTION

Chapter 1 identified the environmental factors which are likely to influence the operation of catering businesses. All organisations, large or small, must work within the constraints imposed on them by these external factors. Inside this framework the organisation has the opportunity to decide its own goals and the strategies it will adopt to achieve them. The strategic planning process may be quite simple or extremely complex, often reflecting the size and scale of the business. For the small cafe owner such goals may be to earn enough money to support himself and his family; but for the large organisation they may include considerations of international market penetration, return on capital investment, brand leadership, manpower planning, and so on.

These strategic considerations must then be translated into the objectives to be achieved by the unit manager. The cafe owner may do this by setting just a few relatively simple targets such as an average gross profit percentage of x per cent or y pounds level of sales revenue. Larger organisations may use similar measures, but there are likely to be many more for them than for the one man business. The range of objectives that may be set can be categorised into 'key result areas' which are the principal outputs of the business. We would argue that, irrespective of whether the organisation is good at setting appropriate and effective targets, the manager's responsibilities are these key result areas. The manager's ability to achieve targets will be influenced by success in these areas and by an ability to interact with the immediate, local environment.

STRATEGIC ISSUES IN MANAGEMENT

Strategy is the consideration of long-term issues. Before examining in detail some approaches to effective management, it is necessary to consider the nature of successful catering businesses. No manager, even if equipped with all the best techniques of operations management, will be able to manage a business that is inherently unsuccessful. One would not advocate, for instance, opening a fast food store on Ben Nevis or an haute cuisine restaurant on Blackpool sea-front. An actual example of an inherently non-viable business appears to be on-rail catering, for it seems that no profit-making catering organisation is prepared to take over on-rail catering from British Rail unless it is subsidised. The importance of strategy is underlined by Drucker, who suggested that 'it is more important to do the *right things* than do *things right*'. Doing the right things means being *effective*, i.e. ensuring that actual outputs correspond to desired outputs; doing things right means being *efficient* i.e. optimising output in relation to input. There are many examples of firms that have been efficient but have failed because they have been in a declining market and have not responded to the environment. In the UK the number of fish and chip shops has halved in the last ten years. Most of those businesses were probably very efficient with low overheads because most of the capital had been written off, self-employed ownership, and good technical expertise. The businesses failed because of the competition from fast food operations which were more effective in promotion and advertising that more closely corresponds to the attitudes and life style of the consumer.

In essence, the creation of an effective catering business unit is a *strategic* issue. For large organisations strategic decisions are made by head office, but for independent caterers, the owner is both the strategist and the operator. Ansoff has made clear differentiation between these two major functions; a strategic manager is 'a change seeker, risk [taker], divergent problem solver, and skilful in leading others into new and untried directions', whereas an operations manager is 'a change absorber, cautious risk taker, convergent problem solver, skillful diagnostician, coordinator and controller of complex activities'.[1] Whatever the size of operation there has to be a mix of these two types of manager.

Although it is not the purpose of this book to examine in detail the issues associated with starting a catering business, it is important to briefly consider the variables that need to be reconciled, in order to produce a concept that will prove successful. For, unless a manager understands the strategic issues facing the business, he or she cannot be effective.

Schaffer[2] proposes a model that illustrates the relationship between the environment, a firm's strategy, its organisation structure and ultimate effectiveness (see figure 2.1).

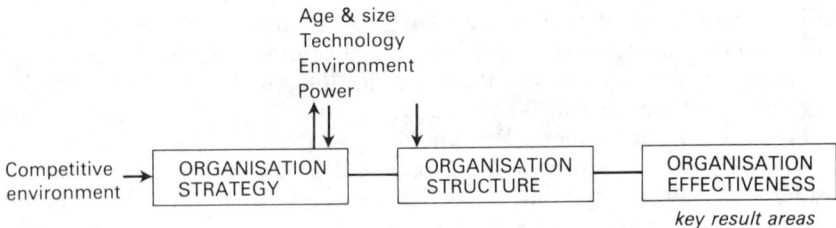

Figure 2.1 *Strategy, structure and effectiveness model.* From *Strategy, Organisation Structure and Success in the Lodging Industry*, Schaffer, J.D.

Although Schaffer's exact description of external environmental factors is not identical to our own, there are clear similarities. The model illustrates that strategy is derived primarily from the competitive environment, although it is influenced by other factors such as those already discussed. This strategy is translated into an organisation structure appropriate for the established strategic goals, which in turn should lead to organisational effectiveness. This chapter examines the process of turning those goals into more specific organisational objectives, whilst chapter 11 considers the organisational context.

Schaffer describes the organisation's competitive strategy as 'the means by which it attempts to link with, respond to, integrate with, or exploit its environment'.[3] He argues that in the hotel sector at least there are three main strategies which firms can adopt, on the basis of their market and their focus. The three strategies are:

- Defender — industry-wide firms which compete on the basis of cost leadership.
- Prospector — this also applies industry wide to firms with a policy of product innovation.
- Analyser — these firms focus on one market segment, and may adopt either innovation or price as their competitive policy.

The implications of this analysis affect the extent to which organisations respond to the environment, the structure they create in order to meet their strategic goals, and most importantly from the point of view of this text the impact these have on the unit manager.

With regard to the degree of response to environmental change, chapter 1 (page 11), has already shown that firms behave differently. Arguably, typical *defender* catering organisations are large chain operations, with a strong brand image and a single product concept, notably to be found in the fast food sector. They are relatively slow to modify their strategic position, and concentrate on operational efficiency through highly centralised quality control procedures. Their tendency is to trade in low-priced market segments. For managers in these sectors, the key result areas of increasing productivity, controlling costs and controlling quality will have priority. There is currently some growth in the UK in *prospector* type organisations. Such organisations are increasingly aware of the need to respond to market changes, so they have pilot catering outlets where new concepts are tried out, for instance, Vittle Inns' Watford operations and Berni Inns' Bournemouth unit. There is a general policy to move their appeal up-market, basing their innovations on a solid reputation. Other organisations' response to the environment, such as that of public sector caterers in both the Health Service and the provision of school meals, has been forced on them. Legislative, external change has made it necessary for them to reconsider their strategic position. The same legislation has meant that contract caterers too have reconsidered aspects of their strategy such as pricing, market segmentation, and product design. The important key result areas for these types of organisation will be increasing volume, assuring service quality and improving employee performance.

Finally, smaller, independently owned and operated catering businesses will tend to be *analysers*. In theory, they have a much more flexible response to the environment and implement strategic change more frequently. In practice, this might not be the case, simply because strategic change implies both a level of expertise and capital investment that many small operators simply do not possess. There is a tendency in a stable environment for such firms to compete on price and act rather like defenders, whilst when they see promising ideas they may adapt and react by trying something new. The types of strategic policy decisions that may be made are illustrated in table 2.1. Further to these three types there are some firms which are ineffective in creating a strategic focus and react to every shift in the environment. Such firms Schaffer terms *reactors*, and typically their organisation structure is inappropriate for their strategy or vice versa.

Table 2.1 *Some major strategic policy options*

Geographic coverage	local, regional, national
Market	
nature	consumer, industrial
development	create demand, increase share
Product design	standard, non-standard
Production process	centralised, non-centralised
Pricing	undercut, match
Credit sales	yes, no
Promotion	
media	television, newspapers
coverage	all year, seasonal
Staffing	
supervision	loose, tight
specialisation	highly specialised, multi-skilled
representation	union, non-union
Finance	
source	equity, debt (long or short term), retained earnings
growth	internal, acquisitions
Organisation	
rewards	fixed, variable with performance
structure	function, geographic, product
co-ordination	formal, informal
delegation	centralised, decentralised
leadership	directive, permissive

THE PRODUCT/SERVICE LIFE-CYCLE

Chapter 1 identified the six stakeholders which will influence a catering organisation. It was recognised that this relationship is placed in the context of a highly complex environment which is changing and evolving over time. The extent to which organisations respond to these changes or remain stable, with a strong brand profile was also questioned. One way to examine the dynamic nature of a product or service is to consider the model of the product/service life-cycle. The typical life-cycle has five distinct stages, stages which can be conveniently termed: innovation; introduction; growth; maturity and decline as illustrated in figure 2.2. At each of these stages

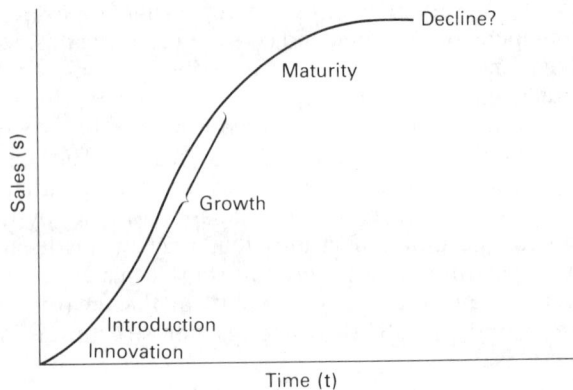

Figure 2.2 *The product/service life-cycle.*

stakeholders may have different objectives, managers will face different problems and new decisions will have to be made.

The *innovative period* covers the point from which the new idea or concept originates up to the point at which it has been successfully implemented. Typically this stage is associated with the entrepreneurial drive of one person or small group of people. An often quoted example is Ray Kroc, the founder of the McDonald's chain, who identified a successful concept and transformed it into a franchisable operation. The management aims at this stage are often very personal in nature and are related to satisfying the drives of the individuals concerned. These drives usually include the need to generate a positive cash flow and the wish to maintain personal control over all aspects of the business. The major problems are how to communicate the new concept successfully to the market-place i.e. the customers, and how to ensure sufficient cash flow to keep the financial backers satisfied and the business operating. The decisions to take are associated with the selection of an appropriate location to launch the concept, the means of raising enough capital to invest in the concept, and the selection of an appropriate system of production and service. Not surprisingly, the involvement of the manager/owner is total and planning-horizons are likely to be short.

Once the innovatory concept has been accepted and implemented, the second stage of the life-cycle is reached. At this point it is possible to introduce replicas of the prototype into new locations. Sasser *et al.*[4] refer to this stage as '*multi-site rationalisation*'. Quite clearly, the major purpose at this stage is to ensure that the success of the original idea can be replicated. Almost inevitably this means that the founder or founders must begin to delegate the management of their units to other people. This can lead to problems in view of the previously stated objectives of the entrepreneurs. It also requires a new approach to control systems as the founder will be unable to keep his finger on the pulse as he has done in the early days of the development.

Assuming that the catering concept is successfully introduced into new locations, the product normally goes through a *growth stage*. This is usually carried out at great speed and in a climate of dramatic change as it is essential from the first to establish a market position quickly before competitors copy a good idea. A good example of this was the steak house concept developed by the Berni brothers over twenty years ago. A second factor in this growth pattern is that a truly successful product which meets market needs can generate so much cash flow that investment in new locations is highly probable. It is usually at this stage that the major issue is whether or not further investment capital should be generated by turning the business into a public company. This obviously has implications with regard to most if not all of the stakeholders. It is also possible that at this stage the business will become a target for acquisition by a larger organisation. Within the growing firm the major problems are to do with selecting new locations, maintaining control and developing sufficient management expertise.

Eventually, the firm will reach the *mature stage*. Growth then slows down, primarily because the firm, probably along with its competitors, has saturated the market for this particular product. The emphasis now changes from generating high cash flow towards minimising costs and maximising the profitability of existing units. At this stage there is the highest level of competition between different operators – at a time when financial backers may be less inclined to invest in the concept. Thus the major issue facing a firm with a mature product is how to prevent the otherwise inevitable decline in sales either by introducing a new concept into the existing market or by introducing the existing concept into new markets. The major breweries have recognised that the market for drinking-out is declining and have attempted to face the situation in a variety of ways, for instance, by revamping the old style public house as theme pubs or turning them into discos to appeal to a younger market.

Quite clearly as the product develops the complexity of the operation increases. More outlets covering a wider geographical area involving a large number of customers and employees in circumstances of growth and intense competition clearly make more complex demands upon management expertise.

Case example 2.1   'The Choux Box'

Chris Lock was a graduate of a hotel school who had some money inherited from his grandmother to invest in his own catering business. Five years ago he bought a dilapidated fish and chip shop just off the High Street of a large town in the Midlands. He recognised that at that time there was a growing demand for fast food products that could be eaten on the premises or as take-away food. The product had to be relatively cheap, maintain its quality over a short period in its prepared state and be consumable without the use of a knife and fork.

He came up with the idea of a fast food based around choux pastry. Choux buns of various shapes and sizes were filled with hot or cold, sweet or savoury fillings. He called his restaurant 'The Choux Box'. During the first few months as he built up trade, he experimented with different fillings and added one or two additional menu items such as salads and hot drinks.

With the opening of a new supermarket next to his restaurant, his sales took off, and he decided to open a second restaurant in a similar location in a town twenty-five miles away. The distinctive style, original concept and friendly service, which was a feature of the 'Choux Box' was equally successful in its new location. Within five years, Chris owned twelve fast food restaurants throughout the Midlands. He believed that the cash flow from these twelve operations would enable him to invest in a new site every three months.

Decide which stage in the product/service life-cycle has been reached by the 'Choux Box' chain and identify which particular issues should be Chris's main concern at this time.

The 'Choux Box' is clearly in the Growth Stage as the concept has been successfully introduced into several new locations. Chris's concerns are fourfold:

- although no other caterer has copied the product concept of the 'Choux Box', competition is growing from other fast food operators.
- this means that competition for sites is increasing at a time when the potential speed of growth is such that sites need to be acquired quickly.
- growth depends upon the continued success and generated cash flows of the original units. Chris must ensure that volume is maintained and performance is carefully monitored.
- the organisation has to be careful to ensure that it can train and develop enough new managers to look after the new outlets.

Whilst it is evident that the life-cycle concept does help to identify the nature of relationships between stakeholders and potential management problems, there is now some doubt as to the validity of the model.[5] Evidence has shown that some products follow the typical S-shape illustrated in figure 2.2, but there are so many exceptions to this that the life-cycle's value, particularly as a predictive tool, is no longer universally accepted.

Examples of exceptions to the stereo typical life-cycle are both theoretically plausible and supported by actual examples. For instance, a new restaurant that opens with very high levels of occupancy and continues to maintain this over a period of years without any further expansion would have a life 'cycle' as illustrated in figure 2.3(a). Many operations do not exhibit the steady growth patterns suggested by the model but go through periods of high and low sales, as shown in figure 2.3(b). It is also possible to imagine an operation whose sales grow steadily at a steady rate, as in figure 2.3(c). An observer who accepted the life-cycle concept in 1975 in the UK would have looked at the hamburger-based, popular catering sector as exemplified by Wimpys and imagined the product to be in the mature stage; within three years McDonald's had totally changed this perception. Likewise, if entrepreneurial companies believed the life-cycle concept they would not now be investing huge sums of money into the steak house concept which observers might have believed was in decline in the late 1970s.

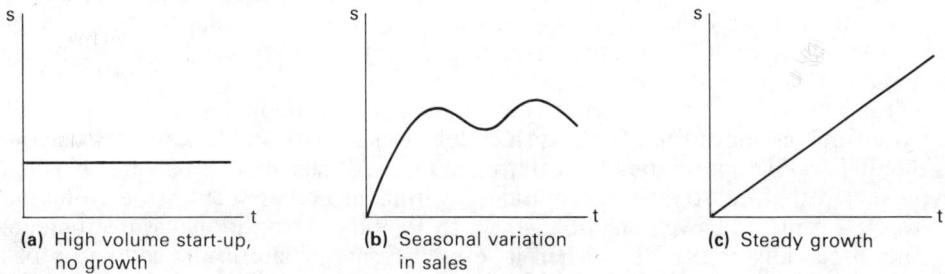

(a) High volume start-up, no growth   **(b)** Seasonal variation in sales   **(c)** Steady growth

Figure 2.3 *Alternative life-cycles.*

Thus, the product/service life-cycle should not be used as a predictive tool to forecast likely future sales. Rather it assists in establishing the extent to which the market potential has been met and in analysing historical sales trends. The life-cycle, after all, only plots volume of sales over a period of time, and as the next chapter shows, these sales are subject to such an incredibly large number of factors that to use past performance for any form of medium- to long-term planning is highly questionable. The origin of the model is from studies of consumer goods, and there are very real problems in applying it to the more complex bundle of products and services provided by the catering industry. If it can be applied at all, it is more likely to be relevant to the product-focused firms we have identified, than other types of operator in the industry.

THE PRO-ACTIVE APPROACH

To what extent do managers have influence over their environment, both the external environment that we have discussed so far and the internal environment of the organisation for which they work? It is certainly true that many factors are far beyond the control of the unit catering manager. For instance, in his review of external influences on the catering industry Tideman[6] included war as a factor that will have a detrimental effect! None the less, managers must be aware of the opportunities available to them to *shape* change, as well as the requirement to *respond* to it. This is equally true of independent operators and large chains. Although implicit in the latter's strategy, if they have a strong brand image, is the assumption that they can influence at least the consumer.

In general, such opportunities are used to greatest effect when caterers work together, either explicitly or implicitly. The explicit attempts to shape the environment are usually clearly identified with organisations of some sort – firms, trade associations, professional associations, and so on.

Large-scale organisations, usually limited companies, are the most obvious example of the way in which managers can exert some influence over events. Firms are able to play such a role because they can influence the environment nationally through their advertising, whilst locally their influence may stem from the size of the workforce they employ. Reichel has suggested[7] that firms should adopt a 'corporate pro-active approach' as part of their long-range strategic planning, and thereby attempt to 'mould the environment in order to create more favourable conditions for their profitability, growth and survival'. This ability of firms to influence the environment is particularly relevant at a local level. A recent press report has shown, for instance, that McDonald's Hamburgers Limited have found that a very large proportion of their planning applications to local councils are turned down in the first place. This has not stopped them from expanding very rapidly, as they have developed an extremely effective public relations campaign aimed at winning over local councillors and residents to their point of view.

Trade associations are theoretically even more powerful lobbies, as they are made up of several or many firms. The British Hotels, Restaurants and Caterers Association is the main body representing the catering industry. It has about 8 000 members and represented the industry on appropriate government bodies such as the Hotel and Catering Economic Development Council. In 1979 the Association was instrumental in the disbanding of the EDC when it refused to participate in the setting up of a tourism strategy sub-committee. None the less it continues to influence government decision-taking through meetings, committees, delegations and media coverage. At the 1985 Annual Meeting, its policy demands included more funding for tourist bodies, relaxation of licensing laws, reduction in VAT and the removal of bureaucratic restrictions.

There are a large number of professional associations in the industry, such as the Hotel, Catering and Institutional Management Association, the Industrial Catering Association and the Hospital Caterers Association. They are primarily concerned with providing services to their individual members, although they too have an influence through representation on such bodies as the Catering Industries Liaison Committee. In addition to organisations and associations, pressure groups can arise to respond to specific changes in the environment. One good example of this is the Hot Take-away Food Action Group (HOTAG) that was formed by fast food operators and popular caterers in response to the 1984 budget proposal to include take-away food in the 15 per cent VAT category.

National groupings are also reflected at local level, where local hotel and restaurant associations may be strongly able to influence local government policy, the local economy, and eating-out habits in the area. This is particularly true in those towns and rural areas where much of the local economy is dependent upon the industry, for instance, the south-west of England, the Lake District, Stratford-upon-Avon, Brighton and so on. It is also at local level that implicit co-operation to modify the environment favourably may take place. We have mentioned previously that caterers may well maintain prices and compete in other ways, in order to ensure margins are maintained. Likewise, some consumer pressure groups have argued that the major brewers, whilst not actively colluding to fix prices, do not use price as a means of competing against their rivals. Other examples of local influence include lobbying the local licensing justices to extend opening hours; lobbying local politicians, particularly with regard to rating levels for businesses; entertaining local journalists in their establishments; and a high degree of contact with local suppliers and other local businesses.

MANAGING DEMAND AND SUPPLY

This pro-active approach can equally be applied at unit level in the local environment. It is particularly evident when examining catering businesses' attempts to optimise their levels of occupancy. In essence managers are manipulating and interpreting environmental factors to ensure that the supply of their product/service is maintained, despite fluctuations in demand. As already described, the catering industry is subject to daily, weekly and often seasonal changes in demand. Sasser argues that service firms can either follow this demand and adopt a 'chase demand' strategy, or ignore actual demand and operate at a 'level capacity' that is above the peak level of demand.[8] Quite clearly, catering is a business that has no option but to chase demand for it is no good preparing a thousand meals a day on the off-chance that demand will be at that level. Nevertheless the catering manager would very much like to be in the situation where he or she could accurately predict and maintain a consistent level of sales if at all possible. Thus management adopts various options for smoothing out fluctuating demand, as well as controlling the supply side to cope with whatever fluctuations there are.

Demand can be smoothed in a variety of ways. Firstly, *differential pricing* may be used to encourage off-peak business. The hotel and catering industry has always priced more cheaply off-peak, but only relatively recently has it seen the advantage of pricing its product at the peak levels and then offering 'discounts' or 'bargains' at off-peak times. Examples of this are happy hours in licensed premises, 'free' aperitifs or wine in restaurants on mid-week evenings, and free coffees for lunch-time diners who finish their meal before 12.30 pm. Secondly, encouraging customers to *book in advance* can level out demand and potentially increase it. A popular eating out spot can therefore manipulate a high demand by offering customers a table reservation earlier or later than they request to ensure the operation is continuously full. Conversely, very popular restaurants do not have reservations at all, for instance, Joe Allans or Chicago Pizza Pie. What they do instead is provide a waiting area next to the bar where people can buy a drink and have a chat whilst they are queuing. Owing to their popularity demand is constant anyway, so the bar provides an extra source of revenue. It is when the customers are queuing up outside to get into the bar that the restaurateur realises the operation is successful. Finally, the manager can *develop the product or service* to encourage new types of business. This has been clearly shown in popular catering with the major roadside restaurants such as Happy Eater and Little Chef, and fast food operators, such as Wimpy and McDonald's, attempting to generate breakfast trade and children's parties.

Given that attempts to smooth out demand will never be 100 per cent successful, the manager must also attempt to control supply to reflect demand and minimise operating costs. The industry has always been relatively effective at this although new ideas and techniques are always being introduced. One way to control supply is to *employ part-timers*, and it is estimated that there are nearly one million people employed in the industry on a part time basis.[9] Sectors of the industry that do this are school meals suppliers, fast food operators, the licensed trade and the banqueting departments of hotels. Secondly, customers can be encouraged to *serve themselves* thereby reducing labour requirements. The introduction of carveries and self-help salad bars in steak restaurants are just two examples of this. Finally, there is the constant search for *greater efficiency* by simplifying service procedures, improving work flows, and so on. It must be recognised that slack periods can also be used effectively for other activities that may be necessary, such as on-the-job training, maintenance of equipment, ensuring the level of hygiene and cleanliness is up to standard, and so on. It is also important to realise that staff who have a high degree of social contact with customers, probably require time in which to unwind and relieve the pressure of the high periods of activity.

PREDICTING THE FUTURE

Although we have said that the product/service life-cycle should not be used as a predictive tool, the manager does need to have some idea of what is likely to happen in the future. The pro-active approach to shaping the environment will only have very limited impact. In the main the manager will be faced with targets in the future that he knows he has to achieve, but uncertainty, to a greater or lesser extent, about the circumstances in which they must be achieved. The manager should, therefore, strive to reduce the level of uncertainty through the application of forecasting techniques.

Chapter 1 considered how the manager may go about collecting information about the environment. Once collected this information may be processed in order to provide some guidance as to likely future events. *Forecasting* should be viewed as part of the information system, and not just as a number-generating technique. In this respect it is amongst the many activities to be considered in the remaining chapters of this book, such as quality control, cost control, and so on. In order to make forecasting effective some strategic preparation should be made:

1. Establish what decisions will be made on the basis of the forecast and what actions may be taken.
2. Analyse the degree of accuracy required, how far ahead forecasts need to look, how often they are needed and what variables need to be included.
3. Select an appropriate forecasting method to meet the criteria established in step 2.
4. Compare the available data with the forecasting method to establish if there is a fit.
5. Develop the specific technique for making forecasts. This is often the first point that is considered, which is why forecasts have a reputation for being inaccurate or too complex.
6. Test the method by comparing forecasts with actual results.
7. Ensure the method is flexible enough to incorporate changes that may take place in the environment.
8. Implement the forecasting system and continue to monitor its performance.

There are essentially three broad types of *forecasting techniques* of increasing sophistication.

Qualitative methods establish forecasts on the basis of personal opinion and 'informed' judgement, often in the same informal way that information about the business may be collected. For instance, a management team might come together to discuss what impact a new hotel in the area may have on their business and plan their future activities on the basis of their conclusions. Alternatively, performance may be based on historical analogy whereby future performance of a particular aspect is based on how a similar aspect has performed in the past. This is often the basis for menu design and development in the catering industry.

Extrapolation   is a statistical technique, called time-series forecasting, that takes the past performance of an aspect and projects this into the future. This method is particularly suitable if the conditions are relatively stable and conditions are unlikely to change in the short term. Even if conditions are changing, there are different techniques available for taking into account trends, seasonality and cyclic change. A trend is a gradual change in conditions over time; seasonality is fluctuations in performance within the space of one year; and a cycle is regularly repeating pattern over a longer period of time.

Causal modelling   derives a forecast based on a series of variables that are thought to cause changes in performance. This too requires statistical techniques, usually multiple regression analysis, to relate the two variables. Such explanatory models will use more than one variable to predict future performance, for instance advertising, price and last year's sales might be used to predict next year's sales.

Case example 2.2   The Olsen & Jose Study[10]

In this study, historical sales figures for two restaurants over a twenty-month period were taken. The restaurants were full-service operations but with a different theme. One was located in a suburban shopping centre and the other on its own site in the suburbs. Once the sales figures had been plotted the question addressed was whether statistical forecasting techniques could have been used to accurately predict the sales in the restaurants. To reach an answer, the sales data for the first ten months were used as a database to predict sales values for the following ten months. The evidence of this study suggests that exponential smoothing, or time-series forecasting techniques have some value in the long run with regards to predicting trends, but are less effective in predicting short-term fluctuations in trade.

OBJECTIVES AT OPERATING LEVEL

Once all the information that is thought to be worth while has been collected and some forecasts of likely future events have been made, the organisation needs to explain to its unit managers how it believes the goals of the organisaion should be achieved. In most organisations this is done by setting targets in a wide variety of key result areas.

Some organisations have systematised the identification of the key result areas and the relative priority that they should have by instituting the idea of 'management by objectives' (mbo). Drucker believes 'without [the] ability to set objectives a man (sic) cannot be an adequate manager'.[11] The advantages that are cited for the mbo approach are that it focuses attention on performance and achievement; managers, their superiors and subordinates have a yardstick against which to measure their performance; managers are motivated by their involvement in setting appropriate objectives and finally mbo focuses on opportunities rather than problems.

In translating strategic needs into objectives, an organisation needs first of all to establish what it is trying to achieve, the nature of the organisation that has been designed to meet these needs, and what are the essential operational characteristics on which success is founded. This reappraisal of fundamentals should be followed by a planning analysis that examines the external environment – the major concern of the early part of this chapter. Using management information systems and forecasting techniques some assumptions can be made about the future that will highlight the strengths and weaknesses of the organisation with regard to its ability to respond to future market conditions. Such analysis will usually indicate a 'performance gap', that is to say a difference between actual and ideal performance that needs to be narrowed by correcting problem areas or improving performance in other areas.

Assuming that the mbo system is operated, at the beginning of the operational year, usually coinciding with the financial or budgetary year, the boss and subordinate manager meet to discuss the objectives for that year. The boss is aware of the strategic goals, budget limitations for the unit and previous results of the operation; and the operational manager should have a clear idea of his or her own abilities and the threats and opportunities facing the operation. Between them, they agree what the operational performance should be, the resources that will be allocated to the operation, how often and in what form performance reports will be prepared, and usually some sort of reward system for achieving or exceeding the target objectives.

The objectives.   These may be of three types. First are objectives covering the usual responsibilities of the manager, which are continual, repetitive and easily measurable. The typical objectives found in the catering industry include percentage of gross profit, wage costs, stock turnover, occupancy rate, and so on. The second type of objective identifies any problem areas and attempts to ensure that they will be solved within the given time period. An example of this might be high levels of staff turnover, whereby an objective of bringing this down to x per cent might be established. Thirdly there are pro-active objectives – those that identify proposed changes which will be introduced into the operation in the next year for which there is a clear indication of what impact these changes are likely to have. For instance, the manager might propose to introduce a salad bar into the operation, with the expectation of maintaining transaction volume and increasing average spend by y per cent.

The features of such objectives are as follows:
1. They are outputs. It was argued earlier that it is by achieving outputs that the manager is judged.
2. They are based on consensus. As such the objectives should provide a range within which the manager is expected to perform. It is suggested that the subordinate set the most optimistic figure, whilst the boss sets the least acceptable figure.
3. There is the expectation that if the manager is achieving the desired level of performance he or she should be left alone to get on with things and not be subject to interference from above. On the other hand, if the manager is below the minimum level of performance he or she is expected to call upon the resources and expertise necessary in order to take corrective action.
4. In addition to this continuous appraisal of performance, a periodic *audit* may take place. In the UK the most common form of audit is a regular stock-take, but in the USA periodic appraisals of all aspects of the business are undertaken including personnel, public relations, purchasing practices, legal compliance, safety, and so on.
5. As part of the objective setting exercise for the next year, the previous objectives are reviewed and discussed.

There are many instances in the hotel and catering industry where objectives exist, but they have not been formulated according to the mbo system. This does not mean to say that managers within their own unit cannot respond to these objectives in the same way as they might if they had had a much greater say in setting these goals. Nor, indeed, does it prevent a manager from operating an mbo system within the unit, in order to delegate responsibility for their achievement to his or her subordinates. Whatever the particular style of approach, objectives must be seen as part of the overall strategic policy of the firm and as a more detailed analysis of some sort of fairly long-range plan. Thus, for instance, the setting of a target gross profit for a catering operation will depend upon whether the firm is seeking fast growth through high turnover, or expects stable conditions in which to maximise profit levels.

SUMMARY

Whilst chapter 1 was concerned with how the environment influenced an organisation's strategy, this chapter began by looking at how these strategic goals may change the life-cycle of the catering product. But the organisation and the manager do not simply react to the circumstances in which they operate, they can, and should, take a pro-active position. To be effective at this, and indeed all other aspects of the operation, the manager needs information and, on the basis of this information, forecasts of what is likely to happen in the future. Once such forecasts have been made strategic goals can be translated into more short-term objectives at which the unit catering manager can aim.

Implicit in the arrangement of this textbook is the relation of such objectives to one or other of the key result areas discussed in the next eight chapters. These are:

increasing the volume of business

maximising gross profit contributions

controlling product quality

assuring the quality of service

improving employee performance

protecting the operation's assets

increasing productivity

controlling costs

The argument presented here is that often they are not stated in such a way as to be of real value to the person required to achieve them or to the organisation itself. Indeed, a recurrent theme of this book is that many of the most common measures and objectives used in the industry, such as gross profit percentage, labour cost percentage, and so on, are inadequate and misleading.

But the fundamental point is that strategy, and hence the relative priority of key result areas (and their measurement), will vary according to the sector of the catering industry, the size and scale of the operation and the stage on the life-cycle. This is why it is more important to be doing the right things, than to be doing things right.

REFERENCES

1. Ansoff, H. I., *Strategic Management*, Macmillan Press, 1980.
2. Schaffer, J. D., 'Strategy, organisation structure and success in the lodging industry', *International Journal of Hospitality Management* vol. 3 no. 4, 1984.
3. Schaffer, J. D., 'Structure and strategy: two sides of success', *Cornell HRA Quarterly*, pp. 76–82, February 1986.
4. Sasser, W. E., Olsen, R. P., and Wyckoff, D. D., *Management of Service Operations*, Allyn & Bacon, 1978.
5. Hart, C. W., Casserly, G., and Lawless, M. J., 'The product life cycle: how useful?', *Cornell HRA Quarterly*, pp. 54–63, November 1984.
6. Tidemans, M., External influences on the hospitality industry, in Cassee, E., and Reuland, R. (Eds.), *The Management Of Hospitality*, Pergamon Press, 1983, pp. 1–21.

7. Reichel, A., Corporate strategic planning for the hospitality industry: a contingency approach, in Pizam, A. *et al.* (Eds.), *The Practice of Hospitality Management*, AVI Publishing Co. Inc., 1982, pp. 49–63.
8. Sasser, W. E., 'Match supply and demand in service industries', *Harvard Business Review*, November/December 1976.
9. HCITB, *Statistical Review of the Hotel and Catering Industry*, CIU, 1984.
10. Olsen, M. D., and Jose, M., 'Time Series Forecasting: a Testing of Applications to the Foodservice Industry', *International Journal of Hospitality Management* vol. 1 no. 3, pp. 151–156, 1982.
11. Drucker, P., *Management*, Heinemann, 1974.

3

Increasing Volume

OBJECTIVES

Identify the need for planned action to increase volume . . . describe a model for analysing consumer behaviour in the catering industry . . . analyse the alternative techniques used for increasing volume in catering businesses . . . explain how to decide which technique should be used in a particular business situation.

INTRODUCTION

Managers who want to increase the profit of their business are faced with two broad options: increase revenue or reduce costs. Usually both of these avenues will be followed, but because catering businesses are predominantly market oriented, the question of increasing revenue is particularly important to managers. In chapter 4 the problem of increasing the contribution made to profit by each customer will be examined. Here we will consider the other aspect of revenue – increasing volume.

In recent years the ability to increase volume has become crucial to management success in a catering business. Firstly, margins have dropped over the last ten years, as menus have become more limited and more convenience food commodities have been used. Productivity has also improved, often coupled with shifts in the level of service. At the same time, the costs of opening a restaurant business have escalated: property costs in major cities have been pushed up by increased competition for prime sites, there is more use of high cost capital equipment, and each new major opening seems to set new heights in fitting-out costs. Variable costs tend to have a downwards trend and the proportion of fixed costs is increasing in many catering businesses – and the importance of improving and retaining sales volume is growing.

There are several reasons why managers may decide to pursue an objective of increasing volume. Firstly, the profit objective for the business may have been increased in order to meet the needs of financial backers or in order to generate funds for future investment. Secondly, external factors may produce a major change in the business's cost structure, such as a major change in employment costs brought about by legislation, or a major refurbishment required by an Environmental Health Officer. Occasionally, a business's cost structure may be changed by a dramatic increase in a particular cost above the general level of inflation, as happened with fuel costs in the mid 1970s. Very often such cost increases cannot be passed on to the customer in terms of price increases as these will meet with price reaction and a consequent drop in profit. Under these circumstances, the most appropriate method of recovering these costs is often by volume increase. Thirdly, managers may decide to put effort into volume improvement in order to counteract the effect (hopefully anticipated) of volume drop. This is often the case with the opening of a competitive establishment. Finally, it is not always prudent to attempt to recover all cost inflation by price increases – either because of consumer price reaction or because of periods of government imposed price restraint as occurred in 1975.

THE PROBLEMS OF CAPACITY AND UTILISATION

Unlike factory products, food-service products cannot be stored – a seat unsold on Thursday remains unsold forever. Managers are faced with the problem of not being able to increase volume on every day of the week, because of the present pattern of business demand. In a typical provincial restaurant peak capacity may be reached on a Thursday and Friday night when customers are often turned away.

The anomaly facing most catering managers is that where demand exists, capacity is usually fully utilised. Most production systems have a limiting factor which determines maximum output. This is usually seating capacity for food-service systems, but may also be dependent on the selection and layout of equipment, on staffing or even on legislation. Catering Managers usually measure utilisation by 'seat turnover' for each meal period. This measure is useful for inter-unit comparisons, but it would be more useful for unit managers to know when their customers arrive and how long they stay. Such an analysis may show up opportunities for volume improvement on the 'shoulders' of the demand pattern – for example in the early or late evening.

Chapter 2 has already discussed how managers can influence volume by the process of demand management. The first step in volume *improvement* is to attempt to increase volume where proven demand exists, in the case of our example on Thursday and Friday nights. It is always worth examining the pattern of demand at maximum utilisation because, by increasing capacity, rapid profit improvement is possible – sometimes without additional expenditure. A check of the number of empty seats when all the tables are occupied will give an indication of what changes are necessary to the seating mix to increase capacity. The possibility of adding extra seating should also be considered. However, the biggest increase in capacity can often be achieved by reducing the amount of time for which the customer occupies the table. This can be done by such techniques as systematically eliminating those dishes with the longest delay between order and service; by speeding up the presentation of the bill and by ensuring that, if appropriate, a separate bar area is used for before and after dinner drinks and for taking orders. All these methods of increasing capacity make changes to the product – by changing the menu, service or atmosphere – and so the possible effects on consumer preference should be considered.

Secondly, whilst it is possible to create space for increased volume by taking reservations at specific times, there is a trend amongst the popular London restaurants to abandon the practice of taking reservations – because this is often counter productive to volume improvement! The demand for business entertaining has brought about the position where some secretaries book tables up to several weeks in advance, just in case their boss may wish to entertain a client on that day. In the event a cancellation or late arrival results in many chance arrivals being unnecessarily turned away. It is easy to understand why many operators are abandoning reservations and providing a larger bar area where customers can take a drink, have their order taken and wait for an available table.

Finally, the pattern of demand for catering products is often unstable and difficult to predict. Some businesses have sales patterns which fluctuate unpredictably from day-to-day and week-to-week. This makes planning and controlling marketing activities very difficult. Often analysis of the pattern of demand can help to give a clearer understanding of the consumers and allow more effective management action. Take, for example, the sales figures for a hotel restaurant, situated adjacent to an exhibition centre, which varied unpredictably from day-to-day and week-to-week. This made it difficult for management to plan and control the operation. Analysis of the demand showed that it came from three main sources – from hotel guests, from chance exhibition-users and from local inhabitants and businessmen. Once the sources of demand were categorised, staff were trained to check the source of each and a regular analysis of demand was undertaken. This in turn enabled management to produce effective volume forecasts and plan and monitor more effective marketing activities.

From the above example it is possible to identify three main categories of demand for catering products. These are:

- **derived demand** – demand for a product which depends directly on demand for a second product (demand for hotel accommodation directly stimulates demand for breakfast in a hotel restaurant).
- **indirect generative demand** – impulse purchase of a product stimulated by the immediate availability of the product (demand for fast food is largely stimulated by the store's location in a street with a high pedestrian count).
- **direct generative demand** – planned purchase, often involving travel (a planned visit to a remote country restaurant). Food and beverage businesses rely on all three categories of demand – and managers need to understand the nature of the present demand for their products, as this limits the type of marketing activities which can be undertaken. This analysis of demand into derived, indirect and direct elements is very useful for preparing accurate volume forecasts.

UNDERSTANDING CONSUMER BEHAVIOUR

When managers attempt to increase volume, they are trying to bring about a change in consumer behaviour, from being non-purchasers to being purchasers of their product. To bring about a change in behaviour in a controlled way (so that there is a reasonable chance of achieving the established aim) it is useful to have some model to aid decision making. This is not easy, as consumers may behave in the same way for different motives. Some people may be using a restaurant because they enjoy trying new experiences, others may be using the same restaurant because they regularly go there and value the security it offers, yet others may be there because they were invited by a friend and did not want to turn down the invitation, yet others may be entertaining business colleagues in order to influence them. So the same behaviour may be caused by different motives. Conversely, the same motive may produce different behaviours. In response to the need to relax, some consumers may buy restaurant meals, others may buy a video, yet others may play squash, and yet others may buy some plants for the garden.

Consumer behaviour is very complex but if effective action is to be taken to increase volume, some method must be found of making sense of what consumers do. The traditional approach to assist in understanding complex situations is to construct a model. A model is an attempt to portray reality in order to make it easier to understand and thereby simplify problem solving. There have been several attempts to derive models of consumer behaviour but there is considerable disagreement between researchers and often results are of little relevance to the catering industry.

The most useful model of consumer behaviour seems to have been produced by Jenkins,[1] who argues that a consumer's attitudes to a product are the most important aspect of their readiness to buy. This is backed up by research at the University of Michigan which shows a closer relationship between intention to buy and actual spending than between personal disposable income and actual spending. Jenkins identifies a continuum of purchase intention consisting of eight stages:
● unawareness of the need for a product or service.
● awareness of the need for a product or service, but no awareness of what is available to satisfy that need.
● awareness of one or more of the products that are available but no knowledge of the characteristics of those products.
● comprehension of the characteristics of one or more of the products available.
● preference for one particular product.
● intention to buy that product.
● purchase of that product and evaluation of its benefits.
● repurchase of that product.

Jenkins' model is practically very useful as it provides a method of measuring customers' attitudes towards a particular product, by assessing what proportion of the target market are at each stage of the market continuum. As an example, a very large restaurant chain wanted to monitor the effect of its national television and newspaper advertising campaign. Before the campaign began, a number of questions were inserted into an omnibus survey which regularly tests a large sample of people's attitudes to a variety of products. The questions were designed to give assessments of the market continuum for the restaurant chain. At the end of the campaign, the same questions were again inserted into the omnibus survey. The result showed the attitude shift which had occurred as a result of the campaign and gave the management useful data to evaluate their advertising campaign.

Changing consumer behaviour (moving consumers up the continuum) involves changing their attitude to the product. Many attitudes are resistant to change – for example, those attitudes concerning acceptable humour, or attitudes to unemployment. In particular, strongly negative attitudes are very difficult to change, and information tends to be distorted or ignored if it is inconsistent with existing attitudes. This chapter is concerned with increasing volume – and that necessitates attitude change – which can be achieved by the use of skilful marketing techniques.

There are several factors which can move consumers along the continuum from unawareness to repurchase. These factors, many of which will be discussed in this chapter, include:
● advertising
● sales promotion
● exterior signing
● publicity
● personal selling
● availability
● price
● packaging
● favourable evaluation of purchase

There are also factors which may halt, delay or regress a consumer's progress along the continuum. These factors include:
● competitive marketing
● attrition
● memory lapse

Finally, there are some factors which may move the consumer forward *or* back along the continuum:

- word of mouth
- social influence
- degree of risk
- unfavourable evaluation of purchase
- personality traits

When Jenkins developed his model, he was mainly concerned with consumer goods. In applying his model to catering operations, it is important to recognise that the purchase of a meal is fixed in time and space – demand on Thursday is not the same as demand on Monday, and demand at Branch X of a chain is not the same as demand at Branch Y. The Catering Manager is faced with the objective of changing consumer behaviour very selectively – by creating the desire to purchase at certain times in the week or at certain branches of the chain.

Repurchase is particularly important as far as catering operations are concerned. Persuading an existing consumer to return, or better still to return at a period of low demand, can be one of the most cost effective methods of increasing volume. Of course, most of the factors which may move the consumer up the continuum have a cost associated with them and the use of these marketing techniques will only be effective if they generate more profit contribution than they cost to incur. For example, a town centre bistro wanted to increase its volume during Tuesdays and Wednesdays. A six-month promotion was organised. Every customer who visited the bistro on Friday or Saturday was given a voucher which entitled them to a free half bottle of wine for every meal for two persons on Tuesday or Wednesday during the promotion period. The cost of the wine was £1.31 and the average profit contribution from the two meals was £5.40. During the promotion period volume increased by 11 per cent on the target days, and when the promotion was over it did not drop back to its original level.

MARKET SEGMENTATION

The market continuum model provides a method of segmenting the market for a food and beverage business. Segmentation is particularly useful if it provides a method of identifying accessible groups of potential purchasers. Of course, in order to take effective action, managers cannot consider individual consumers – and this is overcome by identifying sub-groups of potential consumers who share a common characteristic whose consumer behaviour is fairly consistent within the sub-group and who are likely to be influenced by marketing efforts. These sub-groups are called market segments. Segmentation is used for the basis of much marketing research and for marketing planning purposes – but most managers also adopt a private framework for classifying and understanding their consumers and this is also a form of market segmentation. The basis for segmenting a market is crucial to a manager's comprehension of consumer behaviour and is crucial to their ability to take effective action.

The purpose of market segmentation analysis is to identify sub-groups of the population who will be more susceptible to marketing effort. Specifically, this enables managers to reduce the risk involved in designing new products or reformulating existing products, by ensuring that the attributes of the product meet the requirements of a (profitable) market segment. In addition, segmentation increases marketing efficiency by directing effort and finance towards potentially profitable segments in a manner that is consistent with the characteristics of that segment. It must not be forgotten that segmentation is only a tool for managers to use to increase volume, and not an end in itself. If segmentation does not provide a route to volume improvement, then it is not worth using.

Market segmentation is biased heavily towards the use of demographic data. The unsolicited direct marketing information that lands on your doormat (from, for example, *Which* or Kays Mail Order Company) will probably have resulted from a mailing list prepared by demographic segmentation. The Census provides most of this information – but for most occasional users it is more effective to use an agency to extract this data. The most useful of these agencies for food and beverage businesses is a service called ACORN. This acronym stands for A Classification Of Residential Neighbourhoods and is widely accepted as the practical approach to social classification. The classification is based on census data and includes 41 variables encompassing demographic, housing and employment data. Each census enumeration district (about 150 households) is classified as one of 38 residential neighbourhood types. This classification is apparently far more discriminating than, for example, the Census, IPA or BPM systems as shown in table 3.1 – which shows ACORN discriminating between two types of high status users, mainly ABs in the IPA system.

Table 3.1   *ACORN market segmentation*

ACORN group	I	J
	(inner city)	(suburban)
Typical areas	Kensington	Harrow
	Camden	Solihull
	Bath	Woking
Entertaining		
at home	207	107
Lawn-mower owners	54	145
Guardian readers	355	149

TGI-TNA Monitor/GB average = 100.
Source: *Target Marketing*, CACI Inc International.

Table 3.1 shows how ACORN gives a useful social classification reflecting differences in taste, life style and purchasing habits. ACORN can provide direct mailing lists for a specified target market; profiles of present customers from Postcodes; demographic analysis of a town or specified catchment area and an index of buying power for a specified product in a specified area. The buying power index is used by major breweries in order to decide on the mix of products that should be sold in a particular pub.

An example of the use of ACORN segmentation is found in its employment by Berni Inns – Britain's first steakhouse chain. In the early 1980s they decided to relaunch with three different concepts aimed at different social groups. Berni's marketing manager was faced with the problem of which of the three new concepts – The Burgundy Room, Bistro Marine and Eleven Eleven – should be sited in each of their 260 locations. The ACORN demographics system was used to provide the necessary data to decide on the siting of the new restaurant types, and also which sites should be shelved and where new sites should be acquired.[2]

Before returning to the question of segmentation, it will be useful to explore how consumers perceive catering products. When consumers evaluate how well a product meets their needs, or when they compare two different products, they perceive the products in terms of a number of different characteristics or 'attributes'. The product attributes which are important to a consumer may not necessarily be the ones that a manager thinks are important and often research is necessary to determine what are going to be the most important consumer attributes.

A comprehensive taxonomy of food-service product attributes has been produced by the National Restaurant Association of America in its survey *Consumer Behaviour in the Foodservice Marketplace.*[3] The NRA identifies 15 product attributes which influence consumer choice; these are shown in figure 3.1.

Cleanliness of restaurant
Speed of service
Atmosphere
Convenient location
Cleanliness of toilets
Adequate parking
No-smoking section
Quality of food
Low prices
Variety of food
Friendliness of staff
Consistency of food quality
Availability of children's portions
Availability of salad bar

Figure 3.1 *Salient product attributes for restaurants.* Adapted from *Consumer Behaviour in the Foodservice Marketplace.*

The list is by no means exhaustive, and could well have included other attributes such as the acceptance of credit cards. However, this is the best study available. As expected, the relative importance of these attributes varies according to the type of food-service facility. For example, in the NRA study, a sample of over 3 000 people were asked what were the most important features they considered when selecting a restaurant, by restaurant type. The five most important attributes for speciality restaurants were in order of priority: quality of food; atmosphere; cleanliness; variety of food; friendliness of staff. However, in the case of fast food restaurants, the most important attributes were: quality of food; speed of service; low prices; cleanliness; convenience of location.

In the field of interpersonal relations, it is established that those people who like you do so because of exactly the same attributes for which other people dislike you. We would suggest that the same principle applies to food-service product attributes, as the next case example shows.

Case example 3.1   The Empress Hotel Group

A national chain of long-established hotels, which prided itself on the quality of its hotel dining rooms, was trying to reverse the downward trend in lunch volume. Local press advertising failed to produce any significant change. However, market research interviews showed that the strong nucleus of regular customers appreciated the meticulous silver service and the classical cuisine, and the non-repurchasers (women and younger men in particular) did not like the prolonged, fussy service and the rich traditional food. It was also found that most non-users thought that the prices were higher than they really were. The company decided to introduce a range of daily light inclusive meals of a main course, glass of wine and coffee. The launch was backed-up by national newspaper advertising, stressing the inclusive price, the speed and ease of service and giving examples of the dishes. The new meals fitted well with the existing business and the company achieved a profitable increase in volume.

In this example the biggest risk faced by the company was that some of the existing clientele might trade down from the more expensive à la carte and table d'hote menus to the new inclusive meal. This did happen to some extent, but not significantly because the established consumers were looking for different product attributes. The second risk was the possible result of mixing two very different markets. Customers themselves shape the image of an establishment and one question customers may ask themselves is 'Is this place frequented by the type of people with whom I can identify?' Mixing markets will change the image of a restaurant and this can affect volume. The case example shows that volume can be increased by communicating different product attributes to different market segments, but it is recognised that there are problems associated with mixed markets.

UNDERSTANDING THE COMPETITION

It is not easy for one firm to increase a consumer's total expenditure on eating out – so very often volume increase for one business means volume loss for another. In order to be effective managers need to understand their competition, and make decisions about their business in relation to the competition. The main areas of decision are:
● what product attributes shall we develop and stress in order to win volume from the competition?
● what marketing techniques shall we employ in order to move consumers towards our products, if necessary at the expense of the competition?
The strategic decisions relate to the choice of food-service concept. This should remain relatively stable over a period of several years as changing strategy may involve major refurbishment. Tactical decisions concern activities such as advertising, direct sales and public relations and will vary over a shorter term in response to changes in the market and competitor activity.

Case example 3.2   Scarlett's Hotel

A major London hotel with a multi-million pound food and beverage operation has adopted a systematic approach to profit planning for each of its main outlets. This involves periodic visits by the restaurant managers to competing establishments in order to maintain a regular analysis of the competitors' products. This is supported by the work of a full-time market analyst who maintains market and competitor intelligence for all the hotel profit centres. Every year each restaurant manager (who has full profit responsibility) reviews the strengths and weaknesses of his or her own restaurant in comparison with the identified opposition. They each then prepare a plan for amendments to the product and with the help of marketing specialists, a marketing plan for the restaurant. This system has been in use for fifteen years now and the profit record of the hotel – one of the best in London – supports the approach.

It is important to note that the management devote considerable time to developing their competitive strategy and tactics. Specific resources, in the form of a market analyst, were deemed necessary to make the system work. Senior managers in the business are committed to the approach and have provided the necessary training and development to give the profit centre managers the necessary skills and confidence to participate fully.

Consumers select products which have attributes that meet their needs, but in order to understand the competition fully it is important to know what type of consumer prefers which brand and why. It has been usual to segment markets according to demographic factors such as age, sex, income, occupation and geographic location. However, demographic segmentation is not very helpful in dealing with consumer preferences for a particular brand. Preference for a certain brand is more likely to be due to psychological differences between consumers, particularly differences in values. Certain consumers prefer one brand to another because they believe the salient attributes of the preferred brand are more appropriate to their personal values. Segmentation based on psychological differences is termed 'psychographic segmentation'.

The use of psychographic segmentation in the restaurant business has been the subject of recent market research, by Alfred Boote.[4] Boote surveyed consumers' reactions to a leading restaurant chain and their reactions to its major competitor. He found that traditional demographic segmentation could not explain why one brand should be preferred to another. However, psychographic segmentation clearly separated the two brands. Boote discovered that for the two chains under investigation those consumers who placed great importance on eating high quality meals (a value that Boote termed 'Food Orientation') were more likely to prefer Brand B. Those placing greater emphasis on traditional life style (Rational Orientation) or on relaxing and enjoying themselves (Leisure Orientation) or standing out from the crowd (Individualism) were significantly more likely to prefer Brand A to Brand B. This research also identified the salient product attributes which were perceived as differentiating the brands and were important to the consumers. These were the quality of ingredients and size of portions, cleanliness, comfort, presentation and packaging, the availability of a good steak and a good roast and a varied menu. (These were analysed from an original questionnaire of 47 phrases.)

For Brand A the marketing implications of this were clear. Brand A had to take action to attract more of the consumers falling into the Food Orientation segment – a large segment that currently favours the competitor. This had to be done without sacrificing the values which are important to the existing customers. Any future promotional campaigns should emphasise the salient product attributes and incorporate the values of the main psychographic segments – Food Orientation and Rational Orientation.

TECHNIQUES FOR INCREASING VOLUME

Advertising, direct mail and exterior signing are all attempts to communicate with the consumer, influence their attitudes and change their behaviour. There are two distinct elements to all these attempts at communication – the message that is communicated and the medium used to communicate it. It is a common managerial error to focus on the medium ('What we need is some advertising!') without first being clear about the message. The nature of the message will in fact vary depending on the market continuum position of the people for whom the message is intended.

For unaware potential consumers, the message should contain the basic product information: the name of the restaurant, the menu concept, price range and opening hours. For potential consumers who are aware of the basic information, the message should stress the salient product attributes which make the product preferable to a competitor's. As an earlier case example illustrated, different product attributes may need to be stressed to different market segments. For potential consumers who are convinced that the product is suitable for their needs, the message needs to encourage them to purchase – by showing that there is little risk involved in the purchase (with for example an offer of inclusive-priced meals), by convincing them that their peer groups use the restaurant and by giving incentives to act promptly (by a 'for limited period' offer). For consumers who have purchased the product the message should reinforce the purchase decision (by, for example, giving information about good food awards or details of growth in popularity) and should give them an incentive to repurchase (possibly by an added value offer for repurchasing). These messages are summarised as follows:

Table 3.2   *Messages for each continuum position.*

CONTINUUM POSITION	CONTENT OF MESSAGE
Unaware	Product information
Aware	Salient product attributes
Convinced	Safety of purchase
	Peer users
	Prompt action
Purchaser	Reinforcement of benefits
	Incentive to repurchase
Repurchaser	Reinforcement of benefits
	Incentive to repurchase
	Incentive for loyalty

Choosing an appropriate message is only half of the problem. The most appropriate medium to effectively communicate this information to the consumer also has to be chosen. The choice facing a food and beverage manager includes:
- exterior signing and shop-front design
- direct mail
- personal selling
- newspaper and magazine advertising
- radio or television advertising
- public relations

The choice of media is governed by a number of factors. Media differ in their cost and the normal measure used for comparison is the cost of potentially communicating the message to one thousand people. This can be further refined by assessing the cost of reaching a specific target market (for example, defined in terms of IPA group, age and sex). For printed and broadcast media this information is readily available from publications such as British Rate and Data – but this quantitative measure does not take account of the degree of influence that the media exerts over the consumer. For example, an advertisement in a newspaper that has one hundred pages mainly filled with tightly packed advertisements will tend to have less impact than an advert in a newspaper with mainly editorial content. Similarly, radio advertising tends to be more intrusive (the listener does not have much chance of selectively ignoring subjects that do not interest them) whereas printed media can be easily and selectively ignored.

Decisions also need to be made concerning the frequency of exposure of the message. Intensive scheduling will build awareness very quickly, but awareness drops once the advertising stops. Less frequent advertising over a longer period of time builds more permanent awareness more gradually. Advertisements also wear out – and their effectiveness decreases after prolonged exposure.

Increasing volume depends on careful determination of objectives for increased sales, planning a competitive strategy, and implementing the cost effective tactics –

through the choice of the right message and the right media. The test of success is whether the additional profit generated is greater than the additional costs incurred.

Many food and beverage businesses are situated in areas of high pedestrian and driver flows. High Street fast food businesses provide an excellent example of what good *exterior signing* and shop-front design can do to move a consumer from unawareness to purchase in a matter of seconds. Bright primary colours are combined with pictorial representation of the products, often aimed at children. The high, open doorways and the bright interiors are fast food's most effective means of volume increase. An identifiable logo is also important for High Street sites – and children can spot McDonald's Golden Arches or the Mister Wimpy characters before they can read! An exterior can also say a great deal about salient product attributes, by communicating a wide variety of concepts, including acceptance of credit cards or a young and trendy image. On a day-to-day basis the effectiveness of the exterior of the premises depends on routine cleaning and maintenance of windows and signs and on the care of car parks and landscaped areas.

Case example 3.3   The Queen's Head

The importance of signing was seen in the case of the pub in a Cambridgeshire town which had experienced a dramatic fall in volume after pedestrian routes were changed following the development of a new shopping centre. However, the back of the pub was now on a major thoroughfare whereas it previously been in a quiet street. After a feasibility study was undertaken, the buildings at the back of the pub were converted into a cafe and bar and a new entrance to the original bars was incorporated into the new frontage. This case example shows that when traffic flows change, signing or even moving an entrance is necessary to retain volume. This is paramount in businesses which are situated in intense pedestrian flows – such as retailing and catering on London terminus railway stations.

Shop-front design plays an important part in letting the consumer see what the product is, through the use of large window areas. The development of railway arches into wine bars has been very effectively achieved by building a glass wall at either end of the arch. The resulting design clearly communicates information about the product, image and peer users. Managers of existing units may be able to achieve volume increase by changing lighting levels to facilitate a better view or by removing curtains.

Direct mail is a cheap and effective way of reaching a specific target market. The wider use of microcomputers has brought the use of mailing list software within the reach of most small businessmen – and here we will consider some of the applications of mailing lists for food and beverage managers. The first use is to increase volume by getting additional repurchase from existing users.

A restaurant in the Buckinghamshire countryside always asked for the names and telephone numbers of customers making telephone reservations. From these names and the local telephone directory, the restaurant compiled a mailing list of past users which was stored on the restaurant's microcomputer. When the restaurant ran special promotions to try to fill troughs in demand, it used the mailing list to contact past users.

The most difficult aspect of using direct mail is obtaining a suitable mailing list. Market research agencies can supply local lists, but they are not generally well suited to the requirements of food-service operators. A good list of past users is invaluable. Another method of collecting a mailing list is by couponing, for example, having a weekly draw for a magnum of champagne, which requires a customer from each party eating in the restaurant to complete an entry form with their name and address.

The second use of direct mailing techniques is to contact potential users within a semi-captive market. This technique was used by a hotel that wanted to increase the utilisation of its restaurant by hotel guests. On arrival in the hotel, all first-time guests found a personalised letter in their room telling them about the hotel retaurant and including a voucher for a complimentary after dinner liqueur.

The third use of direct mail is to contact the wider group of non-users. The biggest application of this is in banqueting, where direct mail is used to promote awareness among business houses and local organisations. This is usually followed up by a personal sales call. Direct mail for non-users is also sometimes used by restaurant operators to contact all those people celebrating anniversaries or engagements by using the names from the Announcements column of the local paper. In general it would appear that direct mail to non-users is less productive than direct mail to promote repurchase.

Face to face contact with a prospective customer gives a salesman a more flexible approach to selling than does direct mail. The message can be tailored to meet the prospect's own particular situation, and the salesman's personality and rapport with the prospect are important influences on the consumer's continuum position. *Personal selling* to increase volume, as distinct from personal selling to increase gross profit contribution (see chapter 4), is mainly limited to banqueting businesses in the United Kingdom. For example, a large hotel in the City of London had substantial banqueting facilities which warranted the appointment of a Banqueting Manager and an Assistant Banqueting Manager. Considerable emphasis was placed on customer contact and regular sales visits were made to existing and potential customers in the City. When a potential customer wrote in enquiring about details of the banqueting facilities and prices, these were duly despatched by return of post. Enquiries were then followed up by a personal visit from one of the managers and as a result a high proportion of enquiries were converted into sales.

Personal selling is expensive in terms of time and sometimes in terms of travel and entertainment costs. However, even the managers of individual restaurants can economically undertake some personal selling activities themselves by inviting key people into the restaurant for a meal – for example, secretaries of local firms' social clubs.

The rapid growth in the production of free local newspapers delivered to all households in a certain area has brought press *advertising* within the reach of most food and beverage businesses. Very often these papers have a specific page for small display advertisements for local restaurants and bars and feature an editorial on one of these establishments each week. This type of local advertising is most useful for communicating product information – location, style, opening hours, price range, etc. – to potential customers so far unaware of these details. It is also used to encourage repurchase, by giving details of special promotions. Advertising on local radio stations is also cost effective for independent operators and, increasingly, food and beverage businesses are taking advantage of this medium to communicate product information to a wide audience.

Advertising in the national press and magazines and on television is largely confined to the large chains, particularly fast food operators. Many large chains appropriate about four per cent of their turnover to advertising and promotion – but the industry average is still less than one per cent! It can be argued that until very recently large-scale advertising has not been necessary in the catering industry as each unit's food, service and atmosphere has been enough to create a distinctive product; in this situation it was only necessary to announce the product and its location. Advertising comes to the fore when competing products are very similar – as is the case with shampoos or catfood, for example. Currently the large chain restaurant businesses are mainly concerned with service, decor and cleanliness. However, competition for high street sites has resulted in very similar catering products being located extremely near to each other in competition for the same market. Consequently, advertising is becoming essential to ensure that consumers have a reason to consistently choose one chain in preference to another.

An investigation of television advertising shows that this medium is limited to the large operators – Kentucky Fried Chicken, Berni's, Wimpy, Burger King, McDonald's and Pizza Hut – and that the amount spent on such advertising varies from £500,000 to £5,000,000. Television advertising is also concentrated on certain areas, with a great proportion directed towards viewers in London and the south-east.[5]

Advertising is not a cheap resource and its use should be carefully planned and controlled. Walsh and Hart-Davies[6] recommend the following steps:
- set out your business objectives and then define how advertising is going to contribute to their achievement.
- decide the response that you want to achieve from your audience.
- concentrate on developing a relevant, competitive proposition; then develop the campaign.
- pay attention to the 'image' created by the advertising, as well as the factual content.

Earlier in this chapter the need to measure advertising effectiveness was discussed. It is important to realise that advertising works on a cumulative basis, and to create a successful campaign – such as 'The greatest burger under the bun' – takes continuity and consistency.

Finally, we have discussed advertising as a method of generating volume, recognising also that advertising is an important method of adding value to a product that can be reflected in higher prices and margins – although this has not been the main theme.

SUMMARY

This chapter has shown how the market continuum model provides a useful tool for the diagnosis of volume improvement problems. It is important to remember that depending on the prevalent continuum position – for instance, unawareness or repurchase – various tools for increasing volume will become more or less appropriate. An analysis of the competition is essential to any plans to improve volume, even in the captive or semi-captive market situations such as catering in offices or factories, or at railway stations. Here the consumer does have other choices – to bring their own food, to go to the pub down the road, or to go without. For this type of customer approaches such as personal recommendation and the use of specific in-house promotional material will be most effective.

The need for improving volume has been examined, and the techniques discussed which can help in particular business situations to achieve improvement. Much of the discussion has centred on recent trends in the catering industry, but how will market conditions during the 1990s affect sales volume? The industry is probably on the rising side of an investment cycle and some commentators[7] believe that the growth in the eating-out market does not warrant the level of current and planned investment. The 1990s may well be characterised by increasing competition and subsequent business failure. Under these circumstances, identifying when and how to increase volume will be crucial to survival.

REFERENCES

1. Jenkins, J. R. G., *Marketing and Consumer Behaviour*, Pergamon Press, 1972.
2. Clark, E., 'Berni's Bullish New Stake', *Marketing*, pp. 23–27, 6 January 1982.
3. National Restaurant Association, Consumer behaviour in the foodservice marketplace, in Wyckoff, D. and Sasser, W., *The Chain Restaurant Industry*, Lexington Books, 1978.
4. Boote, A. S., 'Market segmentation by personal values and salient product attributes', *Journal of Advertising Research*, vol. 21, no. 1, pp. 29–35.
5. Walsh, B. and Hart-Davis, M., 'Advertising: not a cost centre but a profit centre', *Fast Food*, pp. 28–32, April 1983.
6. Walsh, B. and Hart-Davis, M., *op. cit.*
7. Brady, J., 'The fast food feast', *Management Today*, pp. 58–65, April 1985.

4

Maximising Gross Profit Contributions

OBJECTIVES

Discuss the usefulness of gross profit contribution as a measure of food-service effectiveness . . . identify the alternative strategies open to catering managers who wish to increase gross profit contribution . . . select a particular strategy for dealing with a particular business problem.

INTRODUCTION

A one per cent change does not sound impossible for a manager to achieve, but it is easy to forget how significant one per cent changes can be to the performance of a catering business. Consider the manager who increases average spend by one per cent, increases prices by one per cent, improves gross profit by one per cent through manipulating the sales mix and reduces food cost by one per cent through recipe revisions! Does our one per cent manager merit a one per cent pay rise?

Table 4.1 *The effects of one per cent improvements.*

	Original	Price increase	Sales increase	Sales mix	Food costs
No. of covers	100				
Average spend	£5.00	+£0.05	+£0.05		
Total sales	£500.00	+£5.00	+£5.00		
Food cost (%)	35			−.1	−1
Food cost	£175.00		+£1.75	−£5.00	−£5.00
Gross profit	£325.00	+£5.00	+£3.75	+£5.00	+£5.00

As table 4.1 shows a manager who can achieve a one per cent improvement in average spend, prices, sales mix and food costs can increase gross profit by almost 6 per cent, without an additional customer setting foot in the door. In our opinion this merits more than a one per cent salary increase!

Chapter 3 examined how managers could increase the volume of a catering business. This chapter focuses on achieving the maximum profit contribution from every customer and, as the above example shows, there is plenty of potential for doing this, even in the most tightly run of businesses.

It should be stressed that this chapter has a much wider scope than merely increasing sales – in fact, managers can often increase gross profit contribution whilst revenue remains the same, or even decreases. For example, a vending machine might sell hot chocolate and coffee, each at £0.18. However, the portion cost of the hot chocolate may be £0.05, whereas the portion cost of the coffee may be £0.04. To increase profit contribution, many caterers would only think in terms of increasing the selling price or reducing the portion cost. An alternative strategy is to shift consumers' preference from chocolate towards coffee, which has a greater margin. The important management skill is the ability to analyse and evaluate the business in order to select the most appropriate strategy for increasing gross profit contribution. Broadly speaking, these strategies involve influencing consumer preference, either by merchandising, by personal selling techniques, or by manipulating the price or cost of the product.

MEASURING GROSS PROFIT PERFORMANCE

There is a general belief that most catering businesses operate on a fixed gross profit margin for all their products. In practice this is not true, because the cost of the product fluctuates, the price may be modified in the light of competition, the production may be modified due to a change in personnel and so on. The result is that there are different selling prices, different portion costs and different profit margins. Caterers know and recognise this complexity which is why most operators rely on an average gross profit return to measure 'success'. The Carriages Restaurant case example illustrates the shortfalls of this particular performance measure.

Choosing the right measure of performance is paramount to effective management. For the key result area of improving gross profit contribution we believe that the best single measure of performance is *cash gross profit per cover*. This is calculated by dividing the total cash gross profit of the business by the number of covers served in a period:

$$\text{Cash Gross Profit/Cover} = \frac{\text{Total Cash Gross Profit}}{\text{No. of Covers}}$$

Case example 4.1   Carriages Restaurant

The proprietor of a small cafe on the east coast is comparing the operating results of two successive weeks. During the first week he ran the restaurant himself, but during the second week his wife was in charge. During the second week, volume dropped because of poor weather. *Who was more effective at generating the most profit from each customer?*

	Week 1	Week 2
Number of covers	1000	900
Average spend	£3.00	£3.10
Total sales	£3,000	£2,790
Food cost	£990	£949

Gross profit per cover for this example is calculated as follows:

	Week 1	Week 2
Gross profit	£2,010	£1,841
Gross profit per cover	£2.01	£2.03
Gross profit percentage	67	66

It appears that the cafe proprietor should consider letting his wife plan the menus and take the orders, because, although volume had dropped during the second week, she had succeeded in achieving more profit contribution from each of the customers who entered the cafe. Note also that the gross profit percentage – which is the traditional tool used to measure management performance in food and beverage businesses – is not in fact a suitable indicator of profit improvement in this case. The reduction in gross profit percentage may have been caused by a wide range of factors, including efficiency, purchase prices, and sales mix changes. As gross profit percentage is such a 'wide' measure of performance, the use of *cash gross profit per cover* is to be advocated as a measure of improved profit contribution. The control of material costs will be addressed separately in chapter 10.

The activities which managers can use to improve gross profit per cover include making selective price changes, increasing average spend through personal selling and merchandising, and manipulating the sales mix through promotion and pricing. The other central aspect of reducing portion costs by recipe development and cost control is touched on in this chapter, but is fully expounded in chapter 9. The first subjects for consideration here are the techniques which are available to enable managers to evaluate the current profit contributions made by menu items and to plan the action required to increase gross profit per cover. These techniques form a group which has developed over recent years and is known as Menu Analysis.

MENU ANALYSIS

The starting point for any manager attempting to improve the gross profit per cover, is an analysis of the current menu items – their popularity, selling prices, portion costs and gross profit contributions. The purpose of such an analysis is to identify those dishes which should be promoted, those which should be repriced, those which should be eliminated or replaced, and those which should be retained. There are a number of different analysis techniques available and they are discussed and evaluated by Hayes and Huffman in *The Cornell Quarterly*.[1] All of these analyses rely on using readily available data for each dish – the number sold, the selling price and the portion cost.

An analysis of the number of each item sold can be obtained as a regular printout from point-of-sale equipment, but if necessary an occasional manual analysis of restaurant bills or waiters' dockets can provide the same information. Each customer will select several items from a menu, and managers are not merely interested in the overall mix of items, but also in the specific per customer sales of starters, desserts, drinks and side orders.

A sales mix does not provide this analysis and a slightly more sophisticated calculation pays dividends. The presentation of this data as a Menu Popularity Index, which shows out of 100 customers how many will select a particular item, as shown in table 4.2 is to be advocated.

The Menu Popularity Index is standardised on one hundred covers and allows easy comparison of one period with another. More important, in this example, it highlights that five customers out of every hundred do not buy dessert and 13 do not buy a starter – clearly indicating the areas for potential additional sales.

The second stage of menu analysis (see table 4.3) is to calculate the 'portion contribution margin' for each of the items. This is done by calculating the standard portion cost (using a costing sheet) and deducting this from the selling price (exclusive of VAT).

Table 4.2   *An example popularity index (based on a sales mix of 200 customers).*

	Sales mix	Menu popularity index
Starters		
Paté Maison	80	40
Soup of the Day	30	15
Prawn Cocktail	64	32
Total Starters	174	87
Main courses		
Sirloin Steak	100	50
Rump Steak	40	20
Fillet Steak	60	30
Total Main Courses	200	100
Desserts		
Apple Pie	90	45
Ice Cream	40	20
Cheese Board	40	20
Total Desserts	170	85

Table 4.3   *Menu contribution margins*

	Price (inc) £	Price (exc) £	Cost £	Contribution margin £	Contribution margin %
Paté Maison	1.10	0.96	0.44	0.52	54
Soup of the Day	0.90	0.78	0.24	0.54	69
Prawn Cocktail	1.60	1.39	0.67	0.72	52
Sirloin Steak	3.90	3.39	1.05	2.34	69
Rump Steak	4.20	3.65	1.25	2.40	66
Fillet Steak	5.40	4.69	1.78	2.91	62
Apple Pie	0.80	0.70	0.24	0.46	66
Ice Cream	0.80	0.70	0.20	0.50	71
Cheese Board	1.00	0.87	0.39	0.48	55

Many caterers, particularly managers whose performance is measured by a gross profit percentage, would respond to this question by suggesting that those items with the highest gross profit margin percentage – soup, sirloin steak and ice cream in this case – are the best to promote. Others, such as the waiter whose service charge or tip is usually determined by a percentage of the total bill, might suggest the highest priced items – the prawn cocktail, fillet steak and cheese. The best policy would actually be to promote those items with the largest cash gross profit margin – the prawn cocktail, the fillet steak and the ice cream. The next best alternatives are the soup, sirloin steak and the apple pie. The third step in menu analysis is to determine what proportion of sales and of gross profit comes from each item. This is done by extending the menu popularity index as shown in table 4.4. The table shows the amount contributed to gross profit per 100 covers by each of the dishes on the menu. For the base of 100 covers, it can be seen that the average spend is £540.68 per 100 covers or £5.41 per cover, and the average gross profit per cover is £3.45. The suggestion has already been

Table 4.4 *Menu profitability analysis.*

	Menu popu-larity index	Selling price (inc. VAT)	Total sales (exc. VAT)	Margin	Gross profit
Paté Maison	40	1.10	38.26	0.52	20.80
Soup of the Day	15	0.90	11.74	0.54	8.10
Prawn Cocktail	32	1.60	44.52	0.72	23.04
Total Starters	87		94.52		51.94
Sirloin Steak	50	3.90	169.65	2.34	117.00
Rump Steak	20	4.20	73.04	2.30	48.00
Fillet Steak	30	5.40	140.87	2.91	87.60
Total Main Courses	100		383.56		252.60
Apple Pie	45	0.80	31.30	0.46	20.70
Ice Cream	20	0.80	13.91	0.50	10.01
Cheese Board	20	1.00	17.39	0.48	9.60
Total Desserts	95		62.60		40.30
TOTAL			540.68		344.84

made that gross profit per cover is the best measure of menu efficiency and it is advisable for a business to recalculate this measure every four weeks in order to assess how effective management has been in improving this key result area.

Note that for this sales mix the sales should be £540.68 per 100 covers. The food cost (sales less gross profit) should be £195.84 per 100 covers. Given this data the food cost should be 36 per cent of sales, assuming that all standards are achieved. This ideal measure is called the *potential food cost percentage* which is an important measure of food cost control. This will be returned to in chapter 10.

Returning to gross profit improvement, different approaches for improving profitability are appropriate for each dish depending on its gross profit margin (£ and %), its share of total sales (£ and sales mix) and its share of total gross profit. A summary of menu analysis findings and recommendations for action is shown in figure 4.1.

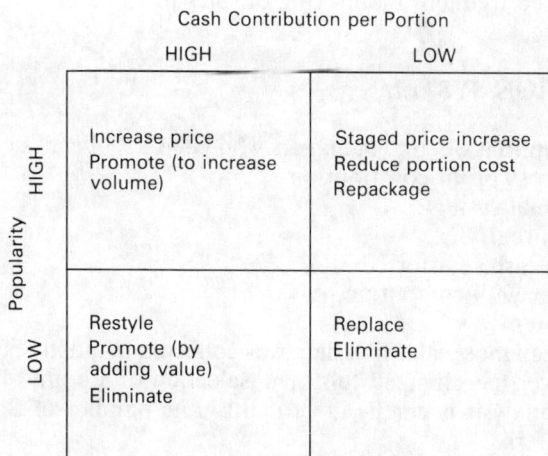

Figure 4.1 *Menu analysis.*

Menu items which are high in both popularity and cash contribution are the most significant in terms of total profitability. The quality, portion size and presentation of these items is of prime importance, and they should be monitored and controlled with great care. The prices of these popular and profitable dishes should be carefully reviewed. The most popular dishes may be price-inelastic – in other words you may be able to increase the price with little lessening of demand. These dishes should be a feature in personal selling routines and other forms of internal promotion, and should be given a prominent position on the menu.

Menu items which are high in popularity but relatively low in cash contribution may also be significant in terms of total profitability because of the high number of dishes sold. Such dishes are often perceived as very good value for money by consumers as there is comparatively little difference between the cost of the materials used and the selling price of the dish. This also tends to result in price-elasticity, and increases in price can bring about a drop in demand. Price reviews for these items need to be conducted with care, and some experts recommend that a staged price increase is more appropriate here.[2] Attempts to increase the margin of these dishes by reductions in portion cost (by imperceptibly changing recipe or portion size) can often be achieved without loss of popularity. The contribution from these items can also be increased by packaging them with other items, such as vegetables, desserts or drinks.

Menu items which are low in popularity and low in contribution should be eliminated from the menu, if possible. Often they are items which are retained because of unquestioned tradition, or because of the requirements of one or two influential customers. Removing these items should shift demand towards more popular and more profitable menu choices. There may be hidden costs associated with these items because of the stockholding and wastage necessary to maintain availability. If for any reason it is necessary to retain such items the price should be increased and the portion cost reduced in an attempt to increase contribution.

Menu items which are low in popularity but have a high margin have the potential for making an impact on profits. Sometimes renaming them, or featuring them in special promotions can help. Sometimes the best approach is to remove them from the menu, particularly if the item requires a lot of preparation or adds to stockholding costs.

To be successful, menu analysis must be undertaken about every three months – and this necessitates the frequent monitoring of sales mix data.

SALES INFORMATION SYSTEMS

There are five broad options open to managers who need to collect sales mix data, as a basis for increasing gross profit contribution:
- using a totally manual system.
- using a simple cash register.
- using an electronic cash register (ECR).
- using a cash register with computing power.
- using computer systems.

Up until ten years ago most sales mix data was collected manually but the advent of cheap computing power has changed this. The selection of a point-of-sale system to undertake sales mix analysis is chiefly governed by the number of registers which a particular machine offers.

Simple cash registers provide a safe place to put money, issue customer receipts, analyse VAT and keep a record of transactions. They may provide a few sales analysis registers (one for food and one for drink for example) but are otherwise limited to these few simple functions. They cost about £600 (in 1986) and do not provide any useful assistance in sales mix analysis.

Electronic Cash Registers can generally be purchased for around £1 000 (1986 prices). ECRs collect, store and report sales data and assist in cash and sales control. Sales are either entered by pressing pre-set keys (one key for chilli and one for fruit salad) or, as a less preferable alternative, by entering a Price Look Up (PLU) number (345 for chilli and 201 for fruit salad). Either mechanism will retrieve the stored price for that item and will increase the register total for that item. This type of point-of-sale system forms an ideal basis for sales mix analysis. The calculation of portion costs and the extension of the sales mix to give gross profit contributions has to be done manually in almost all cases at present.

Cash Registers with computing power will provide the same cash and sales control as an ECR but will also process that information to give inventory control and possibly control of wages and other costs. Purchase prices start at around £1 800. Machines like this have the potential to calculate the profitability of a day's sales mix at the touch of a button.

The three options described above are termed 'point-of-sale systems'. In addition a firm may use computers to run business management systems in the areas of accounting, purchasing, payroll and control of maintenance and personnel activities. These computer systems may be linked to remote point-of-sale terminals to give an integrated system for controlling a large part if not all of the business activities. Purchase prices of computer systems range from £3 000 to £60 000.

All the prices quoted in this section relate to 1986 prices.

PRICE POLICY AND REVIEW

There are two distinct aspects of price determination. Managers have to determine an initial set of prices – either for starting a new business or for completely revising a menu. In addition, managers have to revise existing prices, in order to recover cost increases, increase volume or counteract the competition. There are several different approaches which are commonly used for new business pricing in the catering industry, and these all have different advantages and disadvantages when used in a particular situation.

Mechanical approaches

There are three main mechanical approaches to the initial establishment of price. All of these methods add a certain amount to the portion cost. Firstly, price can be calculated on the basis of cost plus an appropriate margin to give a predetermined gross profit percentage. This can be done using the same percentage on every dish (for example, 65 per cent), or the same percentage for each group of dishes – for example, starters 75 per cent, vegetables 80 per cent, etc. – which should achieve, based on a forecast sales mix, a target gross profit percentage for all sales. In non-profit catering businesses the amount added on may be negligible so that dishes are effectively sold at cost price. A second approach is to base the determination of prices on a ratio of price to cost; for instance starters might be 4:1, main courses 2:1 and so on. Finally, price can be determined by adding a fixed amount of cash (for example, £1.00) to the portion cost of each dish, or differing amounts to each group of dishes (for example, £0.60 to starters, £2.00 to main courses). Whatever approach is taken to initial pricing, the manager needs to consider the effect that a particular method will have on a consumer's perception of the value of the dish, the attainment of necessary profit targets and the ease of use of the method. In addition to these three mechanical methods, some organisations, particularly in the commercial sector, use pricing methods based on managerial judgement. In practice, this means either charging what they think the market will bear, pricing at or below competitors' prices or following the price of the market leader. For instance, the first Happy Eater units under-priced Little Chef by £0.05 on key products until they had established their own market position.[3]

Most catering textbooks focus on the techniques used for new business pricing. Here the main concern is with what managers have to do in order to reprice items on an existing menu. Repricing becomes necessary for a number of reasons:
- as a tactical tool to maximise gross profit contributions, as previously discussed.
- as a method of recovering food or drink cost inflation.
- as a method of recovering other cost increases.

There is a general law of economics that tells us that the higher is the price, the lower is the quantity sold. Imagine that you are selling toffee apples at a fête; the selling price you choose will influence the quantity you sell. From previous experience you may estimate that you could sell 80 at £0.30 each, or alternatively 300 at £0.10, or alternatively 20 at £0.50. Dropping the price below £0.10 will produce few additional sales because of the limited number of people who like toffee apples, and increasing the price above £0.50 will quickly bring the sales down to nil. The optimum price depends on the cost of each toffee apple – in this case £0.09. Now the gross profit made at each price can be calculated, as shown in table 4.5.

Table 4.5   *Effects of price, volume and costs.*

	£0.10	£0.30	£0.50
Selling Price (£)			
Number sold	300	80	20
Total sales (£)	£30.00	£24.00	£10.00
Cost of sales (£)	£27.00	£7.20	£1.80
Gross Profit (£)	£3.00	£16.80	£8.20

In this imaginary example, there is no clear relationship between price and profits – and the same holds true in the catering industry. There are no easy ways to predict the volume which will be generated in response to a particular price change, and planning the price structure in order to achieve the optimum profitability is one of management's most challenging tasks.

Managers need to study the shifts in sales mix which follow a price review, and look carefully at the sensitivity of different items to price changes.

Table 4.6 continues the previous example by showing the sales mix before and after the most recent price review. Examining the effect of these price changes, the following comments are in order. The previous calculation, following the price review, showed that the average gross profit per cover was £3.45. If, for example, the average gross profit per cover was £3.26 before the price review *and* there had been no significant volume drop, then overall the price review would have been successful. As far as individual items are concerned there have been different reactions to the price increases. The number of starters has fallen slightly, with soup proving particularly sensitive. This is not too worrying as soup is a poor cash gross profit contributor in any

Table 4.6   *Effects of price review.*

Item	Previous selling price £	Previous number sold	Current selling price £	Current number sold
Paté Maison	1.05	38	1.10	40
Soup of the Day	0.60	20	0.90	15
Prawn Cocktail	1.50	32	1.60	32
Sirloin Steak	3.75	45	3.90	50
Rump Steak	3.95	30	4.20	20
Fillet Steak	5.20	25	5.40	30
Apple Pie	0.80	45	0.80	45
Ice Cream	0.80	22	0.80	20
Cheeseboard	0.80	25	1.00	20

case. It is encouraging that despite a price increase the sales of the other two starters have not fallen. A possible explanation is that consumers previously identified the price of soup with the £0.50 benchmark and paté at around £1.00 – but after the price review they were both identified at around £1.00. As far as main courses are concerned, the most significant factor appears to be rump steak going through the £4.00 threshold which has shifted sales equally towards the fillet and sirloin steaks. For the sweets no change in price was made, but perhaps the slight decline in sales is due to the overall level of price increase.

Let us consider the effect on sales mix we anticipate the following price changes to have:
(a) Sirloin Steak increased by £0.05
(b) Sirloin Steak increased by £0.15
(c) Apple Pie decreased by £0.20 *and* cheeseboard increased by £0.20
Option (a) – sirloin up by £0.05 – would have little or no effect on volume, whereas option (b) – a £0.15 increase – would take the product through the £4.00 barrier. This could lead to a shift from the sirloin to the rump which, having a poorer gross profit contribution, would lead to a decline in profitability. It is important to remember that moving the lowest priced main course through the £4.00 barrier may have an effect on total volume, especially if competitors price below this level. In the case of option (c) the proposed change is likely to increase the sales of apple pie at the expense of cheese sales. Given the relative margins of these items this will not have a dramatic effect on profitability, but as more customers may choose to have a sweet it is possible that the overall perception of value – and hence the volume – may improve.

There are no ready-made solutions to pricing problems. Each manager needs to assess the effects of price changes in his or her own business and monitor the tactics of the competition. Careful records can provide the data to make more informed decisions, but managers also need to judge the consumer's perception of the price and value of the product.

PERSONAL SELLING

Imagine a customer entering a fast-food store. She reads the illuminated display board above the sales counter whilst waiting in the queue. However, before she comes to a firm decision as to what she wants, she finds herself at the head of the queue, conscious of the people waiting behind her. 'Can I have a burger, please?' our customer asks. In situations such as these, customers are particularly susceptible to personal selling techniques. A young counter assistant says 'Is that a quarter pounder?' Rather than cause further delay or confusion, our customer agrees. Almost at once the counter assistant asks 'Would you like some fries to go with that?' Again agreement! Our customer has spent over £2.00, as opposed to her intended purchases of less than £1.00.

The examples given illustrate the two types of personal selling technique. These are *trading up* – that is, persuading the customer to buy a larger size or more expensive line, and *selling on* – that is, persuading the customer to buy an additional item. The choice of a fast food restaurant for the example is no accident as this business relies on gaining the maximum gross profit contribution from each customer who sets foot through the door.

Opportunities for personal selling do not arise by accident. They require careful menu design. A fast food burger menu contains many created opportunities for trading up and selling on:

Burger, Quarter Pounder, Half Pounder
Regular Fries, Large Fries
Regular Coke, Large Coke

Whatever a customer initially asks for, opportunities exist for increasing the sale.

However well the menu is designed selling still depends on the skill and motivation of the employees. One of the critical factors appears to be how employees perceive their jobs; if they see their main objective as serving food then this is likely to limit the effort they put into sales promotion. Developing the right attitude – that salesmanship is the primary function of food-service staff – depends on good selection in the first instance, and subsequently on good training and supervision. The My Kinda Town restaurant chain has a particularly effective approach to personal selling. Employees are selected for their appearance and interpersonal skills – food-service experience is not considered of great importance. Sales and service procedures are laid down in a manual and employees are taught the house style of service and how to sell at each stage of the meal. The unit managers carefully monitor staff performance during each meal period and then give staff feedback on performance, highlighting missed selling opportunities.

Although My Kinda Town achieve very effective selling skills from their staff other businesses have adopted the same approach with less success. The problem with this intensive behavioural sales skills training is that some employees will adopt this as a lifeless routine. Social skills and sales skills depend very largely upon sincerity (however this may be motivated), and staff who are told what to say and when to say it without additional incentives will not be fully effective over a long period of time.

In order to motivate staff to sell effectively, many operators have adopted incentive programmes. This has been facilitated by the growing sophistication of point-of-sale systems. Employees need to be convinced that the rewards they obtain are linked to performance, and this usually means being able to identify the sales mix achieved by each individual employee. As an example, consider the employees working in a steak restaurant who each key into an electronic cash register in order to obtain a customer's bill. The service charge of 10 per cent is distributed among the staff in proportion to their sales. What effect does this scheme have on the behaviour of the employees? We would suggest that there will be a tendency for employees to try and steer the 'best spenders' to their own station, serve them as quickly as possible and not worry too much about increasing average spend or selling the most profitable items. Of course, it is relatively easy to achieve an average spend of say £6.00 and this will bring a commission of £0.60. However, is it worth the employees' effort to increase the spend to £6.50 when this will only bring another £0.05 in commission? This type of *direct commission* is unlikely to produce an increase in average spend and there is a real risk of losing repeat business.

In fast food stores a similar scheme operates, whereby the sales per hour for each employee are monitored and the top performer earns a bonus. This *inter-employee competitive bonus* has the effect of stimulating rapid service, which is of course desirable in this instance, and it further encourages the employees to use personal selling techniques to increase average spend. In other types of catering business it may be undesirable to encourage rapid service; furthermore, the competitive nature of the incentive may adversely affect teamwork.

Another approach is to use an *inter-unit competitive bonus* as Travellers-Fare have done. Cash prizes or vouchers for chain stores are awarded to employees of the unit which succeeds in achieving the biggest percentage increase over the previous year's sales during a specified week. The week selected is generally a notorious slack period or one immediately following a price increase. In this case, teamwork and in-house co-operation are fostered and this incentive scheme has been shown to achieve cost effective profit improvements.

Such inter-unit competitions are suitable for large groups, but what can the managers of small catering businesses do to provide a sales incentive? The best tactic in this situation is to provide an incentive that will encourage employees to increase the average spend. For example, if a restaurant achieves an average spend of £5.00, employees whose weekly average spend meets the norm for the restaurant of £5.00 should be paid a low commission rate, say one per cent or £0.05 per cover. When an employee succeeds in raising their average spend to £5.50, they merit a higher commission rate of two per cent or £0.11 per cover. A further increase to £6.00 merits four per cent or £0.24 per cover. This type of *incremental commission scheme* recognises that employees have to put considerable effort into increasing average spend and rewards them accordingly. From the employers' point of view it is only necessary to reward achievements and if no increase in average spend is achieved then no payment is made. Consequently a well-designed incremental commission scheme can be entirely self-financing.

The success of personal selling will depend very largely upon the effective nature of supervisors and management. A well-designed menu, well-trained employees and a good incentive scheme will only produce profit improvement if supervisors set good examples, develop employees' sales skills and provide encouragement.

MERCHANDISING

The role of sales promotion and advertising as tools for increasing volume has already been discussed. Here the concern is with selling to the customer once they have walked through the front door. Merchandising is influencing the customers' purchasing behaviour, at the point-of-sale. In practice this involves the use of menus, tent cards, light boxes, wall posters, displays of food and drink (such as buffets, self-service counters and trolleys) and other types of display material.

Merchandising material will only be effective if it influences purchase behaviour towards buying more profitable items. Many people organise a Beaujolais Nouveau promotion in November – but if it merely shifts sales from other more profitable wines, it does nothing to improve average gross profit per cover. (It is accepted that promotions such as Beaujolais Nouveau may have the effect of stimulating interest and generating volume, but they should be planned with specific marketing objectives in mind.) So, where a choice of several items exists, those items which contribute most to gross profit should be merchandised.

Secondly, where purchase of additional items is possible – for example, side orders of vegetables, liqueur coffees or apéritifs – these should be merchandised. This merchandising has to be co-ordinated with personal selling activities so that the employees and the printed material reinforce the same message.

Finally, merchandising can be a costly activity, particularly where custom produced colour printing is involved. Of course the merchandising promotion must generate more contribution to profit than the cost of producing the promotional material. This sounds obvious but it is easy to allow over-enthusiasm to get the better of pragmatism!

SUMMARY

Increasing the average gross profit per cover requires all the professional caterer's skills of menu design, pricing, staff selection and training, design of incentive schemes, recipe formulation and merchandising and sales techniques. Approached systematically it is possible to produce substantial improvements in even the best managed of businesses.

Several different tools have been examined which may be used for increasing gross profit contribution. The most important of these are menu analysis, personal selling and merchandising, and price determination and review. One further tactic for increasing gross profit contribution is by reducing the portion cost. In our section on menu analysis we suggested that this was particularly suitable for low margin/high popularity items – but of course this needs to be done in a way that will not detract from the item's popularity. There are four methods of reducing portion costs. Firstly, a cheaper commodity can be substituted for a more expensive one in a recipe. Secondly, by reducing the quantity of a commodity which is used in a recipe. Thirdly, by purchasing more effectively, and fourthly, by reducing over-production, wastage and pilferage. These topics will be examined in chapters 5 and 9.

Managers who wish to improve the gross profit per cover of their business, irrespective of the orientation of their business, will start by analysing the exact nature of the problem. Menu analysis is the diagnostic tool which is most suitable for this purpose. Its use is becoming increasingly widespread in all sectors of the catering industry and the first computer programs for menu analysis have now appeared.[6] Following the diagnosis using menu analysis various remedial actions may be necessary. In practice, the choice of approach may be restricted by a variety of factors such as the size and scale of operation, industry sector, level of market orientation and cost structure. For instance, in the hospital sector, cost reduction will be the most frequently adopted approach to patient feeding. In strongly branded chain restaurants, the unit manager is unlikely to be able to review price or reduce material costs (although this will of course be done at corporate level) and so action will focus on personal selling and effective merchandising. It is only the independent commercial operator who will be able to utilise all of these tools.

REFERENCES

1. Kasavana, M., *Computer Systems for Foodservice Operations*, Van Nostrand Reinhold, 1984.

2. Hayes, D. K., and Huffman, L., 'Menu analysis: a better way', *Cornell HRA Quarterly*, February 1985.
3. Jones, P. L. M., *Food Service Operations*, Holt, Rinehart and Winston, 1983.
4. Docker, J., *High Tech High Touch*, UB Ltd, 1985.
5. Rogers, A., 'Price formation in hotels', *HCIMA Review* no. 4, 1976.
6. Kasavana, M., *op. cit.*

5

Controlling Product Quality

OBJECTIVES

Identify the characteristics of 'quality' . . . identify the factors that influence product quality management . . . analyse product quality control procedures . . . analyse and correct poor quality performance.

INTRODUCTION

There is no doubt that quality in the catering industry is an important issue. Many organisations overtly use this word frequently in their advertising and promotion, McDonald's and Kentucky Fried Chicken for instance. Indeed a major advertising campaign by Burger King was based on their belief that '[McDonald's] have always been vulnerable on product quality . . . and that's a terrible vulnerability for a number-one company'.[1] More recently large hotel chains have instituted quality programmes, such as Ladbroke Hotels' Quality '85 campaign.

Quality is important in the catering industry due to a combination of factors, some have always existed and some are more recent trends. Any industry that markets a product in a highly competitive market, competing for the consumer's disposable income, needs to be aware of quality issues. Since quality relates to consumer's needs and expectations, the standards adopted by the industry are mostly established by its customers. In the 1950s and 1960s, the standard of catering was said by many to be relatively low, so much so that in 1967 Derek Cooper wrote his book the 'Bad Food Guide'. The improvement in quality standards seen in the UK is a result of the way in which consumers' expectations have changed. There has been a growth in 'consumerism' in general, which has resulted in customers expecting to receive products and services that are acceptable. An example of a successful consumer pressure group is the Campaign for Real Ale (CAMRA), which has had a significant impact on the licensed trade. Consumers' expectations have also been raised by competition from abroad that has introduced products into this country of a higher standard than those previously offered. This is particularly true of fast food, where McDonald's have completely revolutionised popular catering on Britain's high streets. Companies have also been able to produce higher quality products because technology has developed that assists them to do so. In the catering industry much of this is derived from advances in food technology that have resulted in higher quality raw materials. Today British consumers have also travelled more widely than ever before, due to package holidays and cheaper transportation. They have returned from foreign countries with new ideas and standards about food and restaurants now reflected in the types of dishes offered on menus. Finally, catering organisations themselves have fuelled higher quality expectations amongst customers by using the concept of quality as a marketing tool, as identified above.

WHAT IS QUALITY?

Quality has sometimes been confused with 'the best'. Dictionaries define quality as 'the degree or standard of excellence of something', and naturally enough caterers do not wish to think of providing a product that is sub-standard. This is particularly true if caterers tended to have a product-oriented view of their business. The provision of quality is therefore a technical problem. The meal itself is seen as the product, and the problems of quality control are therefore associated with ensuring high and consistent standards. Today, many more caterers are consumer oriented and therefore take a much broader view of quality. The modern concept of quality is 'fitness for purpose'. This shifts the evaluation of quality away from the provider, i.e. the caterer, onto the consumer. Caterers no longer need to provide the best, but the best that the consumer's money can buy. Thus quality is no longer just a technical problem, but a behavioural one too. The caterer has to be aware of the consumer's attitudes and perspectives in order to be able to provide quality.

The definition of quality that we shall adopt is that of the British Standards Institute:

> The totality of features and characteristics product or service that bear on its ability to satisfy a given need.[2]

In the case of the catering industry, we have identified that 'the totality of features' of the catering experience comprises two main elements – the tangible 'product' and the service element (see page 2). Ensuring quality of the product is a technical characteristic that can adopt and adapt methods and ideas used in other manufacturing processes. Quality in this sense is therefore capable of scientific measurement or 'an orderly classification of a product's chemical and physical characteristics'.[3] Service quality management is, however, a different matter. This feature of catering is the least tangible aspect of the experience and relies heavily on consumers' perception. Since this is extremely difficult to measure, other and more innovative ideas are needed in order to ensure consumers' service needs are satisfied. Such ideas tend to be based in the behavioural rather than natural sciences. But it is important to remember that technical controls can be exercised over service attributes, just as behavioural evaluation can be applied to food and drink.

Some experts would no doubt argue that to separate product quality from service quality is the antithesis of quality management as a whole. There are many different approaches to quality, each of which is supported by its own jargon. It is now becoming accepted that for quality to be effectively introduced into an organisation it has to be totally integrated into *all* activities of the firm. This belief originated with the Japanese who took up this idea of 'total quality control' in the 1950s. At the end of the 1960s, Juran a leading expert in this field, recommended that a more apt description of the approach is 'company wide quality control'. Finally, there is the school of thought that believes 'control' is too narrow, and that 'quality management' is more appropriate. Whilst, in 1985, Hart and Casserly advocated that 'total quality management' combines all the elements needed to 'imply that quality is a discipline to be implemented throughout an organisation, and it suggests the complete dedication essential to making a quality programme work'.[4]

Such an organisation-wide approach does appear to lead to the most successful application of quality principles. However, it is important to focus on the practical aspects of how the unit manager, when faced with a 'quality' problem, can put it right. For diagnostic purposes, therefore, this chapter looks at product quality and service quality is considered in chapter 6. This approach also tends to look at the two main attitudes to quality, namely quality *control* and quality *assurance*. Quality control tends to focus on error detection, it seeks to put things right. Quality assurance concentrates on error prevention, in other words it seeks to ensure that things are right in the first place. The origins of quality control procedures lie in manufacturing industry, and hence it is appropriate to look at this with regards to catering production. Quality assurance can be applied to production, but it is of particular relevance to the provision of service, since in providing a service it is very difficult to put things right once they have gone wrong. Therefore, the phrase 'quality control' will be used, for the most part, in this chapter, and 'quality assurance' in the next.

CATERING AS A MANUFACTURING INDUSTRY

In order to understand quality control in the catering industry it is fruitful to examine the evolution of quality concepts in manufacturing industry.

Prior to the development of mass production techniques, craftsmen were the designers and manufacturers of the product, and the only assurance of quality was that the consumer could inspect the goods before purchase. Mass production was made possible by new technologies and for the first time conformity was necessitated, not to meet consumer needs, but simply because the parts of the product had to fit together when finally assembled. In the factories, foremen controlled quality, simply by sorting the batch into good quality, seconds or scrap. Gradually foremen were given more supervisory roles, and inspection was carried out by 'inspectors'. The need for accuracy in this work was significantly increased during the First World War, for munitions that were the wrong calibre or 'dud' meant the difference between life and death. Quality control was so poor at the beginning of the First World War that the government sent its own inspectors into the factories. It was at this time that statistical techniques were used whereby a sample of the batch was tested in order to evaluate the acceptability of the whole batch.

As manufacturing advanced and accuracy of measurement improved, there was less human inspection of the product and a growing reliance on instruments to effect quality control. The increasing sophistication of aero engines and metal airframes which suffered from metal fatigue resulted in an emphasis on prototype development – testing of all component parts rather than just a sample and testing to destruction. There was also a move towards customers giving detailed specifications to their suppliers which covered every detail of the product and requiring the suppliers to demonstrate that they had effective quality control procedures. To eliminate human error and to foster innovation and quality awareness, the Japanese introduced the concept of quality circles. A further reduction in human error is now being made by the use of computers and robots during the manufacturing process.

King[5] has summarised the manufacturing quality control system as follows:
Design quality level;
  Define customer requirements
  • Identify desired quality characteristics

Set product standards;
  Design product to meet standards
  • Drawings
  • Raw product specification
  • Equipment specification
  • Production-line design
Check conformance
  Output
  • Testing
  • Inspecting
  Process
  • Raw product
  • Equipment monitoring
Correct non-standard output
  • Rework or scrap rejects
  • Analyse rejects for cause of failure
  • Adjust production system

Quite clearly there are major differences between catering and manufacturing, although the growth of the technocratic approach, strongly-branded, product-oriented large chains, and complex food-service systems demonstrates that in certain sectors the catering industry has some similarities with manufacturing industry. The major difference between catering and manufacturing is that catering includes the manufacturing process as well as the distribution, sale and service of the product to the consumer – often within the same building. Thus in many respects the catering industry is still in the 'craftsmen era' – the caterer, albeit he has researched his market and designed a product for which he or she hopes there will be demand, presents this product to the consumer, sight unseen, on a take it or leave it basis. In some respects, self-service may be regarded as providing the opportunity for better quality provision. Whereas in a silver-service restaurant, the customer is in the situation described previously, whereby he or she has to take what is placed in front of them, in the cafeteria, the customer can inspect the food and select from a wide range those items which most appeal. Such inspection and selection suggests that, in terms of the evolution of quality control, the cafeteria is further up the evolutionary ladder than the silver-service restaurant.

There are some sectors of the catering industry where closer parallels with manufacturing can be drawn. Contract catering is a sector where the client, representing the consumers, does negotiate prior to a delivery which also includes in its purchase agreement clauses about the quality of provision. As in manufacturing, this may include stipulations about suppliers, types of commodities and standards of provision. This is particularly an issue in those public sector catering operations that are being put out to tender. Here the major opposition to privatisation has focused around the contention that the quality of provision will fall if contracted out. There are, therefore, extremely detailed and complex specifications established prior to tender to ensure that this should not happen.

DEFINING QUALITY STANDARDS FOR THE CATERING INDUSTRY

If it is accepted that quality must satisfy a given need, it is necessary to understand how a consumer judges whether or not a particular restaurant will do this. There are three main criteria:

Availability.   The catering product can only satisfy consumer needs if it is available for purchase when consumers experience this need. This means that not only must the restaurant be open at the right times, but also that it must be located in the right place geographically. For consumers in a hurry for a snack, this means open all day in a high street location; for consumers seeking a special meal experience, this may mean open only in the evenings in some tucked away spot.

Grade.   Consumers naturally compare every experience, or potential experience, with previous experiences. They evaluate situations and create expectations with regards to the 'grade' of experience they wish to receive. For instance, consumers are likely to grade the quality of an up-market expensive restaurant more highly than a middle of the road not-too-expensive operation.

Conformity.   As well as an expectation of the level or grade of product they will receive, customers also expect conformity. That is to say they expect the product to be the same whenever and wherever they experience it. For example, a customer who has used a fast food restaurant in one town will go to the same operator's unit in another town, with the expectation that the experience will be the same as in the original restaurant. If for some reason the experience does not meet these expectations, the operation will be graded down in the consumer's mind, whereas if the experience exceeds expectations, the operation will be upgraded.

Successful quality management is therefore concerned with identifying the grade of provision required by a group of consumers; ensuring the operation conforms with this grade by designing and implementing a quality management system; and operating the unit at a time and place that makes it available to the consumers. The role of market research in identifying consumer wants and how to promote sales through emphasising the most important characteristics of the operation has already been discussed in chapter 3, so the primary concern of this chapter is how to ensure conformity of provision of the food and drink product.

The first stage in quality management is to determine the level of quality that will satisfy the target market. An example of a mismatch was encountered when a large brewing conglomerate developed an innovative restaurant concept for twenty-to-thirty-year olds. The concept was based around American specialities such as chilli con carne, New England king prawns and so on. In keeping with the concept, a featured dish was deep fried potato skins, well known and popular in the United States. Research following their introduction into this country, however, showed that consumers' perceptions of this dish were very unfavourable as potato skins are usually thrown away as waste.

Since food is only one aspect of the total meal experience, there is a tendency to concentrate on those aspects of the operation for which consumer preferences can be easily measured. A great deal of work has been done on interior design, for instance, and the impact that colour and pattern can have is well documented. Food preferences, however, are not easily measured and little or no definitive research has been done. This is due to the complexity of the investigation, lack of methodology available, and the need for collaboration across a wide range of expertise, such as behavioural sciences and physiology. Khan[6] suggests that the main factors influencing a person's choice of food include the intrinsic characteristics of the food such as odour, texture and taste; extrinsic factors such as time of year, state of health, age and sex; personal factors such as emotional level, influence of others and level of expectation; socio-economic factors which relate food choice to income and cultural factors, including religious dietary restrictions.

The caterer's response to all these factors is essentially entrepreneurial. Unable to predict accurately consumers' response to new food ideas, the caterer relies on the collective past experience of the industry to develop the concept, product range and quality level of the food, incorporating any new ideas on a trial and error basis. In effect there is a huge database of possible food products stored in recipe books from around the world. From this database a menu is assembled and modified by the creative flair of the catering team. The selection of which particular items to place on a menu is based on an evaluation of the needs of the market and nature of the planned meal experience. The selection process is almost certainly constrained by cost – both in terms of capital cost, which may restrict the range of equipment available or skill level of the staff employed, and also in terms of producing a meal at a price that ensures value for money for the particular market segment.

As well as selecting specific dishes, the caterer also has to determine the breadth of the product range (the number of dishes on the menu) and the frequency of change to this range. We would suggest that there are three criteria that are the major influences on determining the approach to quality management. The level of *dish complexity, range of dishes* and *frequency of change* strongly influence the production system employed and hence the expertise of food production personnel. Those operations with a narrow product range, relatively simple dishes and fairly stable menu employ relatively unskilled personnel, use technology-based production systems and usually rely on high volume sales output. Quality control procedures reflect this by being procedural, systematised and reliant on measurement by machine rather than human perception. On the other hand, operations with complex dishes, extensive menus that are quite often changed by introducing specials or dishes of the day require highly skilled personnel and flexible food production systems. Such restaurants rely much more heavily on sensory perceptions and value judgements of the personnel in achieving quality standards.

PLANNING PRODUCT QUALITY CONTROL PROCEDURES

The strategic policy of the business is established from market analysis and organisational goals. Within this, there should be a policy statement concerning the quality of provision. This general statement must then be translated into standards of performance. Such standards of performance will range from an unwritten policy established and monitored in person by the owner or manager of the operation, up to highly detailed documentation specifying exactly the quality that is required at each stage of the process. The quality control system will reflect this range too. The owner or manager without written specifications is likely to inspect the finished product at the hot plate on an accept or reject basis, whereas the operation with detailed documentation, often made up into a Standards of Performance Manual, will have specific control procedures to monitor performance at each stage. It is obviously the larger, chain operations that have such manuals. This is illustrated in figure 5.1.

It can be seen from figure 5.1 that the quality of food and drink depends upon the effective control of the products through four main stages of operation: selection and purchase; storage; preparation and processing; holding and service. For each of these stages there are two elements to the control procedures.

Firstly, there is the specification of the exact standards of performance within each stage; secondly, there is the monitoring of performance to see that these standards are achieved. It should be noted that quality cannot be improved at each stage, it can only be maintained or deteriorate. To achieve a high quality meal product, control must be applied to *all* stages of the catering process. The selection of poor quality raw materials will result in a poor quality meal, despite good storage, cooking and

Stage	Control procedure or documentation	How performance is monitored
Food Purchasing	Purchase Specification	Inspection on delivery
		Sampling of bulk deliveries
Storage	Specify storage conditions	Sampling of stored items
	Stock rotation procedure e.g. FIFO	Stock control checks
		Stock write-off procedure
Preparation/ Processing	Controlled issue by requisition	Equipment maintenance
	Standard recipe	Sampling
	Production scheduling	Observation of staff performance
Holding and Service	Specify holding conditions	Equipment checks
	Dish layout specifications	Screening
	Standardised service procedures	Observation of staff performance

Figure 5.1 *Catering quality controls.* Adapted from *The Restaurant – a Place for Quality Control and Product Maintenance.* Jones, P., Major.[8]

handling procedures. Likewise, good quality commodities can be ruined by poor storage conditions, incorrect cooking or mishandling.

In some cases there are control procedures that will apply to all stages which we shall call general standards of quality control. These include the use and practice of safe and hygienic methods, the maintenance of a safe environment, vermin and rodent control and so on (page 118). In other stages, specific techniques and methods are applied in order to ensure quality control, and these will be examined in more detail later in the chapter.

Selection and purchasing

To achieve quality, there are five basic steps to be carried out each associated with the purchasing function.
● Write purchase specifications.
● Appraise suppliers.
● Select supplier.
● Place the order.
● Inspect delivery.
These activities have to be placed in the context of the objectives of the purchasing function, which may not all be attainable at the same time. As well as maintaining quality the operator probably also requires to obtain the lowest possible purchase price, maintain the unit's competitive position, minimise investment, and make sure all commodities and supplies are always available. Our research indicates that the priority order of these five main objectives varies from sector to sector. Managers with purchasing responsibility were asked to choose the most important objective of two pairs of objectives in order to establish their ranking. The results for the hospital sector and the fast food sector were as follows:

Hospital catering management	*Fast food operators*
Maintain quality	Maintain quality
Minimise purchase costs	Maintain competitive position
Assure regular supply	Minimise purchase costs
Minimise investment	Minimise investment
Maintain competitive position	Assure regular supply

Probably every catering organisation uses the concept of *purchase specifications*. In small, owner-operated restaurants these may not always be written down or be formal documents but a preference expressed by the restaurateur for a particular cut of meat or brand of goods. At the other extreme, in large-scale catering based on the bulk supply of commodities, the purchaser specification for one item may be several pages long. Whatever the nature of the specification, the two fundamental points are that it achieves its function of helping to assure quality and it is an appropriate management tool in terms of its sophistication and cost.

The type of information contained on a specification may include
– intended use for the commodity
– name of commodity
– type, grade, brand
– size, weight
– order quantity parameters
– cost parameters
– applicable standards based on legislation or trade practice
– edible yield
– packaging
– inspection procedure on delivery
– supply procedures.

The factors that will vary the style and detail of the specification include company policy, cost of producing specifications, food production system employed, storage facilities available, level of staff skills, nature of menu, style of service in operation, and the competitive nature of the market.

Purchase specifications also quite clearly have purposes other than establishing the quality level of goods to be supplied. In highly complex production processes it is very important to ensure that raw materials match the process, i.e. have fitness for purpose. Indeed, with the growth in the technocratic approach, the use of highly specialised and computerised equipment, the right grade and size of commodities may be crucial. For instance, deep fat fryers that are pre-set and thermostatically controlled, require the correct size and weight of French fries to operate effectively. As well as this, specifications also facilitate the contractual agreements made between suppliers and users, since they should eliminate any misunderstandings. The specification also provides for consistent performance over time, which may be very important in a business such as catering with very high levels of staff turnover. A chain operation in particular can survive such labour problems if its purchase specifications, (indeed all its quality control procedures), are comprehensive, relatively easy to operate and can be monitored by one or two skilled staff. Lastly, purchase specifications are of value in ensuring the lowest cost of supply, since detailed specifications should ensure that the cost difference between competitive tenders is a true cost difference, rather than one based on the supply of a poorer quality commodity.

This is not to suggest that specifications do not also have problems and disadvantages. Firstly, creating specifications is costly since it requires expertise and probably some testing and evaluation to ensure that the specification is going to be of value. Secondly, partly because of the cost and partly because once something is written down it is liable to be accepted without question, specifications can create a rigid perspective of the commodity market. This rigidity may be undesirable for a variety of reasons. It may prevent changes being made to the menu in response to changing consumer tastes; it may continue the supply of a commodity for use in a dish for which it is not the best option; it may ignore food technology developments that make an alternative product available; it may ignore the installation of new kitchen equipment requiring a different commodity specification and it may result in a reluctance to use new or different sources of supply of the commodity. Thirdly, the specifications may have deficiencies in some way that detract from their value. Such deficiencies may arise because the specification is too vague or too detailed. Specifications that are too vague can result in too many suppliers being able to meet the criteria so that supplier selection becomes almost as indiscriminate as picking up a telephone directory; suppliers obtaining a contract for supply over a period of time with inadequate specifications for a commodity which must be paid for during the period of the contract; and thirdly, a vague specification provides no reliable means of assessing the quality of commodities delivered. Specifications that are too rigorous on the other hand may result in no suppliers or only one supplier being able to meet the criteria. This will mean that there is no competitive tender possible; no standards of delivery laid down, limitations on quantity, cost parameters and so on. All these add to the cost of supplying the commodity and hence to the cost to the user of the commodity. Moreover a commodity that is higher in quality than that required by the operation is being purchased at a premium.

The food supply industry quite clearly has a close, even integral, relationship with the catering industry. Changes in the nature of raw materials and the distribution of these products will therefore have important consequences for the catering manager. There certainly have been changes with regard to raw materials, as was seen in chapter 1, and in the future there are likely to be changes in the sources of supply.

There are many potential sources available to the caterer, ranging from the original producer, through markets and wholesalers, to retail outlets. These are examined in chapter 8. When it is practicable, all possible sources should be investigated to identify their ability to provide and deliver regularly the quality of materials specified. Whatever source of supply is the most suitable or available, there is still the question of *selecting the supplier* or suppliers that will provide the right quality at the optimal price. In most cases, certainly in cities and large towns, there are likely to be several wholesale butchers, greengrocers, cash and carry warehouses and so on. It may be desirable to use the minimum number of suppliers, to minimise costs and time, so therefore some sort of selection process is needed in order to determine the nominated suppliers. There are broadly two purchasing policies or buying plans, each with its own approach to supplier selection.

For large organisations, with high-volume purchase requirements, it is usual for suppliers to tender for the supply contract. The catering company draws up detailed specifications of all its commodity requirements and asks suppliers to 'bid' for the contract. This tendering document will also include details of method of delivery, frequency of delivery, accounting procedures, credit arrangements and so on. It is usual, so long as all the suppliers who are asked to tender are deemed to be equally competent and trustworthy, to then select the cheapest quotation. In return the caterer will agree contractually that all supplies for the specific commodities will be purchased from this supplier for a period of time, usually between three months and one year.

The second approach is to select a list of 'nominated' suppliers from whom commodities may be purchased. This buying plan is more flexible than contracted suppliers, and allows the caterer some choice as to which supplier to use. This means that commodity prices are likely to be more volatile, since the caterer will be paying the market price as opposed to a contract price, but on the other hand the caterer can switch from a poor supplier to a new supplier much more quickly.

The most important factor affecting quality management at this stage in the purchasing process is the *person placing the order* with the supplier. So far, the quality controls have been pre-determined, probably by experts, and are technical in nature, i.e. purchase specifications, supplier selection, tender documents, and so on. However, quality can only be assured if at this stage the person placing the order complies with the system established. This is usually achieved by ensuring all orders for supplies are made in writing using the correct purchase order book. Even when telephone orders are made to suppliers, the procedure necessitates that a supporting, written purchase order is made out. As chapter 10 will show, this documentation also plays an important role in effective cost control.

The final stage in the purchasing process is the receipt of goods and *delivery inspection*. Good receiving procedures are fundamental to quality control. These procedures must be designed to ensure that the following are achieved

- the commodities meet the purchase specifications
  e.g. grade, weight, standard, brand, packaging, etc.
- the delivery agrees with the purchase order
  e.g. time/date of delivery, quantity, price, etc.
- the supply is from a nominated or contracted supplier
  e.g. proper documentation, driver identification, etc.

In order to achieve this, competent personnel equipped with the suitable equipment should be located in appropriate surroundings and provided with the relevant documentation. All too often this is translated by some operators as meaning employing a retired person as a doorkeeper, giving him a spike on which to place all the invoices, a set of broken scales which are never used to weigh supplies and instructions to send back any cases that look damaged or broken. Whilst it is not always possible, because of the physical environment, to have ideal inspection arrangements, it is essential that the caterer creates cost-effective procedures that will ensure the level of quality that is required is actually maintained.

The ideal procedures require personnel, either doorkeepers, storepersons or chefs, who are diligent, honest and knowledgeable about the commodities they will have to receive. Where cost prevents the full-time employment of a person of such calibre, then management must take responsibility for carrying out spot checks of goods delivered to ensure that some sort of quality control is being achieved. Whoever checks deliveries should have available accurate scales to weigh goods, thermometers to check refrigerated and frozen products and tools to facilitate opening for inspection all types of packages and cases. The goods inwards area should be well lit, secure, preferably on the same level as the delivery point from vans or lorries, and located near to the stores area. Finally, the personnel should have copies of all purchase specifications and purchase orders against which to check quality and quantity.

The exact procedure to follow will vary from operation to operation, and commodity to commodity. The minimum level of inspection is likely to be a visual check for any defects, such as split packaging or the presence of insect filth; counting of each item and the weighing of some commodities, particularly meat, fish and fruits and vegetables. More detailed procedures might include the testing of specific attributes of commodities such as syrup density using a refractometer, fat content of minced meat using a fat percentage measuring kit, and sugar content using a hydrometer. It may also be thought appropriate to take samples of some commodities for a more detailed analysis. Such analyses need to be carried out by specialist laboratories and are therefore only likely to be carried out by chain operators purchasing commodities in bulk. The factors that contribute to the procedures established are as follows

- the purpose of inspection to reject or accept delivery.
- the necessity to establish the continued conformity of supply.
- the type of commodity under inspection.
- the size of the order.
- the frequency of delivery.

Storage

Following selection and purchase, raw materials are stored on the premises until needed. The same level of detailed control can be exercised over this stage in the process, in order to ensure that materials are used whilst at their peak of quality. For fresh produce this may be within a few hours of purchase, whereas frozen, canned or dehydrated products' quality will not deteriorate over a period of weeks or even months. To achieve this the storekeeper must ensure that materials are stored under ideal conditions, in which temperature, humidity and light levels are controlled and monitored. Assuming storage areas are correctly designed and maintained, the level of monitoring need not be sophisticated, although recording thermometers and warning signals may be advisable for refrigeration. As well as storage conditions, material must be shelved and stacked correctly to avoid damage or cross-contamination by bacteria or odours. Finally stock rotation procedures, to ensure old stock is used before new, are an integral part of quality control at this point. This is greatly facilitated by the now common use of date coding on most products.

Preparation and production

Just as purchase specifications are designed to maintain raw material quality, so standard recipes are designed to ensure dish quality. They should provide details of both ingredients and method, as illustrated in figure 5.2, in order to ensure a consistent, accurately costed end product. The advantages of standard recipes are very similar to those we identified for purchase specifications (on page 65).

Standard recipes should be supported by effective production scheduling, the provision of the necessary measuring devices, a preventative maintenance programme for equipment, sound on-the-job training, and random monitoring of performance. Testing of the end product may be purely sensory, relying on expertise of skilled personnel to smell and taste the food, or be scientific testing using swabs, contact tape, samplers or rodac plates.

Holding and service

Following production, it is usual for the food to be held in its semi-finished or finished state for a period. In à la carte restaurants this period may be very short; in fast food each prepared item has a specified shelf-life before it is dumped, for instance seven minutes for unbagged French fries; whilst in cook–chill this holding period may be for

CATEGORY – STEWS/CASSEROLES

Card No. 51

DISH – CURRIED LAMB WITH RICE

Portions 100

INGREDIENTS	AMOUNT		UPLIFT		METHOD
	Imperial	Metric	Imperial	Metric	
Diced Shoulder of Lamb	19 lbs	8.5 kgs			Start preparation as for Curry sauce. Add meat to fried onions and cook. Continue as for curry sauce.
Curry Sauce (See Card No. 186)	2 gals	9 lts			Plain boil, wash and drain the rice, reheat the rice in fresh boiling water, drain and place in a hot bain-marie container.
Patna Rice	7½ lbs	3.5 kgs			

STANDARD PORTION – SERVED

	Imperial	Metric
Meat/ Sauce	8 ozs	220 gms
Rice	3 ozs	90 gms

GARNISHES/ACCOMPANIMENTS

Mango Chutney
Coconut

EQUIPMENT FOR SERVICE

½ size deep Bain-Marie container
8 oz. Ladle
Unperforated Serving spoon

COST RECORD

Date ... ...

Price per Portion ... ...

Figure 5.2 *Standard recipe from an industrial catering company.*

a maximum of five days. There is no doubt that it is at this stage that cooked food is most likely to deteriorate or become a health hazard. To avoid this rigid procedures are required, as outlined by the *Guidelines on Pre-Cooked Chilled Foods* issued by the Department of Health and Social Security.

After holding the food is served to the customer. An important aspect of quality is portion size. This can be assured by proper adherence to all the procedures so far mentioned and by reference to a dish layout specification. This may include details of portioning, as well as an illustration of what the dish should look like on the plate. It is at this point that sensory evaluation techniques may be employed to check quality conformity. This is most likely in organisations that have used sensory evaluation in the planning and devising of their dish recipes. There are two broad approaches to sensory evaluation. The first relies on untrained 'consumers' and is used mainly to evaluate consumer acceptance of newly devised menu items. The second relies on a trained testing panel and would be used for initial product development and quality control. In the case of quality control the panel would carry out a series of tests, either discriminating between items or describing their characteristics. A discrimination test is usually applied to recipe modifications and requires panel members, who might well be made up of volunteer consumers, to differentiate between three food samples, one of which is different to the other two. If they are unable to pick out the modified food item, then the modification may be incorporated into the standard recipe for that dish. This type of test may also be used to evaluate the acceptance of a convenience product.

Paté	Ingredients	Portion size	Preparation
	Paté	1/6th of a lb	Place washed leaves of lettuce onto a 6″ plate
	Toast	1½ slices	and put a slice of paté in the middle. Garnish with
	Lettuce	3 leaves	2 slices of tomato and a sprig of parsley as shown
	Tomato	2 slices	in the photograph.
	Parsley	1 sprig	Service and presentation
	Butter	10 grams	Serve hot toast, cut into fingers, with butter.
			Offer pepper mill.

Figure 5.3   *Example of dish layout specification.*

For quality control purposes, however, descriptive tests are the main technique applicable. These examine specific sensory characteristics such as taste, aroma, texture, consistency and so on, and rank these attributes in some way. In typical catering operations this testing is, of course, carried out by the chef, but for a variety of reasons he or she may not be the most suitable person to do this! On the other hand it is unlikely that an operation can afford to employ a sensory analyst on a full-time basis. Thus, most valid testing is only viable when developing new dish items for large-scale operations.

PERFORMANCE FAILURE

So far this chapter has concentrated on technical approaches to quality control, but it must be remembered that the catering industry, compared with many other industries, is labour intensive. Successful performance depends on people. Failure to achieve the desired level of quality is therefore most likely to be caused by human error, since the human being is the most variable 'component' of the majority of systems. This is not necessarily a disadvantage for, as chapter 9 will illustrate, this variability means that employees are able to respond to the wide range of expectations and needs that consumers may have. At the same time this can mean that operatives are almost certainly not able to maintain competely consistent standards of performance.

Their mistakes are potentially of three types, each of which can be remedied in different ways. Firstly, there may be random error. Such error will be infrequent and conform to no consistent pattern. These characteristics make it extremely difficult to analyse and investigate the cause. In any business where there is a high degree of human interaction there will almost inevitably be changes in performance, perhaps because a member of staff is not well, or has personal problems, etc. Management must attempt to identify the reason for poor performance, but accept that if it is random and infrequent there is little that can be done. Secondly, error may be sporadic, that is to say be clearly identifiable as conforming to a pattern but not in evidence all the time. Such errors are often caused by external influences creating circumstances that induce errors – unusually high peaks in demand, a combination of individual staff members who in a team work less effectively together than other combinations of the same staff, and so on. The prevention of this type of error depends on identifying the cause and removing it. Finally, errors may be systematic, that is to say fairly frequent and conforming to a clear pattern. This suggests that there is something fundamentally wrong with the operation and the quality control system.

There are five main factors that will influence human performance. The *environment* in which employees work is influential. In terms of the physical surroundings such as the level of noise and lighting, decor, size of work area have an effect; and also the intangible environment of the worker culture – compatibility between personnel and management/employee relationships. Secondly, the *equipment* provided for achieving the work must be suitable and efficient. Likewise, *job instruction* must be accurate and appropriate, both in terms of training and the level of supervision exercised. Fourthly, *job design* is of importance. This may have physiological effects whereby the job is performed under conditions of discomfort, fatigue, restricted movement, or whatever; and psychological factors associated with the degree of monotony, speed of performance or level of potential criticism. Finally, the nature of the *individual* performing the task will be critical. Their experience, aptitude, intelligence and motivation must conform with the nature of the task being undertaken. All of these factors are examined in more detail in chapter 7, which looks at improving employee performance.

It is usual when there is systematic human error that either one or more of these five factors is the cause. Certainly, errors will continue where any one of these five factors is poorly planned or organised. Excellent recruitment of staff and effective training will not prevent poor quality products if the equipment is defective or inadequate. Likewise, well-planned environments and well-equipped facilities will not in themselves guarantee consistent performance if staff are poorly motivated or unsuited for the work they are given. In attempting to improve performance, technology has often been introduced to reduce human error (as well as for other reasons). This technological response is not without problems however. One large catering organisation experienced this when it began to introduce electronic point-of-sale equipment into its bar operations. The company's experienced bar staff's performance was consistently poorer in terms of stock and revenue control. At first it was assumed that the computerised system had identified errors (and perhaps fiddles) that the older system had not. In fact the EPOS system had induced more errors, simply because the bar staff found it too slow. They were used to adding up the price of a drinks order in their head as they served it and then entering the total on the till. With the EPOS till, each item had to be entered separately and then totalled, which slowed down the service. It also reduced the level of job satisfaction experienced by staff. The company

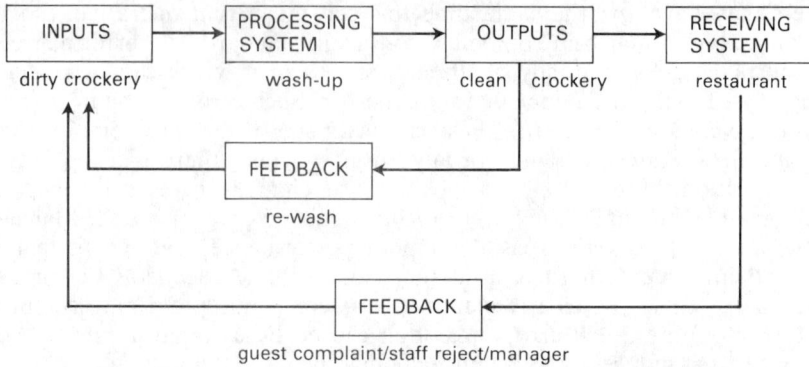

Figure 5.4   *A wash-up systems diagram for quality control analysis.*

found that re-training was not effective, and so has instituted a policy of recruiting and training inexperienced bar staff to work in bars with EPOS systems. In this case they have found that it is advantageous to employ staff who cannot add up.

One approach to analysing the cause of poor quality is to develop a systems diagram of the processing and receiving systems. An example of one particular sub-system is given in figure 5.4. The figure illustrates that there are two possible points at which quality control can be exercised, immediately after processing or at the end-user stage or receiving system. Quite clearly, it is preferable for the control of the processing system to be carried out immediately by the person carrying out the processing. This has the advantage of giving some responsibility to the operative concerned, minimising the risk of poor quality product reaching the customer and allowing for immediate corrective action. If dirty plates reach the restaurant there is the disadvantage of creating tension between wash-up and restaurant staff, or even worse of losing custom.

This diagnostic technique assists the manager in identifying the cause of poor performance. By looking at each sub system and strengthening the feedback loop for each sub system, quality can be enhanced. In the case of the wash-up, poor quality can be caused by environmental factors, particularly the peaking and troughing of demand for the wash-up facility; poor equipment, which may need servicing or replacing; poor procedures, whereby the operative has not been instructed how to differentiate between acceptable and unacceptable standards; poor job design, such as not being given responsibility for quality control or a sense of pride in the work and, finally, the wrong person may have been employed to do the job. This systems approach can be applied to any of the activities of a catering operation, such as stores, cash control, the vegetable section of the kitchen and so on.

SUMMARY

This chapter began by looking at what is meant by quality and the relationship between quality and market orientation in the catering industry. Quality management is an organisation-wide approach to ensuring consumers are provided with a satisfactory product or service. Quality control is post-operational and is applied primarily to the product component of the catering package. Quality assurance is pre-operational and designed to prevent poor performance. Quality itself is based on the consumer's perception and hence the caterer needs to be concerned with providing value for money and popular items to their customers. In particular, quality must be consistent, in the sense that an operation provides a total meal experience and that over a period of time this standard must be maintained. There is no infallible formula for identifying successful concepts, only past experience and flair can be used to establish the right grade of quality. The factors that affect the approach to monitoring this quality are the complexity of the menu items, the range of the menu, and the frequency with which the menu is changed.

It was the conclusion of this chapter that relative to manufacturing industry, the catering industry is not very advanced in its approach to quality control, although the shift to technocratic methods and the growth of large-scale chain operations is narrowing the gap. Part of the reason for this is the cost of implementing a quality control programme in an industry that traditionally is price sensitive, has low margins and employs highly skilled, but individualistic, operatives.

At each stage of the transformation process from raw materials to end product, there are a range of options available to the caterer in order to control quality. During selection and purchase there are purchase specifications and delivery inspection procedures; during storage stock rotation, stock write-off procedures and stockroom regulations play their part; at the production stage standard recipes, production scheduling and measuring equipment help to control quality and finally, at the point-of-service, dish layout specifications and portion control procedures help to ensure the customer receives what he or she is expecting.

Despite these procedures, because of the high level of human input, it is still possible to have performance failure. Chapter 5 explored the reasons for this and suggested that a systematic analysis of the relevant part of the operation would help to identify the nature of the corrective action that needed to be taken.

Finally, it must be emphasised that quality should not be seen as an isolated, separate element of the organisation's policy, but as a fully integrated part of the organisation itself. Quality management is concerned not only with creating procedures, but also an environment in which they are carried out scrupulously and enthusiastically by the staff of the unit. In the next chapter, in looking at quality assurance of the service provision in catering, we examine approaches to creating such an environment.

REFERENCES

1. Hart, C. W. L. and Casserly, G. D., 'Quality: a brand-new, time-tested strategy', *Cornell HRA Quarterly*, pp. 52–63, November 1985.
2. Bentley, T. J., *The Management Services Handbook*, Holt, Rinehart and Winston, 1984.
3. Thorner, M. E. and Manning, P. B., *Quality Control in Foodservice*, AVI Publishing Co. Inc., 1983.
4. Bentley, T. J., *op. cit.*
5. King, C. A., 'Service oriented quality control', *Cornell HRA Quarterly*, pp. 92–98, November 1984.
6. Khan, M. A., 'Factors affecting consumer food preferences and their utilisation in hospitality management' in Pizam, A. *et al.* (Eds.) *The Practice of Hospitality Management*, AVI Publishing Co. Inc., pp. 455–464, 1982.
7. Wyckoff, D. D., 'New Tools for Achieving Service Quality', *Cornell HRA Quarterly*, pp. 78–91, November 1984.
8. Jones, P., 'The restaurant – a place for quality control and product maintenance?' *International Journal of Hospitality Management* vol. 2, no. 2, pp. 93–100, 1983.

6

Assuring the Quality of Service

OBJECTIVES

Analyse problems of service provision . . . identify the cost of quality management . . . compare and contrast alternative approaches to service quality assurance . . . investigate alternative measures of guest satisfaction . . . explain what is meant by 'quality audit'.

INTRODUCTION

In a 1984 survey,[1] three out of five consumers said that what irritated them most about restaurants was poor service, and a 1985 Gallup Poll found that 83 per cent of restaurant customers would not go back to a restaurant if they had received bad service.[2] The last chapter looked at procedures, methods and techniques for ensuring the quality of food and drink. This chapter is concerned with the quality of service. The obvious question to ask is why does service need different techniques to food and drink? As was the subject of discussion in chapter 1, the meal experience is made up of these two components, and it is the service element that provides many of the characteristics of the catering product – intangible, simultaneously produced and consumed, heterogeneous and reliant on consumer contact. Such characteristics create circumstances that product-oriented quality control procedures are unable to deal with, for instance, how does one measure the effectiveness of employee–customer interaction? Any approach to quality management must address itself to these characteristics and the implications that they have for an appropriate procedure.

THE NATURE OF SERVICE

Before going on to examine how to control the service experience, let us look in more depth at what is meant by service. Nightingale[3] has developed a systems diagram of the service system as illustrated in figure 6.1. The diagram illustrates the relationship between how customer satisfaction is achieved from the consumer's point of view and how an organisation attempts to ensure that this takes place by designing the 'right' customer service system. It is assumed that from the customer's viewpoint everyone has their own set of *consumer quality standards*, which are derived from previous experience of the operation or from other service experiences. For the service provider, the design of the *customer service system* is based on reconciling

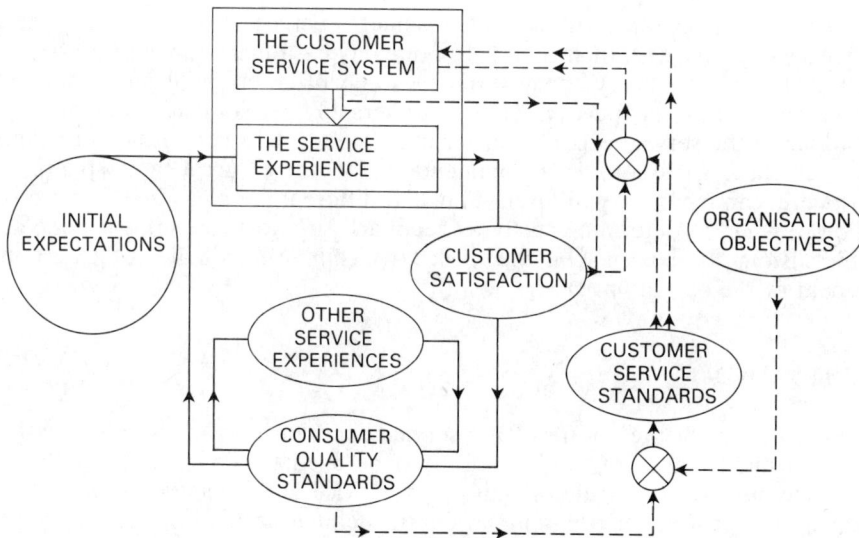

Figure 6.1 *The service system.*

consumers' quality standards and the organisation's objectives. This balancing of the two perspectives results in '*customer service standards*' from which the service system can be designed. The point at which satisfied (or dissatisfied) customers have been served provides the opportunity to modify the service system in the light of customers' reactions. As in the last chapter, quality assurance is a two-stage process concerned with establishing standards and monitoring the system to ensure they are achieved.

PROBLEMS OF ASSESSING QUALITY OF SERVICE

At each point in the service system (see figure 6.1) there are potential problems. These fall broadly into three main areas: the ability and opportunity of management to set the right customer service standards in the first place; the nature of the service experience; and the measuring of customer satisfaction. Management may not establish the *appropriate standards* for a variety of reasons. Firstly, they probably judge themselves as experts in their chosen profession and may therefore think that they know better than the customer what is required. Secondly, the evaluation of consumer satisfaction is extremely complex, as we shall see, and few managers are trained in these skills. In particular the wrong signals may be used to interpret whether quality standards are right, for instance the level of verbal and written complaints. Finally, operational managers have many different roles to fulfil and they may not have the time to spend on detailed quality standard setting.

The *nature of the service* does not assist management. In most catering operations the customer may have contact with several members of staff during the experience. On top of that the number of interactions between customer and staff may be over one hundred during the course of a two-hour dinner. Such interactions range from catching the eye of the waiter whilst he is serving someone else to a chat with the manager about the weather.

Lastly, there are problems with actually *measuring customer satisfaction*. For one thing customers themselves may not be able to actually say whether or not a particular aspect of the service pleased them. Consumers' perceptions of identical service experiences will vary with their mood – on one day customers may wish to be served quickly as they are in a hurry, the next day they may be entertaining guests and expect to be served at a leisurely pace. Even if customers do have some idea of what is good and bad about the service experience, for many people it is very difficult to express. One often hears restaurants recommended for their 'great atmosphere', but 'atmosphere' can mean very different things to different people. Finally, there is the question of when to determine customer feedback. In most cases this is done at the time the customer is experiencing the service, which in itself will affect the customer's judgement of the operation.

QUALITY AUDIT

One way to examine the nature of the service experience in an establishment is to conduct a 'quality audit'. Quality audits can be used either to test hypotheses or substantiate hunches about the organisation's service effectiveness; or as a part of a total quality improvement programme. Juran[4] defined an audit as 'an independent evaluation of service quality to determine its fitness for use and conformance to specifications'. As will be shown, such an audit attempts to overcome the problems identified above by ensuring objectivity through independence from the organisation and by expert and articulate evaluation of the experience through observation and participation. Prior to any such audit taking place, management and auditor will discuss and agree the objectives, methodology, scheduling and reporting procedures of the study. Such an audit does not of itself control or assure quality, it enables management to assess the effectiveness of its quality management.

In the case of hotels, it is generally accepted[5] that the nature of the service is so complex that an audit cannot be made of the entire service experience. For catering establishments this is not necessarily the case, but even within one operation at different times of the day the nature of the service may change, for instance morning coffee, lunch break, afternoon tea, evening meals. Therefore, it is necessary to establish the objectives of the audit. A commonly used method is Pareto analysis, that is to say every possible problem is listed and then ranked in its order of importance. A second technique, advocated by Wyckoff, is 'fishbone' analysis which helps to identify cause and effect. The effect is identified and major categories of cause – material, personnel, procedural, equipment and 'other' – are the spine (see figure 6.2). Then from these headings, component factors are identified.

Once the objectives are established, the next step is for the auditor to adopt the consumer's frame of reference, that is to say 'adopt the customer's mentality'.[6] This is done by familiarisation with the profile of typical customers in terms of their age, background, occupation, income and so on. From this some judgements can be made concerning their life-style and likely attitudes towards the service provision. Some attempt will also be made to assess the purpose and importance of the service, i.e. meal, to the customer, for instance is the meal a substitute for a meal at home or an opportunity to entertain guests or a celebration of some sort.

The next stage is to conduct the audit itself. There are two main methodologies, both of which are usually applied. The first is to observe guests experiencing the service, and the second is to participate as a guest in the experience. Whilst it is possible for the auditor to be introduced to employees and have his or her role explained, in most cases this is not done. The reasons for this are to stop staff changing their behaviour because they know they are being observed, to allow the auditor to

DELAY IN TAKING
CUSTOMER'S ORDER

Equipment

not enough pads

Procedure

order taker slow
order written in full
distributes check to
kitchen/cash desk

Material

Personnel

too few order takers
undertrained
poorly motivated

Other

customers too slow
too many customers

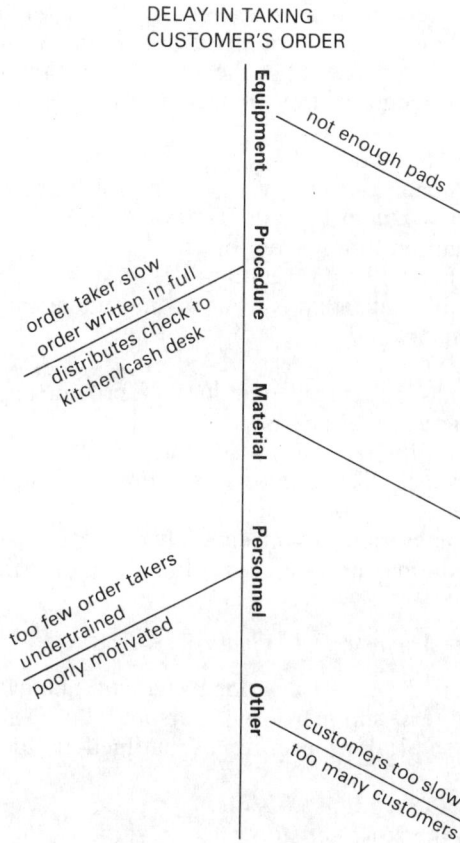

Figure 6.2 *Fishbone analysis of cause and effect.* Adapted from *New Tools for Assessing Service Quality.* Wyckoff, D.D.

have the same experience as real customers and to prevent distrust as to the purpose of the exercise being created. The only disadvantage in this is that the exercise involves a detailed recording of the experience which may involve note-taking, tape recording, photographs, checklists and chatting to other customers. In small outlets such behaviour would obviously be out of place, although it is not unknown for business people dining alone to carry on working.

Once the observation/participation period is completed a detailed report of the study is written, and an analysis of the findings is made. It is usual to identify each of the contributory factors that lead to guest satisfaction and then to rate them in some way. This can be a rating on a serial classification scale or semantic differential scales. The former would grade items along a scale as being, for instance, excellent, acceptable, moderately acceptable, and so on, often giving a numeric score to each, such as excellent = 1, acceptable = 2, and so on. Another scale can be the better-and-worse-than continuum:

| Worse than expected (−5) | Just as expected (0) | Better than expected (+5) |

For each of the factors rated the audit would give the basis for any deviation from the best or expected score. For instance, a rating of 'acceptable' with regard to transaction time at a check out might be the result of the average length of time being 30 seconds longer than the standard length of time expected or laid down.

The *advantages* of quality audits are:

> they are consumer-oriented.
>
> auditors take a consumer's perspectives but can explain themselves to management in a way that management can understand.
>
> they are independent and therefore objective.
>
> they are capable of providing a wealth of detail.
>
> they collect actionable data, that is to say management can act to correct below-standard performance.

The *disadvantages* are:

> in terms of statistical sampling an audit does not provide any valid evidence of the level of satisfaction of real guests.
>
> there may be bias on the part of the auditor.
>
> the auditor's experience, like each other customer's, is unique and may provide misleading evidence.
>
> an audit can only be carried out infrequently owing to its complexity and cost.
>
> the detail of the audit may provide results that do not see the wood for the trees.

Case example 6.1   The 'Friendly Fish' Chain

One particular approach adopted by a national chain of take-away-food restaurants is to use a so-called mystery shopper. This person follows a detailed routine for evaluating a store. A typical procedure, as outlined in the company's 'Quality Manual', is as follows:

(i)   Park as close to the store as possible.

(ii)   Before entering the store set stopwatch to zero.

(iii)   After entering the store check the toilets before joining the service queue.

(iv)   Start stopwatch as soon as you join the queue.

(v)   Order the items specified but also purchase some items suggested to you by the operative. Start second stopwatch when order is placed.

(vi)   Upon receiving order stop both stopwatches.

(vii)   Drive away from store, checking on exterior.

(viii) Park away from store.

(ix)   Use probe thermometers to measure temperature of all food items.

(x)   Note on report details of visit including salesperson's name, time of visit. Record temperatures of food.

(xi)   Staple receipt to the report.

(xii)   Move on to next store.

ALTERNATIVE APPROACHES TO QUALITY ASSURANCE

Chapter 5 showed the industrial/manufacturing model of quality control (see page 60) and briefly discussed how this can be applied to the quality control of the tangible products of the meal experience, food and drink. Implication thus far has suggested that this manufacturing model is inappropriate for quality control of the service element. As we shall see this is not necessarily the case. There are many examples of catering' businesses which adopt this approach to all aspects of their operation, including service provision. This is partly a reflection of the increase in the technocratic approach to catering discussed in chapter 1 whereby routine, mechanistic systems are used to control and monitor the business. We shall call this the *traditional, control approach*. However there is a growing opinion amongst some experts, Wyckoff[7] and Jones[8] in particular, that this approach to quality control leads to too much standardisation and an impersonalisation of the service element – 'customers now ask where the service has gone from service industries'. We shall describe the alternative approach to quality management as the *quality assurance approach*.

It is easy to assume that one approach, usually the most recent, is better than another, and that in this case the assurance approach is superior to the traditional approach. However, it is instructive to apply the principles of quality management to assessing quality procedures themselves. The main principle is that of 'fitness for use', that is to say, in this case, the quality procedure should satisfy the needs of catering management. It is clear from the wide diversity of catering outlets that these needs will vary enormously. Two criteria in particular that differentiate between sectors are the extent to which catering is conducted back-of-house and the extent to which the service is customised. Those sectors that have little or no front-of-house contact with guests are typically hospital tray service systems, self-service cafeteria and fast food outlets. In such styles of service, the number and time duration of interactions between staff and customers is extremely low. On the other hand, in waiter or waitress service restaurants there is a much higher percentage of personal service. Such operations can also 'customise' their provision to a certain extent, that is to say they can speed up or slow down the service, produce a meal to the customer's specification, such as cook a steak rare or well-done, and generally provide the sort of experience that each customer is looking for. However, those sectors identified as having low front-of-house contact, are also unable to customise their service very easily. They are dealing with a high volume throughput that depends upon a standardised product. It is possible for instance, in a fast food store, to ask for a hamburger without the relish, but if every customer asks for their own customised hamburger the whole basis of the fast food concept would be destroyed. Wendy's, though, have used this customisation of their product as one means of differentiating themselves from other fast food chains.

It is possible to take these two variables – the level of front-of-house contact and the degree of customisation – and place them in a matrix (see figure 6.3). It is the contention here that for routine, low-contact catering operations quality control is appropriate, whereas for customised, high-service operations the assurance approach is more viable.

THE COSTS OF QUALITY MANAGEMENT

It is sometimes believed that improved performance will result from an 'up-grading' of the operation, for instance by the promotion of a 2 star establishment to a 3 star. This is not necessarily the case of course, since it will depend entirely upon whether or not there is a market for the up-graded unit, i.e. whether the new unit design satisfies a need. It is probably also true to say that in order to be achieved such an up-grading will require a degree of capital investment and increased operating costs. On the other hand, 'higher quality of conformance, can often be attained by a reduction in costs'.[9] The reason for this is that making sure that an operation conforms to the established quality standards may cost more, but it results in greater savings from the reduction of

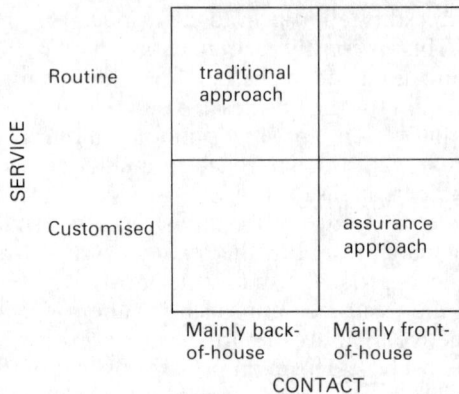

Figure 6.3   *Quality management in relation to level of contact and service.*

waste. It is also likely to result in a greater degree of consumer satisfaction, which may lead to a higher level of repeat business.

This can be seen in more detail in an analysis of the cost of implementing quality management. Wyckoff believes 'the total cost of quality is made up of four components'.[9] These are:

(1)   Prevention costs   – those expenses associated with creating quality performance standards, i.e. staff training, preparing purchase specifications, recipe development, etc.
(2)   Assurance costs   – expenses of inspection, measurement and data collection and analysis.
(3)   Internal failure costs – expense due to waste or loss before the item reaches the customer.
(4)   External failure costs – expenses relating to defective items reaching the customer, i.e. free drink to placate customer, and so on.

If it is accepted that, strategically, the quality level matches the consumer's needs, then the key requirement for operational managers is to achieve this level of quality at the lowest possible cost.

Table 6.1   *Cost comparison of two approaches to quality management.*

Cost component	Cost factor	Traditional approach	Quality assurance
Prevention	Cost of premium	–	high
	Meetings with suppliers	–	high
	Employee training	–	high
Assurance	Receiving inspection	–	high
	Chef's inspection	high	low
Internal failure	Rejection of commodity	high	low
	Server rejections	high	low
External failure	Customer rejection	high	low
	Placating customer	high	low
	Lost future business	high	low
	Total cost of quality control	high	low

Adapted from: *Hypothetical Comparison of Two Cost Control Strategies*, Wyckoff, D. D.[9]

The two basic approaches to assuring quality have been identified. The traditional 'control' approach starts off on the basis of purchasing commodities at the lowest possible cost and then inspecting these commodities in order to reject those that do not meet acceptable quality standards. The quality 'assurance' approach is the application of the more recent ideas about quality and relies on the idea that paying a premium price for a highly specified, good quality commodity is more than offset by subsequent operational savings, as well as higher levels of job satisfaction amongst staff and less risk of customer dissatisfaction. This is illustrated in table 6.1.

THE TRADITIONAL APPROACH TO SERVICE QUALITY MANAGEMENT

King[10] believes that the manufacturing quality control system, (outlined on page 60), can be adapted for application in a service context. She is quite clearly supported in this view by those catering organisations that, in their standards of performance manuals, adopt such an approach to service standards. As well as standards of service, King also advocates a behavioural control system, recognising that the key element in effective service is the behaviour and interaction of the staff with the customers. It is our view that, since service and staff performance are so inextricably linked, such control systems should be seen as one system, rather than two systems operating in tandem. It is extremely unlikely that service quality will be achievable with unsuitable, ill-trained staff, or that good staff will provide the right level of service without some sort of guidance.

The traditional approach is illustrated as follows:
Design Quality Level
    Define customer requirements
- Identify desired quality characteristics
- Identify desired behaviours
- Define desired image

Set product standards
    Design the service delivery system
- Document procedures
- Outline range of flexible responses
- Plan space use
- Select equipment

    Design organisation
- Recruitment standards
- Training programmes

Check conformance
    Output
- Customer complaint analysis
- Solicitation of customer feedback
  - comment cards
  - surveys
- Quality audit
- Observation of transactions

    Process
- Statistical analysis
- Employee morale measures

Correct non-standard output
- Appease customer with complaint

- Determine cause
- Take corrective action
- Involve employees

Designing quality level

Quality levels are established by detailed market research surveys of customers' needs and wants, an analysis of successful performance by competitive operations and the business goals of the organisation.

Setting product standards

Based on established quality level, product standards can be either tangible or abstract standards. Not surprisingly tangible standards are easier to set, measure and correct in the event of poor performance. They include such things as the length of time a customer queues at a fast food counter, how long it takes to make and serve a cocktail, what extra time is involved in using the customer's name when addressing him or her, and so on. Abstract standards are more concerned with human interaction and are based on interpersonal skills and communication skills. Such standards may require staff to use eye contact during a transaction, to stand in a certain way to suggest that attention is being paid and to solicit customers' opinions at appropriate moments during the service period.

In setting product standards the operation is also designed to facilitate practices that will lead to conformity. This involves providing equipment and a work environment that makes conformity possible. For instance, if the time for a payment transaction at a cash desk was established at no more than 30 seconds, the cashier must be provided with point-of-sale equipment that can operate within that time limit. Equally, a cashier must be recruited who is capable of achieving this proficiency and must then be trained in the skills needed for the desired performance.

King states – 'procedures must be thoroughly defined and documented, specifying how each task should be performed'. The advantages of such documentation are that responsibility for conformity can be assigned to staff and supervisors; it provides the basis for training new staff; it can be the framework for an analysis of how to achieve higher levels of productivity; it prevents confusion and misunderstandings between staff; and it is likely to support cost control procedures and provide management accounting data.

Table 6.2   *Possible service quality standards.*

Procedural Dimension	Convivial Dimension
– accommodation	– attitude
– anticipation	– attentiveness
– timeliness	– tone of voice
– organised flow	– body language
– communication	– tact
– customer feedback	– naming names
– supervision	– guidance
	– suggestive selling
	– problem solving

Reproduced from *Defining What Quality Service is for You*, Martin, W. B.

One particular approach is advocated by Martin.[11] He divides service quality into two dimensions. The procedural dimension is the technical systems involved in delivering products to the customer, and the convivial dimension is the server's ability to 'relate graciously to the customer'. For each dimension there are standards which should be ranked by the manager in their order of importance, (see table 6.2). Once ranked, each standard can be assessed and monitored by key indicators. For instance, a key indicator of timeliness might be 'customers greeted within 30 seconds of entering unit'; of attentiveness – 'customers ask for specific members of staff'; and of appropriate body language – 'eye contact made when talking to customers'.

Checking conformance

The first, and most important source of information about conformity with standards is the customer. This can be received in three ways: unsolicited complaints and compliments; customer comment cards and guest surveys. The nature and suitability of these three approaches are discussed later in the chapter. Another approach, already discussed, is the quality audit.

Of great importance here is employee involvement. For King this means that conformance must be supported – by recruiting the right sort of staff; training staff in behavioural as well as technical skills; providing good staff facilities to maintain morale and ensuring effective supervision by supervisors who can reduce stress to the employees and who lead by example with regard to interpersonal behaviour. In this regard King's approach has some similarities with quality assurance.

Correcting non-standard output

However well designed the quality control system, there is always the possibility that things will go wrong. Murphy's law states that anything that can go wrong, will go wrong. Appropriate reactions to poor performance are considered later in this chapter.

Case example 6.2   Racy Joe's Fast Food Chain

Racy Joe's is a chain of fast food units serving a range of burgers, fries, drinks, and desserts. There are 13 units in the chain and turn-over exceeds £3,000,000 in a year. The maintenance of food quality standards is essential to the business success of this type of operation, and a comprehensive policy of quality assurance has been devised which covers the product from its purchase to its consumption. The company has appointed a Quality Assurance Officer to assess and report on food quality and, where appropriate, suggest ways of overcoming problems associated with the maintenance of food quality. The Quality Assurance Officer is responsible to the Marketing Manager but monitors quality throughout the company sending reports to the Purchasing Officer, Food Technologist, Operations Manager and Unit Managers, as suitable. It is the purpose of this case example to consider the quality assurance activities concerned with one very important commodity – the beef patty used to make the burger itself.

Racy Joe's considered that quality control must cover their suppliers' activities as well as their own. In addition to preparing a precise purchasing specification for the beef patties, Racy Joe's required the manufacturer to conduct a series of quality control tests. Some of these concerned the meat before it was processed, such as a serology test, a grid analysis of the lean meat, chemical fat analysis, pH tests, microbiological evaluation and cooking tests. After processing a second series of tests was carried out by the manufacturer on the finished patties before they were frozen. These included cooking tests (to assess weight loss, distortion and taste) microbiological evaluation, and fat and moisture constituent analysis. Further tests were carried out on the frozen products. Racy Joe's Quality Assurance Officer made occasional visits to the manufacturer and ensured that the tests were being correctly carried out and the results acted on as necessary.

The procedure for cooking and garnishing the beef patties, was clearly laid down in Racy Joe's operating manuals. Many of the quality aspects were governed by the equipment – such as the chain broiler. The Quality Assurance Officer carried out further checks in the Racy Joe's units. These included the temperature and microbiological condition of the deep-freeze storage, the operating conditions of the chain broiler, the condition of the patty as it came out of the broiler (internal temperature, surface temperature, weight, distortion), the operating condition of the make-up table, the condition of the patty as it left the make-up table (internal temperature and surface termperature), the operating conditions of the storage chute and the condition of the burger taken from the chute (correct make-up, external temperature and internal temperature).

The final aspect of quality control was concerned with consumer evaluation. Periodically a survey was undertaken by a research agency with the intention of assessing consumers' perception of the product, and their ranking of its value compared with competitive products. The results were treated as the overall assessment of the quality of the product.

This case example shows the comprehensive approach which can be taken to quality control – the business function concerned with ensuring that quality standards are met. The findings of the Quality Assurance Officer were used as part of the control process to keep the performance of suppliers, manager and staff in line with objectives. The company was also able to measure and discuss quality – so it became a regular feature of management meetings. Individual managers were assessed and remunerated on, amongst other things, the quality performance of their units. Finally, the planning of such activities as staff training, preparing equipment and food purchasing specifications, and product reformulation was based on factual, systematically collected data.

THE ASSURANCE APPROACH TO SERVICE QUALITY MANAGEMENT

Almost by definition, this approach is less formal and mechanistic than the manufacturing based quality control system. Rather than impose a system upon the operation, 'these new methods give caring workers the tools for self-improvement in delivering service quality – and substantially reduce the need to denigrate service quality by sacrificing customisation, choice, flexibility, and personalised service'.[12] By its very nature then, stressing as it does customisation and personalisation, there is no *one* specific assurance approach. It is more a question of philosophy than of a system. The principles of this philosophy are

- recruit the right people.
- employ imaginative ideas and responses to problems.
- take a questioning attitude towards all aspects of the operation.
- adopt a total commitment to quality.

Such principles are fine in theory, but how can they be put into practice?

Mill[13] suggests that service employees should be flexible and be able to see the customer's point of view, or 'empathise'. He suggests that personality tests , such as the 'Central Life Interest Inventory', 'Self Monitoring Scale', or 'Selling Orientation – Customer Orientation Scale', might be an appropriate way of selecting such people. The advantages of such tests are that they have some external validity and are an objective evaluation of applicants. Less formal methods have increasingly been criticised, although the recruitment interview is undoubtedly the most widely used method of selection. There seems some irony in the idea that an organisation that is looking for flexible, empathic staff should use a test to select such people.

With regard to the business environment, most employees can easily identify what the business is but may have a very wide range of views about the most important aspect of that business. Quality can be brought to the forefront of their thinking by an overt use of the word from the moment of recruitment, right through the induction period and during any on-the-job training – as in McDonald's. Equally, since this concept may also be consistent with the image the operation wishes to create in the consumer's mind, it can become part of an advertising slogan. This emphasis on one feature of the operation can then become central to the shared value system of the organisation, in recognition of which management praises high quality performance, promotion or bonuses are seen to relate to the quality of work done, the physical resources, such as equipment and work environment provide the necessary tools to achieve quality and are of high quality themselves, and so on. It will be difficult for management to convince their workforce of the need for quality front-of-house if their changing rooms are filthy, their work clothes ill-fitting and management themselves do not appear to care about timekeeping, personal appearance or standards. Therefore, both management and staff can help to set standards by behaving as role models thus contributing to the cultural climate. This means management and supervisory staff must clearly express opinions and display behaviour that is quality-conscious, and staff who are particularly adept must be seen to be rewarded. Such members of staff become 'heroes' to whom other members of staff can relate and look up to, they make success human and attainable, and potentially motivate their fellow workers. This can be further supported by the rites and rituals that arise in any organisation. These might include the manager buying a drink after work for the employee who has been the most quality conscious worker of the week, or the informal presentation of awards to staff during a training session.

Training can have a role to play in developing the service quality too. In the main, such training focuses on increasing staff awareness of customers' needs. Methods include transactional analysis, used notably by British Rail and the Carlton Tower Hotel,[14] whereby staff are instructed in identifying three main ego-states and are trained to interact accordingly; hospitality clinics, in which staff are encouraged to visit another catering outlet, complete a report form on their experience and then discuss this experience with other employees and 'wait training' [*sic*], which informs staff of the customers' attitudes towards time in general and speed of service in particular.

As well as creating the appropriate climate in which quality can thrive, there is a particular technique that is meant to result in total commitment to the idea – namely the *quality circle*. A quality circle is 'a group of four to ten volunteers working for the same supervisor who meet once a week, for an hour, under the leadership of the supervisor, to identify, analyse and solve their own work-related problems'.[15] The features of such circles are that they are entirely voluntary, intensely practical and unbureaucratic. The growth and development of the circles depends entirely on the employees and is not dictated by the organisation. The way in which each circle works should be as follows:

• a list of problems originated by brainstorming.

- problems outside their own work area rejected.
- those problems that are possible to solve selected.
- problems ranked in priority order.
- the problem analysed.
- relevant data collected.
- problem solved.
- this solution sold to management.

For this concept to be effective it is essential that some guiding principles are followed. Much of the criticism of quality circles has come from organisations who have implemented the idea without fully adopting these principles. Firstly, membership of the circle is entirely voluntary. Thus management cannot even set up the first circle, they can only explain the idea to supervisors and workforce and then hope that their staff will take up the idea. Since there is no obligation to return every week, quality circles will only continue if the workforce continue to volunteer. Secondly, particularly in the early stages, circles should only address themselves to solving problems within their own work area. It is usually the case that poor performance is blamed on other sections of the workforce, but this is not the concern of the members of a quality circle. Thirdly, the circle itself will determine its mode of operation, although the organisation can provide support with regard to training and expertise in techniques such as brainstorming, data analysis, and so on. Problem solving requires staff to become experts in a very difficult area of expertise, so that they may also need to be introduced to some of the techniques we have mentioned previously such as Pareto analysis, flow charting, fishbone analysis, and so on. Fourthly, the circle will only be effective if it is accepted by management and given any information that it thinks it requires to solve problems. Companies and management are often reluctant to divulge information which they regard as confidential, simply because it gives them a psychological edge over others, but 'facts and figures distinguish quality circles from suggestion boxes'. Finally, the organisation must have a realistic time perspective with regards to how long it will take for the idea and the groups to be effective. It is likely that at least two years are needed before quality circles might start to consider problems at the interface between themselves and other employees. 'Every operator who has reported successful circles . . . has stressed the fact that it has been a long-term growth experience for everybody involved'.[16]

The reported benefits of quality circles are numerous. Most importantly they change attitudes within the organisation: staff are better motivated, supervisors gain confidence, problem solving is more competent, communication at all levels is improved, and there is the creation of a problem-solving, rather than blame-shifting, ethic. As well as these unquantifiable results, organisations have found that the solutions that circles generate can in some cases save them thousands of pounds per year. Added to this even a better motivated workforce has resulted in less absenteeism and lower rates of staff turnover.

Case example 6.3   As You Like It Restaurant

Peter Jones was responsible for setting up and operating a quality management system, but in this case the assurance approach was adopted. The restaurant concerned was in Brussels and aimed specifically at the British residents of that city, the majority of whom were aged from 25 to 40, single or married with young children, and employed in professional jobs with high remuneration. This market group clearly wanted a British meal experience, or at least they wanted to eat typically British meals with such dishes as meat pies, deep-fried fish, puddings and so on, which were unavailable at that time except in pseudo-British pubs. Quality was clearly an issue for three reasons; firstly, this meal experience was a substitute for 'home-cooking' – 'just like mother used to make', secondly, the level of competition and quality standards of other restaurants in Brussels is extremely high, and thirdly, the restaurant's market position was more up-market than the pubs and hence the product had to be of higher quality.

It would be pleasant to recall that quality was achieved by a thorough process of investigation and implementation. In fact, as is the case with many small-to-medium, owner-managed restaurants, quality was a result of the application of some basic principles and trial and error. The basic principles included the daily purchase of fresh commodities from local markets, careful stock rotation, preparation of all dishes as close to service time as possible or on an à la carte basis, and monitoring guest satisfaction by frequent dialogue between all members of staff (manager, chef and waiting staff) and the customers themselves. What emerged was that quality derived from other much more subtle interactions which became part of the worker's culture and the customer's ambiance. Firstly, the restaurant was very informal. Its customers wanted somewhere to relax and feel at home in, where they could meet other British people and chat if they wanted to. There was no pressure of time, particularly in the evening and closing times were fairly fluid. It was not unknown for the personnel of the restaurant to socialise with customers outside the restaurant and therefore both staff and customers alike contributed to the overall ambiance. The restaurant layout made it possible for staff to see into the kitchen and to talk to the chef whilst she was working. Menu ideas were developed from frequent discussions with the chef and waiting staff, all of whom were British, and from requests from the customers. At least two of the dishes which became favourites were demonstrated to the chef by customers donning an apron and going into the kitchen themselves. A high level of repeat business meant that all the staff knew the personal likes and dislikes of customers, both with regards to the food and drink they liked, and the way in which they liked to be treated.

It is obvious to ask the questions – was there any quality control at all and was the restaurant a success? The only answer can be that customer complaints were on average less than five a week, which represented less than one per cent of all customers. In this style of restaurant, and in its particular location, this was regarded as very good: Belgian customers, unlike British people, do not hesitate to complain if something does not meet their requirements and the natural British reserve was removed by the particular nature of the relationship established between staff and customers. There was also a high level of repeat business. At lunch-times in particular, customers would eat in the restaurant very regularly. Finally, in a highly competitive eating-out market, the restaurant was operated for over two years and eventually sold as a going concern.

MEASURING CUSTOMER SATISFACTION

It has been explained that customer satisfaction may be monitored in three main ways: unsolicited complaints and compliments, comment cards and customer surveys. Of these, only the first two represent an active segment of all customers, i.e. those prepared to comment verbally or in writing. A customer survey, however, obtains opinions from a much broader range of customers and as such is preferable as a means of ensuring quality management has been effective.

Using unsolicited complaints and compliments is not a very satisfactory way of measuring satisfaction for a variety of reasons. They can either be expressed at the time the customer is experiencing the service or afterwards, usually through a complaint letter. In fact one survey found that 60 per cent of all complainants who sent a letter of complaint had already expressed their grievance in person at the time.[17] It is unlikely that management will keep any valid record of verbal complaints, simply because the recording of them would be impractical, so that it is usually written complaints that form the basis of evaluation. Such complaint-registration ignores the customers who are only moderately dissatisfied, maybe annoyed enough not to use the establishment again but not sufficiently to write in complaint. The ratio of complaints to compliments received is often used as a measure of quality control. However the same research showed that, using both letters and comment cards, actual complaints and compliments received did not reflect the true ratio of happy and satisfied customers. One in three compliments were expressed but only two in seven complaints, so an operation that had registered approximately an equal number of complaints and compliments, would in fact have more dissatisfied customers than satisfied ones.

Comment cards have also come in for a considerable amount of criticism. Lewis and Pizam have described most of them as meaningless, unreliable, product-oriented and statistically invalid.[18] Typical faults included asking customers to rate food as excellent, good, fair, poor. In this instance, whilst a rating of 'poor' will clearly indicate dissatisfaction, management are unable to identify the exact nature of the problem. Another format is to ask yes/no questions such as 'was your food properly prepared?' In this case it is easy to see that a customer might answer yes to this question, even if he or she did not actually like the food. A slightly more effective means of asking customers for their opinion is to ask if the provision met their expectations or not. At least here, there is an attempt to match service with customers' wants. Once again, however, a respondent who replies that the service did not meet expectations could mean that whilst it was not as good as expected, it was still satisfactory.

Lewis and Pizam have identified the factors that a satisfaction index should achieve and say that it should:
- measure the dominant trends in consumer satisfaction.
- provide straightforward information.
- not be so long as to discourage customers from responding.
- tell the organisation if the guest will return or not.
- meet the specific needs of an operation.
- be easy to analyse, so that prompt action can be taken.

In order to meet these requirements they suggest the following methodology. Firstly, detailed interviews should be conducted with customers of a business to discover which variables were important in creating satisfaction or dissatisfaction. This potentially long list of variables should then be factor-analysed to arrive at a smaller number of main factors or dimensions, so that the final survey is not too long. In the event that a particular dimension is found to be rated badly, it can be examined in more detail by separating out the original variables to investigate the exact nature of the problem in a subsequent survey. The most important step is then to use regression analysis in order to weight each of the dimensions according to their importance in contributing to an overall level of satisfaction, for example, in a restaurant food might have a weighting of 0.4, whilst the toilet facilities might have a weighting of 0.1. The significance of this weighting is seen when guests are asked to rate the dimensions on a five point scale, as illustrated in table 6.3.

Table 6.3 *Hypothetical satisfaction index for a restaurant.*
A

	Weighting	Rating	Possible score	Weighted rating	Possible weighted score
Food	0.4	5	5	2.0	2.0
Convenience	0.25	4	5	1.0	1.25
Service	0.2	3	5	0.6	1.0
Professional staff	0.1	2	5	0.2	0.5
Cleanliness	0.05	1	5	0.05	0.25
	1.00	15	25	3.85	5.00
Satisfaction level (%)		60		77	
		(without weighting)		(with weighting)	

B (reversed rating)

	Weighting	Rating	Possible score	Weighted rating	Possible weighted score
Food	0.4	1	5	0.4	2.0
Convenience	0.25	2	5	0.5	1.25
Service	0.2	3	5	0.6	1.0
Professional staff	0.1	4	5	0.4	0.5
Cleanliness	0.05	5	5	0.25	0.25
	1.00	15	25	2.15	5.00
Satisfaction level (%)		60		43	
		(without weighting)		(with weighting)	

Adapted from *The Measurement of Guest Satisfaction* by Lewis, R. C. ands Pizam, A.[18]

Table 6.3 illustrates the importance of weighting each factor. Both example A and example B have a total rating of 15, representing a satisfaction level of 60 per cent. However, after each factor is weighted in example A the customer has a satisfaction level of 77 per cent, because the most important factors are rated highly, whereas in example B the customer's satisfaction is only 43 per cent, since the most important factors are rated poorly. Whilst, admittedly, this methodology provides both reliability and validity, it does require that a detailed survey of the particular operation be made in order to establish the weighted factors which to a certain extent counteracts the ease of administration and analysis that the method affords. The detailed preliminary survey can only be administered once in several years, and there must be concern as to how long the factors identified, and in particular their weighting, will remain valid over a long period of time, in what is recognised to be a highly dynamic market.

DEALING WITH CUSTOMER COMPLAINTS

However good a quality system, it is inevitable that some customers will complain. As well as monitoring the level of complaint for feedback purposes it is important to take action to resolve the complaint as soon as possible. Studies by the American Management Association[19] suggest that the satisfied customer tells three friends or acquaintances about his or her good experience, whilst dissatisfied customers moan about it to eleven people. A calculation shows that if 22 per cent of customers leave dissatisfied, more people will be told how bad the restaurant is than will be told how good it is.

Whilst the nature of the catering operation does present a whole host of problems already discussed in this chapter to a certain extent these characteristics make complaint resolution somewhat easier than in other businesses. Firstly, it is often possible to put things right straight away, face-to-face contact enables an apology to be offered and, if need be, some form of reparation, such as no charge for an item or a free drink, may be offered. Thus it is possible to extinguish dissatisfaction before the customer has the opportunity to complain to others. Indeed, swift and efficient response can actually reinforce satisfaction and loyalty. In particular, customers who complain need to be convinced that management has taken action to ensure that the cause of the complaint has been removed, not only from their point of view but forever. Dissatisfaction can often be aggravated by a response that suggests a standard reply, without any action to resolve the cause for the original complaint.

SUMMARY

This chapter began by examining the nature of service using Nightingale's model. The problems of assessing service quality standards are associated with management misperceptions, intangibility of the service experience and the measurement of guest satisfaction. One way to analyse the quality within a unit is by a quality audit.

The two main approaches to service quality management were then considered and called the traditional and assurance approaches. In as much as both approaches are utilised within the catering field, we can assume that there are advantages and disadvantages to both approaches. In fact, what can be seen as an advantage of one approach is often a disadvantage of the other. To be positive, therefore, only the respective advantages of the two approaches need be discussed. The stated advantages of the traditional approach are as follows:
1. All members of the organisation are working to clear guidelines, so there is no confusion over standards of performance.
2. All customers are treated equally.
3. The control system provides a framework for the analysis of problem areas which can often lead to increased productivity.
4. An effective and appropriate system is transferable from one unit to another within a chain operation.
5. Staff can be transferred from one operation to another without any loss of quality awareness.
The stated advantages of the assurance approach are:
1. Staff have a sense of pride in their work, which is reflected in less absenteeism, lower levels of staff turnover and greater participation in the operation of the business.
2. Customers are treated flexibly by staff who are responsive to their mood and needs.
3. Staff participation may lead to problem solving with economic benefits to the organisation.
4. Consumer awareness means that the operation can quickly respond to changes in demand.
5. Staff are flexible and responsive to change.
In conclusion problems with regard to measuring guest satisfaction and identifying the desired characteristics of a measurement technique were analysed.

REFERENCES

1. 'Tastes of America', *Restaurants & Institutions*, p. 102, 5 December 1984.
2. *Gallup Monthly Report on Eating Out* vol. 4 no. 3, March 1985.
3. Nightingale, M., 'The hospitality industry: defining quality for a quality assurance programme – a study in perceptions', *Service Industries Journal* vol. 5 no. 1, pp. 9–22, 1985.
4. Juran, J. M. and Bryna, F. M., *Quality Planning and Analysis*, McGraw-Hill, 1980.
5. Haywood, K. M., 'Assessing the quality of hospitality services', *International Journal of Hospitality Management* vol. 2 no. 4, pp. 165–177, 1983.
6. Haywood, K. M., *op. cit.*
7. Wyckoff, D. D., 'New tools for achieving service quality', *Cornell HRA Quarterly*, pp. 78–91, November 1984.
8. Jones, P., 'The Restaurant – a place for quality control and product maintenance?', *International Journal of Hospitality Management* vol. 2 no. 2, pp. 93–100, 1983.
9. Wyckoff, D. D., *op. cit.*
10. King, C. A., 'Service Oriented Quality Control', *Cornell HRA Quarterly*, pp. 92–98, November 1984.
11. Martin, W. B., 'Defining what quality service is for you', *Cornell HRA Quarterly*, pp. 32–38, February 1986.
12. Jones, P., *op. cit.*
13. Mill, R. C., 'Managing the Service Encounter', *Cornell HRA Quarterly*, pp. 39–43, February 1986.
14. Venison, P., *Managing Hotels*, Heinemann, 1984.
15. Robson, M., *Quality Circles – a practical guide*, Gower Publishing Co. Ltd., 1983.
16. Faulkner, E., 'Will quality circles work in American foodservice operations?', *Restaurants & Institutions*, pp. 149–151, 15 September 1983.
17. Lewis, R. C., 'When guests complain', *Cornell HRA Quarterly*, pp. 23–31, August 1983.
18. Pizam, A. and Lewis, R. C., 'Measurement of guest satisfaction', *Cornell HRA Quarterly*, November 1981.

7

Improving Employee Performance

OBJECTIVES

Identify the impact employee performance has upon catering operations . . . analyse approaches to evaluating performance . . . compare and contrast alternative approaches to improving employee performance.

INTRODUCTION

The catering industry is highly labour intensive. With one million full-time and one million part-time workers it is one of the largest sectors of the UK labour market. In addition, this book has identified a major characteristic of the catering industry in the provision of a 'service'. The combination of these two factors result in catering managers having to spend a great deal of their time in managing their employees. A survey[1] carried out in Northern Ireland, suggests that the most common problem facing hotel and catering managers is 'getting a suitable workforce'. The general conclusion of this is that managers in all types of business rate their problems in terms of sales, then finance, then personnel, whereas managers in catering rate personnel ahead of these other two problem areas. Indeed, throughout the other chapters of this book the approaches, techniques and procedures discussed probably all involve the training, participation and performance of staff. All too often staff are seen as a means to an end, for instance, costs can be reduced by shedding extra personnel, sales can be increased by developing their personal selling skills, quality performance depends on the workforce, and so on. But it is the contention here that employee performance is not *just* a means to an end, but an important key result area in its own right.

In some respects, it can be argued that the idea of improving staff performance is the most important key result area of all. A manager who is unable to achieve this is likely to find that performance standards in all the other areas discussed cannot be met. But the concern in this chapter is not so much with the impact that staff performance has, but more with identifying why this is important in its own right. In many organisations managerial effectiveness in this area is measured by factors that seem intrinsic to other chapters of this book, for instance, labour cost percentage (chapters 9 and 10), level of customer complaints (chapter 6), and so on. This is largely due to the fact that measuring improvements in employee performance is difficult except through their performance of their work. This chapter examines the importance of improving staff performance and the ways that this can be measured.

MATCHING OBJECTIVES AND PERFORMANCE IN
CATERING OPERATIONS

In broad terms there are two main areas for concern – the performance of individual members of staff, and the collective performance of the staff as members of a team. All too often it is assumed that achieving the best from an individual will improve the operation's performance, but it might not; whilst it is equally fallacious to believe that good teamwork is a result of maximising each individual's potential. In reality, of course, this distinction is very difficult to see and hence manage. Interrelationships are complex enough between two people, so that for even a small team, the number of possible interactions and communication channels is extremely large.

Catering managers should be concerned with individual performance for a variety of reasons. Firstly, poor employee performance will have direct consequences for the overall performance of the operation as measured by both its management, probably in financial terms, and by its clients, probably in service terms. Secondly, it will have consequences for the team's performance, particularly in terms of morale. Thirdly, it will take up a manager's time in many possible ways, such as counselling and disciplinary interviews, tribunals, recruitment and selection of replacement staff, and so on.

Poor team performance is a more serious problem and clearly has major implications for the effectiveness of the operation. The manager of a team that is performing well below standard is in effect not 'managing' at all. In essence, the very concept of management is the placing of someone in a position to control the behaviour of subordinates. This is often referred to as 'achieving results through other people'. All too often, managers hand blame for poor teamwork onto other people. The classic instance of this is the unit manager who believes that 'industrial relations' is the Personnel Manager's problem.

The nature of both the role that catering staff play and the relationship that they have with the consumer creates some specific problems associated with this industry. This applies primarily to front-of-house staff, but has implications for all employees. With regard to their role, waiting staff typically have three quite separate functions to perform. They are customer relations experts; technicians and administrators. Such roles are often in conflict and the employee is continually being asked firstly to indentify what particular function is necessary and secondly what priority the standard action should be given. Take, for instance, the case of a counter hand serving a customer in a cafeteria. Administratively she has been told to ensure that strict portion control is adhered to and technically she has been trained to serve using the correct equipment and techniques. What does she do if the customer asks for a different size portion – either smaller or larger?

Such conflicts are partly related to the relationship some catering workers have with the customer. In non-service industries, the workforce has little or no contact with consumers. The relationship between management and workforce is therefore quite straightforward. In service industries, particularly those sectors with high contact, the relationship is three way or 'triadic', as illustrated:

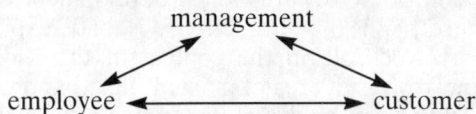

The result of this can be another conflict of interest derived from a sense amongst the workforce of working for the customer rather than the catering company. The irony of this is that quality management often attempts to heighten the sense of customer awareness amongst employees, so that great care must be taken to ensure that such conflicts are managed effectively.

JOB DESCRIPTIONS

Chapter 2 discussed how organisational objectives are influenced and determined. Once such objectives are clear, then the task of the manager is to translate these into individual targets for each employee within their particular job category. The way in which this is usually approached is to not start with the individual person, but with the job to be performed. This should result in a job description which specifies the contribution that each individual job makes towards the overall business objectives. However, as has already been seen, all too often such job descriptions actually comprise a list of component tasks without making explicit how these fit with the business goals. This is illustrated by the job description for a food and beverage manager in a major international hotel chain in figure 7.1.

JOB PROFILE: FOOD AND BEVERAGE MANAGER

The Food and Beverage Manager will concentrate on the short-term and long-term needs of the operation in the confines of the corporation's needs and objectives. Therefore, he is the principal agent of pro-active change.

He will personally supervise the daily Food and Beverage operation in its entirety, including:

- Quality and consistency of service and product.
- All cost factors.
- Cleanliness of all Food and Beverage areas.
- Final selections and training of staff.
- Production of departmental profit.
- The implementation and exercise of all policies and procedures.

The Food and Beverage Manager will be actively involved in financial planning, including:

- Preparation of monthly and annual forecasts and budgets.
- Development of recommended concept changes.
- Development of profit potential.

Figure 7.1   *Typical job description of a hotel food and beverage manager.*

The reason why job descriptions typically describe tasks is to facilitate the allocation of individual duties within the operation and translate delegated authority within an organisation structure down to individual operatives. It is further influenced by the requirements of employment legislation to specify in detail the requirements of the job.

One way to write job descriptions appropriately is to identify the outputs and the standards required. This means informing all personnel in the unit of management's focus on the key result areas discussed in this book. Staff are not merely required to perform tasks, but to contribute towards sales, development of customer relations, cost reduction and control, and so on. Unless this is made explicit to them, how can they perform their perceived role in the context of the wider organisation? For example, if we select the key result area of maximising gross profit through increasing customer average spend this can be disseminated down through the organisation by setting individual targets for each type of operative staff. Thus, for the wine waiting staff, their job description might include such items as specifying target spend per head on wine, volume of sales per customer or percentage of total custom that purchase drinks before their meal. This 'sales' type of target, linked with others related to standards of quality and control, will help contribute to the departmental objectives.

Even when job descriptions have been written effectively, there may still be problems relating to the effective supervision of the workforce by first-line managers. Research suggests[2] that there is often a mismatch between what managers think their staff want, and what the staff regard as important. Managers rank as most important the following three factors:

- higher wages
- job security
- promotion in company.

In fact their staff ranked most highly the following:

- full appreciation of work done
- feeling of being in on things
- help with personal problems.

Quite clearly organisations have to consider not only 'technical' and systematic approaches to performance improvement, but also behavioural considerations.

A MODEL FOR ANALYSING EMPLOYEE PERFORMANCE

At the end of chapter 5 some of the reasons for poor performance of staff in the context of quality control procedures were discussed. Performance is influenced by the individual job holder, design of job content, and the approach adopted by management to communication and review of performance, in order to ensure the achievement of business goals. Failure at any stage of this process will result in employee performance falling below the expected level. This is illustrated in figure 7.2 which identifies most of the common reasons for poor employee performance.

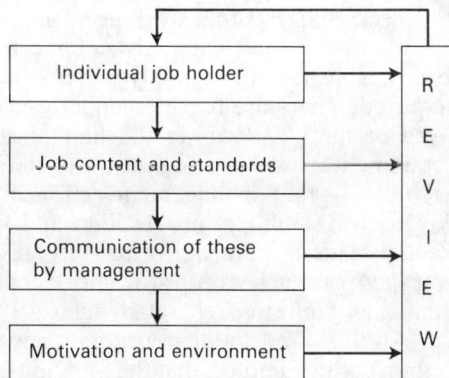

Figure 7.2 *Influences on employee performance.*

With regards to the *individual job holder*, there are three main factors that can result in poor performance. Firstly, the intellectual capability of the employee may be inappropriate for the job requirements. Most operative jobs do not require a high level of intellectual ability, and over-qualified people may prove to be as much a problem as under-qualified staff. This is particularly true where tasks are repetitive and systematised. Bright individuals may attempt to innovate and modify working procedures which then conflict with their colleagues and the organisation. Secondly, there must be match between the role to be played by the member of staff and their physiology. Physical strength is the most frequently quoted example of this, but in the catering industry dexterity is probably more important and this is rarely tested in the selection process. This would also include problems associated with dependency on alcohol and drugs. The former has unfortunately always been associated with an industry which involves the sale and consumption of alcoholic beverages. A third factor is the emotional characteristics of the employee. This is particularly important for front-of-house staff in contact with the customer, as so much of the service element relates to the sense of well-being generated by the staff. Emotional factors can include a wide variety of aspects, ranging from the psychological health of the individual, to the strength and commitment of the employee to work as opposed to social and family life.

Throughout the last fifty years, the trend in most industries has been to analyse in detail each *job* and to break it down into its smallest possible component parts. In manufacturing industry this has led to the idea of mass production techniques, with each individual repetitively carrying out only one or two operations. Previous chapters have shown how, for a variety of reasons, this trend has not become widespread in the catering industry, although fast food and hospital tray-serve systems are examples of where such ideas have been put into practice. This operational orientation can conflict with both the overall organisational goals and the intrinsic needs of most individuals for a sense of work satisfaction. On the other hand work may be deliberately organised so that a group or team is needed to perform it effectively. This can result in a wide range of factors that affect performance, most noticeably those relating to the establishment of group norms different to those of the organisation.

Poor performance may also result from poorly defined *standards* or a failure to communicate these to the workforce. It follows that once the content of the job has been determined and the individual selected to do the job, management must define some work performance standards. They key to success in this area is to define the standards appropriately. Kreck[3] suggests that work performance standards should be 'practical, reliable, relevant, observable, explicitly defined and measurable'. Once such standards have been established, the employee must be fully informed of the operational standards required. There are two elements to successful *communication* – informing the employee of the standards in the first place, and then providing feedback as to their attainment or otherwise, on a regular basis. Any mismatch between the two may require further management action in the form of training, encouragement, redeployment, disciplinary proceedings and so on.

Finally, lack of *motivation* leads to poor performance. This word is often used in textbooks and motivation theorists such as Maslow and Herzberg have had a major impact on management thinking. Unfortunately, many managers find it very difficult to relate theory to practice. All too often, poor performance is described as being the result of a lack of 'motivation', which implies that the individual employee is to blame. Much of the manager's time should be given over to thinking more positively about their role in generating enthusiasm amongst employees for the job they are required to do. Managers may perceive employees as having motivational problems and these may arise from a wide range of causes such as a lack of interest in their work, differing cultural or personal values, conflict between work and family life, and a sense of frustration at having no responsibility or sense of achievement in their work. Additionally employees will suffer from poor morale if they feel that they are unable to contribute to the improvement of their work methods and environment. Mill[4] suggests that 'a different strategy is required to correct poor performance' according to the cause of employee failure. For each stage in the process of improving employee performance different systems can be suggested that require an appropriate action plan, as illustrated in table 7.1.

Table 7.1   *Poor worker performance and appropriate solutions.*

Process	Symptoms	Action plan
Individual	Poor attitude	Redeploy/dismiss
	Poor skills	Improve selection
Job content	Good skills	Job enrichment
	No inclination to work	
	High conformity	Job enlargement
	Low responsibility	Job enrichment
Communication	Low organisational clarity	Management by objectives
	Low standards	
Motivation	Good skills	Job enlargement
and environment	No inclination to work	Job enrichment
	Low team spirit	Climate of trust
	Few rewards	Positive reinforcement

Adapted from *'Upping the Organisation'*, Mill, R. C.[4]

EMPLOYING THE RIGHT SORT OF PERSON

The influence that employees' physiological, psychological and emotional make-up will have on their work performance is already known. Hence it is important to carry out a detailed analysis of the precise attributes that are required to perform a particular job function. This should include not only evidence of previous experience relevant to the duties involved, but also an assessment of the compatibility of the prospective individual with the likely physical environment, level of customer contact, fellow members of the team, manual and mental requirements, and demands on personal time. This analysis will provide a database from which decisions can be made regarding location and style of job advertisements, role and nature of written applications, type of selection method, suitability of assessment procedures, and so on.

Case Example 7.1   The Pasta House

A chain of Italian restaurants, selling home-made pasta dishes in fairly young, trendy surroundings, was expanding rapidly in the more prosperous areas of London. Most customers were aged between 20 and 35 and were usually single, although dining together in couples or small parties. Owing to the availability of suitable premises, several of their operations had food production areas located in the basement which meant that waiting staff were required to climb stairs frequently. The management philosophy of the two owners was highly entrepreneurial, and far from being technocratic or systematised. Waiting staff each ran their own stations and were responsible not only for all the service of their tables, but the billing and cash reception too. At the end of service, their takings were reconciled against their checks and any overage was assumed to be 'tips'.

The management identified the following as key characteristics of the 'ideal' member of the food-service team:

- is aged between 18 and 30.
- is physically fit and healthy.
- has good interpersonal skills.
- has an ability to handle cash and basic numeracy skills.
- has an outgoing personality.
- is available to work evenings and weekends.
- has own transport or lives within 10 minutes' walking distance of unit.

To find such suitable applicants, the owners chose to place recruitment advertisements in the classified advertisements section of magazines aimed at young people. They did not use the catering press, since previous experience was not required, nor the London evening newspaper as its readership was too wide. Their advertisements stressed two aspects of the job, namely the 'fun', 'trendy' nature of the operation and the fact that it was relatively hard work. The advertisement also pointed out that reward was directly linked to performance.

Since little or no writing skills were required, applicants were not asked to complete an application form, but instead they were required to telephone. At this stage some preliminary screening took place by asking prospective applicants questions such as had they worked in a restaurant before? where did they live? did they have their own transport? had they held a previous job that involved handling cash? and so on. As well as satisfying the manager as to some of the criteria he was looking for, this provided an opportunity to assess the interpersonal skills of the applicant. If the person was thought suitable, they were invited to an interview. This comprised three elements − firstly, recording factual information about the applicant and their background; secondly, a ten-minute test of numeric ability and finally, an interview designed to investigate the interpersonal skills and outgoing personality of the applicant. Whenever possible this was done during the opening hours of the unit so that the applicant was able to see the operation in action and meet other members of staff.

It is interesting to note that this selection procedure did not display any concern for the operational or technical expertise of the applicants. The management were confident that if they selected the right type of person, then they would be more than capable of learning the necessary skills of serving at table.

DESIGNING THE JOB

Implicit in the Pasta bar case is the idea that the role of the employee must fit with the nature of the catering business. All too often job titles tend to constrain management's thinking about the role that an employee should or could be playing. Wherever possible the job should be organised so that the employee can appreciate the contribution they are making to the success of the operation, rather than breaking it into small components the purpose of which is hard to indentify with end-product. In those operations where specialisation is a necessary factor in effective production, notably fast food, managers recognise that there is a need to 'multi-skill' employees and move them around the unit to perform a variety of tasks. This has the additional benefit of creating a flexible workforce that can respond to fluctuation in demand and temporary changes in the availability of staff.

There are basically five methods of enriching jobs. Firstly, the grouping of work should be 'natural', that is to say, what a person is asked to do should be relevant to some clearly identifiable stage in the process or clearly indentifiable section of the business. The traditional kitchen brigade is based on this concept, so that the Chef Patisseur produces pastry not only for his sweets but also for the Chef Rotisseur's pies. Secondly, tasks should be combined so that people complete a 'unit' of work. For instance, producing twenty salads is a more meaningful work process and job experience than washing lettuce for one hundred salads. Thirdly, the worker should be encouraged to have contact with the consumer of the product. For service industries, and the hotel and catering industry in particular, such contact is quite common, although possibly chefs might be persuaded to have greater consumer contact. Fourthly, workers should be encouraged to plan and control their own work, rather than have it controlled by others. This is known as 'vertical loading', which should not be confused with 'horizontal loading' which is simply giving the employee more to do. Finally, more and better ways should be made for the worker to receive feedback on his or her performance.

The extent to which jobs can be redesigned and enriched has often been exaggerated, with examples given more often being the exceptions that prove the rule. Much of the work in this area is based on Herzberg's motivational theories and concepts of job enrichment and job enlargement. The principle applied is one of building into a job more challenges and opportunities for achievement and therefore appealing to a person's higher order needs. Successful examples of these ideas have been seen in car production plants, such as Volvo, and other assembly-type operations that used the traditional production line methods. Its application to the catering industry is however questionable.

Firstly, some employees may not have a strong need for achievement and are quite content simply being told what to do and how and when to do it. If job enrichment were introduced it may well cause stress and anxiety in the workforce and hence lead to even lower levels of performance. Secondly, many employees are quite satisfied with and motivated by extrinsic factors, particularly money. This is often true of part-time employees who go out to work specifically to supplement the family income. Since the catering industry has nearly one million part-time employees, it should recognise this factor. Thirdly, the catering industry has many characteristics which mean that most employees do not carry out highly repetitive tasks. Fourthly, most catering employees can see the result of their labour. The chef in the kitchen sees the completed dish and the waitress meets the satisfied consumer, and both of these people probably derive a great deal of satisfaction from this. Finally, it is a fact, however undesirable, that the industry has high levels of staff turnover. Hence the opportunity for promotion and advancement is often present, so that employees are rarely in any post for any length of time. It seems likely that staff move from one employer to another not because they are doing a different job but because pay or conditions are perceived to be better, or simply for a change.

There are some conditions when job enrichment may be of value to an organisation. Such conditions arise when the quality of work is of prime importance, the job requires a lot of organisation and judgement, the organisation is seeking creative decisions, staff clearly have strong higher level needs and there is not an acute morale problem caused by non-job factors, such as low pay or poor supervision. Such conditions are rare in the catering industry, although possibly the food production area of a Michelin restaurant is a good example of one situation where they do occur. Finally changes to work practices may be the result of work study seeking productivity gains (see page 127).

Case example 7.2   Breakfast at the Victoria

Serving breakfast to hotel guests at the four star Victoria hotel was disliked by most of the restaurant staff who were rostered to do it two or three times a week. Although the hotel had very high food standards and the breakfast menu was extensive with items cooked to order, customers often complained or walked out in dissatisfaction, usually because of slow service. For several weeks, employees had been requesting that extra staff be put on to speed up the service. Staff also complained that there was no 'atmosphere' in the restaurant at that time in the morning and it needed brightening up in some way.

The food and beverage manager thought through the problem and decided that the focus of attention on good food and top quality service was inappropriate for breakfast service. Customers, often businessmen, wanted the typical full English breakfast, but above all they wanted it quickly and without continual interruption from waiting staff taking their order, serving their juice, beverage, cereal, etc. The style of service was changed. After the guest was seated, the waiter approached with a pot of hot coffee. For those customers who wanted coffee (the majority), this was served immediately. At the same time the guest was directed by the waiter to the breakfast buffet where nearly all of the breakfast menu items were now on display for self-selection. The customer could therefore help himself to whatever he wished at whatever speed he chose. Those guests requesting tea or some hot beverage other than coffee the waiter would usually be able to serve whilst the customer was selecting his first item from the buffet.

COMMUNICATING STANDARDS

It is all very well designing the job, but unless the employee is made aware of the expectations management have of him, there is no guarantee that the job will be performed correctly. Communication has three components: a statement of the standard required, training, and a review of actual performance in order to provide feedback.

Large organisations with standard products place great emphasis on detailed manuals of performance including specifications for presentation and production of dishes, completion of documentation, interpersonal behaviour, and personnel practice and procedures. As well as using written material in an attempt to personalise the nature of communication, many multi-site operators are now producing video taped material for induction and training purposes. It is important that the type of communication is matched with the particular feature being developed in staff. Thus written communication may be very suitable for disseminating knowledge, but entirely inappropriate for skill development. The amount of new information generated must also be suitable for the level of employee at which it is aimed. Management who send a barrage of departmental memos to their staff will soon find that few staff read them.

Smaller organisations rely on face-to-face communication, with little being committed to paper. Standards are often only known by the manager who relies on personal supervision and coaching to ensure that expectations are actually met. The great advantage of this is that such 'standards' are much more flexible and responsive to consumer needs than are formal systems. The latter are often decided by committee and can be out of date very quickly if there is a change in the market conditions.

As the catering industry involves a large number of staff carrying out practical or technical operations, much of the communication process involves training. There are four main occasions when training may be required. Firstly, upon the employment of a new staff member when it will comprise an introduction into the organisation and the work place together with specific technical inputs particular to the operation. Secondly, in times of change when either new legislation, technology or procedures necessitate the re-training of existing staff. Thirdly, when staff performance does not match required standards and management are satisfied that they have the right person doing a well-designed job. Finally, it may take place when it is desirable to develop the individual staff member beyond the present requirements of the position that they hold, in order to prepare them for a future appointment.

Training can take many forms, ranging from a simple piece of technical training given on a one-to-one basis lasting only a few minutes up to a complex management course involving role plays, case studies and simulations lasting weeks. Whatever the size of the catering organisation, in many respects the nature and role of training will be the same. However, small organisations are unlikely to have the resources available nor the need for highly specialised training staff and for developmental training courses. Thus they are likely to concentrate on technical skills, and may buy-in the necessary expertise for more advanced types of training. Large organisations, particularly those that are growing, have a much greater need to develop their personnel in-house, in order to provide a pool of appropriately qualified staff.

Feedback is the third component of effective communication of standards. In the catering industry there is usually a high degree of contact and interaction on a daily basis between supervisory management and staff. Typically feedback here is ongoing and informal. If a manager sees a member of staff failing to perform up to the required standard the member of staff is likely to be told about it immediately and hopefully told how to take corrective action. But it is equally important for good performance to be recognised by feedback as promptly as poor performance. In addition to this, there are many more formal systems of providing feedback such as weekly staff meetings, staff probationary period reviews, monthly budget reviews, and annual staff performance appraisal interviews.

The most important point to bear in mind with regard to performance appraisal is that the basis for assessment should be made as objective as possible. All results should be measured against pre-determined standards and performance objectives. Due regard should be made to any external influences – those outside the employee's control – likely to affect performance. For instance, a sales target for service staff may be affected adversely by the weather or a new competitor opening up sooner than was anticipated at the time when objectives were set. The great danger of the nature of on-the-job appraisal and feedback typical in catering is that it is prone to personal, subjective influences, such as favouritism, halo effects, racial bias, sexual prejudice, and so on.

The nature of the feedback and style of the review, will be influenced by the timescale of any decisions involved, seniority of the management inolved and the complexity of the performance under review. This is illustrated in figure 7.3. The outcome of any appraisal must lead to a *jointly* agreed job improvement plan and new targets and objectives for the next period of operation.

Assistant Managers Monthly Assessment

Assistants name: ....

Branch: ....

Month: ....

Date: ....

Areas of Work	A	B	C	D	E	Weakness	Managers Comments
1. Front of House Skills							
Seating & Greeting		✓					
Supervision of Waitresses			✓				
Knowledge of company standards		✓					
Hospitality		✓					
Liaison with Staff							
Liaison with Customers		✓					
2. Kitchen							
Knowledge of Products		✓					
Preparation Methods			✓				
Storage		✓	✓				
Safety				✓			
Ability to train subordinates in simple preparation methods							
3. Bar Foods							
Preparation Methods				✓			
Portion sizes				✓			
Knowledge of applicable products			✓	✓			
Ability to evaluate				✓			
GP Margins				✓			
4. Barwork							
Knowledge of drinks		✓					
Service methods & preparation		✓					
Cocktails			✓				
Knowledge of beers & wines		✓					
Speed of service		✓					
Knowledge of prices		✓					
Ability to supervise staff			✓				
Knowledge of procedures & dangers				✓			

Figure 7.3 *Steakhouse chain assistant manager review form.*

CREATING THE RIGHT CLIMATE

Motivation of staff becomes an issue when the manager believes he has selected the right person, designed an interesting and relevant job, specified and communicated the standards required, provided the appropriate training and yet, in appraising performance, finds that there is still a shortfall. An implicit assumption in this book is the idea that no amount of 'motivational' expertise will be effective in the long term if any of these other factors are absent. There are many motivation theories, so their use here should be clarified. Maslow talks of the higher level needs of individuals, such as social needs, recognition and self-fulfilment; Herzberg's model is concerned with the 'motivating' factors and McClelland's concept is of n(Ach) or need for achievement and n(Pow) or need for power. Whilst, recognisably, there are differences in these theories, in terms of practical application to the work situation, they all stress that effective motivation stems from appreciating the individual needs of people far more than just a work-related role.

There are basically two ways of controlling behaviour. One can either impose sanctions, which is McGregor's theory X viewpoint, or give rewards, which tends towards theory Y. Sanctions can take the form of simple rules and regulations, formal disciplinary procedures, removal of privileges and benefits and, in the worst case, demotion or dismissal. The form which sanctions may take is often explicitly stated by organisations. This is partly because some organisations are highly centralised and formal and partly because employment legislation requires organisations to formally record certain information or make known in writing to employees their legal rights. However, sanctioning can be carried out informally by managers – often more effectively than by following laid-down procedures. Such action would include rostering members of staff unfavourably, allocating undesirable tasks to individuals, withholding information from employees who are out of favour and so on. However, it is arguable that sanctions are the best way to achieve the best from staff.

One particular approach to motivation is 'operant conditioning'. Whilst this is regarded by some theorists as out-dated, when one looks at what managers actually do they do seem to adopt attitudes and carry out actions that show remarkable affinities with the operant conditioning model. There are four main courses of action. Positive reinforcement and negative reinforcement attempt to reinforce the desired behaviour, whilst extinction and punishment attempt to reduce undesirable behaviour.

Let us consider the example of the employee who is habitually late for work. A manager using *positive reinforcement* would employ tactics designed to encourage the worker to arrive on time. Such tactics might include a chart showing the days when the worker arrived on time, greeting and praising the worker when arriving on time, or a more formal system of paying a good time-keeping bonus. *Negative reinforcement* involves tactics that reward the worker if he is on time but not applying some sort of punitive action, so that he avoids reprimands or pay deductions for lateness. *Extinction* works on the idea that people tend to repeat behaviour that they have learned leads to positive consequences. By withholding positive reinforcement, it is hoped that the worker will gradually reject his bad habits. This might be expressly carried out by withholding a pay rise on the grounds of poor timekeeping. Finally *punishment* means applying sanctions, such as reprimands, pay deductions, whenever the worker is late.

Research has suggested that rewarding desired behaviour i.e. reinforcement is much more satisfactory than sanctions against undesired behaviour. Mitchell[5] states – 'Almost all the studies [of operant conditioning] show that reinforcement procedures, properly administered, can significantly change employees' behaviour in the desired direction'. Further research has shown that the way in which positive reinforcement is applied has important consequences. Thus, the manager can reward a worker every time he carries out the desired behaviour (mass reinforcement), or according to some type of schedule (partial reinforcement). The former tends to wear off over time as people begin to forget that it is related to a specific action. The most successful application seems to be linked to providing the reward at certain intervals. In the given example this may be a bonus if the worker arrives on time for a certain number of consecutive days, which would gradually become longer as the employee became better at time keeping. This may be helped by a random element, so that reward is not too predictable, such as praise from the manager every so often. This random element may be systematised, so that instead of receiving positive reinforcement regularly, an average frequency is established and then applied with different time periods between each reinforcement, as in the case study below.

Case Example 7.3   Positive Reinforcement in a Steak Bar

A major restaurant chain had undergone some sales training for its waiting staff aimed at their using scripted sales techniques in an attempt to increase sales of starters and sweets. Cliff Goodwin, the manager, analysed his sales records for the previous month and decided to reward staff who successfully promoted additional sales. He had used incentives of this type before but after a good initial response had found that improvement was not maintained. Previously the system was based on the highest spend per head on starters and sweets, and the prizes were always being won by one or two outstanding waiting staff. This demoralised those staff who had made improvements since their efforts were not being rewarded.

To overcome the problem he adopted the following system. He was required by his sales budget to achieve an average sale of five starters/sweets for every four main courses served. He therefore set a target of six starters/sweets per four meals sold. At the end of each month, all staff who had reached this basic requirement had their names put into a draw to collect a voucher for the local hairdresser or fashion store. In addition the names of the staff who had qualified for the draw were put on the staff notice board. Thus the monthly draw introduced a random element in the positive reinforcement of sales targets. The impact of this approach was immediate and sustained. Moreover, the manager exceeded the expectations of his employing organisation.

As well as being appropriately timed, rewards must also be at the appropriate level. Using Maslow's model, lower level needs are satisfied by extrinsic factors, such as wages; whilst higher level needs, such as the need for achievement, are satisfied by factors intrinsic to the work, for example, how challenging it is. The implication of this is that higher needs cannot be satisfied until lower needs are met. So that more responsibility is unlikely to make up for poor rates of pay.

ACHIEVING THE BEST FROM TEAMS

So far the concentration of this chapter has been on motivating the individual. Now the problem of motivating teams and developing team spirit must be considered. Such work groups usually result from a deliberate organisational decision to place workers together in order to meet operational needs. This is traditionally based on the functional nature of the task to be performed by the group. It is often at the interface between groups that conflict arises and results in energy being diverted into group rivalry rather than being used to pull together to achieve organisational aims. The catering industry depends upon teams of staff, usually sub-divided into two main groups – production and service teams. Ever since Whyte's study[6] attention has been given to how the social interactions between these two categories can be made to work effectively.

Berger and Venger[7] identify the signals that may indicate poor team work – 'These include low productivity, poor service quality, a decrease in customer satisfaction, hostility and conflict among group members and an increase in the number of requests for transfers'. Further to this it might be suggested that poor team spirit may exist if there is poor co-operation both between management and staff, there are high levels of absenteeism and poor timekeeping, and individuals place blame on others for any unsatisfactory performance.

In the study of working groups, the often quoted Elton Mayo clearly defined two types of group that exist within an organisation. The formal group is set up by the organisation to satisfy strategic aims and the informal group is set up by the group members who have some affinity for each other. Informal groups can work for the organisation, but at other times will work against it. One of the skills of management is to match the different needs of the two types of group. Where mismatches occur, the organisation may suffer from a wide variety of malaises, as illustrated in table 7.2.

Table 7.2   *Relationship between formal and informal groups.*

	Purpose	*Structure*	*Progress*
Formal	Financial return for effort and investment	Jobs, roles, accountability, delegation	Policies tasks and procedures
Informal	Satisfaction of personal/social needs	Influence based on knowledge, social skills and friendship	Interpersonal, group, inter-group
Problems arising from mismatch	Low productivity, poor standards	Authority without power	Red tape, finger-pointing, buck-passing

Groups often fail to work as a team due to a breakdown in the informal relationships, rather than for formal, work-oriented reasons. Hence management need to adopt informal methods to solve this problem. This might include emphasising the value of teamwork when recruiting new staff and meeting with employees, featuring the ability to work as a team member in job descriptions, encouraging staff to socialise together and involving other members of the organisation in decision making. Often informal groups are beneficial in terms of satisfying social needs, which the formal structure cannot do, and in providing extra channels of communication. Chapter 6 showed how managers can attempt to use such informal relationships and communication to create a 'culture' aimed at meeting unit or corporate goals (page 84).

Many attempts have been made to describe the characteristics of an effective team. Generally the team members depend upon each other to achieve the organisation's formal goals, trust each other, have common objectives, make decisions by consensus, are strongly committed and solve conflict by working through the problem. It is noticeable that such an analysis bears strong resemblance to the guidelines for effecting quality circles within organisations (page 85). Communication within the team is a key factor whereby group feelings can be expressed freely, members can be open with one another, and will listen to each other.

Casey[8] questions whether it is essential for work to be carried out in groups at all. He suggests that large numbers of management decisions are made by individuals and not by teams. He also suggests that the need for a team approach is influenced by the levels of uncertainty affecting the decision. As shown in figure 7.4 team work only

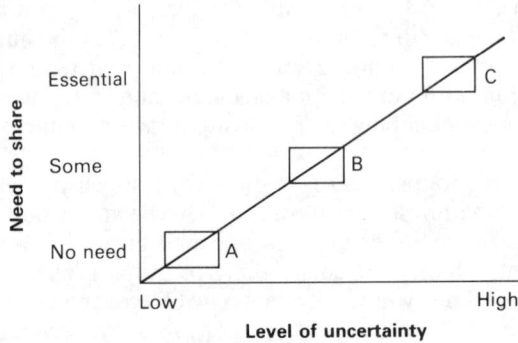

Figure 7.4   *Model of influence of uncertainty on teams.* Adapted from 'When is a team not a team?', *Personnel Management*, Casey, W., 1985.

really becomes necessary in times of great uncertainty when problems are complex and bewildering and there is doubt about the type of expertise required.

Casey suggests that 'simple puzzles' (box A), such as technical issues relating to one member in the group, can be resolved without any help from other group members. Whereas 'complex puzzles' (box B) which no individual group member can solve on their own will require group members to co-operate and negotiate with each other. Management problems (box C) are the most complex and require discussion amongst the management team of the organisation.

SUMMARY

The size and complexity of the catering workforce requires catering managers to spend a large amount of their time and effort on getting the best out of their staff. In particular, catering staff are placed under stress by the three, sometimes contradictory, roles they have to play and the triadic nature of their relationship with management and customers.

The industry has attempted to solve these problems by writing detailed job descriptions. These, however, tend to say what people must do without clearly explaining why and how the tasks are to be achieved effectively. It seems advisable for managers to examine the four main influences on job performance: the individual job holder; the job itself; how the standards associated with the job are communicated and the level of motivation amongst staff. For operations of relatively small scale and for simple operational procedures the effective analysis and execution of these four factors is likely to be informal, unsophisticated and reliant on the interpersonal skill of the manager. In larger, more complex units a more formal system is likely, with the personnel function having a role to play in terms of the documentation and procedures associated with selection and training. This does not absolve the unit or catering manager from taking responsibility for this key result area.

Whatever the size of the unit, this chapter provides a framework for analysing poor performance and suggests practical alternative solutions for a variety of contexts. It also identified teams as an important component of the organisational structure of most catering firms and examined the nature of such teams. Stress was placed not only on the formal purpose of groups but also on the role that informal groups play, particularly in the social climate of the operation.

REFERENCES

1. Lamour, R., 'Problems faced by managers in the hotel and catering industry', *International Journal of Hospitality Management* vol. 1 no. 1, 1982.
2. Zacerelli, H.E., 'Is the hospitality industry turning its employees on – or off?', *International Journal of Hospitality Management* vol. 4 no. 3, 1985.
3. Kreck, L.A., 'Evaluating training through work performance standards', *International Journal of Hospitality Management* vol. 4 no. 1, 1985.
4. Mill, R.C., 'Upping the organisation', *Cornell HRA Quarterly*, February 1985.
5. Mitchell, T.R., *People in Organisations*, McGraw-Hill, 1982.
6. Whyte, W.F., *Human Relations in the Restaurant Industry*, Wiley, 1948.
7. Berger, F. and Venger, R., 'Building your hospitality team', *Cornell HRA Quarterly*, pp. 82–88, February 1986.
8. Casey, W., 'When is a team not a team?', *Personnel Management*, January 1985.

8

Protecting Assets

OBJECTIVES

To define a catering manager's responsibilities for protection of assets . . . to discuss the management of cash in catering businesses . . . to review stock management principles applied to catering operations . . . to examine the value implications of employees in catering businesses . . . to examine the techniques necessary to protect and maintain premises and plant.

INTRODUCTION

So far in this book the key result areas which are the basis for effective performance in catering management have been examined. Another key result area is the protection of the assets of the business. There are three obvious types of asset which catering managers need to protect – stock, cash and premises. Catering businesses have large amounts of capital tied up in stocks of food, beverages and materials and these are subject to wastage, spoilage and pilferage if not carefully managed. The second type of asset – cash – requires very careful control. Cash is often called the life-blood of the business, and certainly if its flow is restricted the business may suffer a sudden and painful death. The third type of asset – the premises themselves – represents a substantial investment – which of course needs to be properly cared for and maintained. These three areas of asset management require the catering manager to employ the skills of cash flow management, stock management, security controls and planned maintenance of premises and equipment. In addition to cash, stocks and premises, employees will here be considered as assets and the costs associated with unnecessary employee wastage examined.

CASH MANAGEMENT

The new business failure rate in the catering industry is not due to lack of hard work or good ideas. Rather, it seems, it is often due to poor cash management – failure to match the receipt of cash against the payment of bills. The following case example demonstrates why the success of a catering business depends on its cash management.

Case Example 8.1   The Old Leather Bottle and Silver Spoon Restaurants

Two similar restaurants, The Old Leather Bottle Restaurant and The Silver Spoon Restaurant, each made a profit of £100 per month as shown in table 8.1

Table 8.1   *Profit for The Old Leather Bottle and Silver Spoon.*

Net sales		1000
Food costs	350	
Gross profit		650
Wages	250	
Other costs	300	
Total operating costs		550
Profit		100

Although the restaurants made the same profit, the cash flow in each business was controlled differently. The Old Leather Bottle accepted credit cards for the payment for all meals and consequently did not receive the cash until the following month. On the other hand cash was paid for all expenses. As a result a summary of The Old Leather Bottle's cash book looked like this:

Table 8.2   *Cash book for The Old Leather Bottle (£).*

	Month 1	Month 2	Month 3
Cash in	–	1000	1000
Cash out			
food, etc.	350	350	350
wages	250	250	250
other costs	300	300	300
Total cash out	900	900	900
Cash flow	−900	+100	+100
Cash balance	−900	−800	−700

The Silver Spoon had made very different arrangements. All customers paid cash, instead of using credit cards. Wages were paid in cash, but the payment of bills for food and all other items was delayed for one month. Their cash book appeared as follows:

Table 8.3   *Cash book for The Silver Spoon (£).*

	Month 1	Month 2	Month 3
Cash in	1000	1000	1000
Cash out			
food, etc.	–	350	350
wages	250	250	250
other costs	–	300	300
Total cash out	250	900	900
Cash flow	+750	+100	+100
Cash balance	+750	+850	+950

After three months trading, The Old Leather Bottle had been forced to borrow £700 from the bank (paying interest of course) in order to carry on trading, whereas The Silver Spoon had £950 cash in the bank which could be invested or used to help the business expand. There is an important lesson here: good profitability is no guarantee of satisfactory cash flow – and these two key areas need to be controlled separately.

The starting point for effective cash control is to set a *cash holding limit* which represents the largest amount of cash that will normally be kept on the premises. This is not only important for cash control purposes, but also has implications for the insurance and security of the premises. The cash holding limit is the minimum quantity needed to allow for floats, cash payments and petty cash and for the payment of wages. In practice, most catering businesses keep cash payments to an absolute minimum: they are administratively inconvenient and, of course, adversely affect cash flow. It may be necessary to pay wages in cash, as manual employees have the right to cash payment at present. This involves retaining two or more days' cash in order to make up the wage packets for distribution to staff which necessitates different cash holding limits for different days of the week. Some firms, with their employees' agreement, have successfully introduced comprehensive credit transfer or cheque wages payments. This aids administration and improves cash flow.

Until the cash is in the bank, a catering manager needs to be concerned with physical cash security. There is always the possibility of theft by employees, customers or outsiders. The cash register, with its associated control procedures, is the focal point for the prevention of employee cash theft. Security World suggest there are four ways for employees to steal from a cash register.[1]

- failure to ring up when the exact amount is tendered.
- under-ringing.
- ringing 'No-Sale' instead of entering a transaction.
- operating on an open-drawer.

Although no-one has yet found a cost effective method of eliminating all employee cash theft it is possible to limit this by taking several wise precautions. The first step is to locate the till in such a position that is impossible for any employee to pocket cash undetected: this means that employees have to wait to take their thefts out of the till and thus management has an additional opportunity to exercise control. Secondly, it is essential to have a clear policy regarding areas of till operation such as over-rings, no-sales, open-drawer operation, destruction of discarded receipts, employee purchases, etc., in order to limit the opportunities for doubtful practices; of course, the manager must ensure these procedures are followed. Thirdly, it is useful to have a series of spot till checks, where a substitute cash drawer and float is supplied by the manager, the till is read and the cash is taken away for counting and comparison. Finally, the use of a detective agency or a 'shopping service' to undertake secret checks on employees can be of considerable use.

Guests who steal are even more difficult to deal with. The manager who attempts to handle customers who walk out without paying or provide doubtful credit needs to be absolutely sure of the legal aspects of such actions. Interested readers are referred to Alan Pannett's book on this subject.[2]

STOCK MANAGEMENT

Hotel and catering businesses require a wide range of products and services – from a glass of mineral water to a dance band. Purchasing is therefore a complex activity, given the large number of commodities and materials that must be procured – often in relatively small quantities. Even with an apparently simple purchasing decision – say the purchase of some frozen peas – a manager has to appreciate the implications that this purchase may have for the business. Firstly, the peas will need to be paid for and this will affect the *cash flow* of the business. Secondly, the peas will need to be stored and *storage costs* can be considerable. Thirdly, the peas become an asset of the business and management has a duty to protect and preserve these assets from *deterioration and pilferage*.

When commodities or services are purchased, there are several different terms of supply which might be negotiated: payment may be made some time, often weeks, after the delivery has been made; at the time of the delivery, as in the case of cash and carry purchasing; occasionally, payment may be made before the delivery occurs or discount may be made for payment within a certain time period. Within the limits imposed by the purchasing agreements, payment of accounts should be delayed as long as possible as this represents an interest-free unsecured loan to the business.

Managers in catering businesses must keep careful control over suppliers' credit. The most useful way of measuring this is by monitoring the *average credit taken on purchases* (ACTOP). If, for example, the average amount of credit taken is £6 000 and the total purchases for the year are £104 000, then the ACTOP is:

$$\frac{\text{AVERAGE CREDIT OUTSTANDING}}{\text{TOTAL ANNUAL PURCHASES}} \times 52 \text{ WEEKS}$$

$$= \frac{6\ 000}{104\ 000} \times 52 \text{ WEEKS}$$

$$= 3 \text{ WEEKS}$$

So in this business the management have succeeded in obtaining the equivalent of enough interest-free loans to pay for three weeks' purchases.

By monitoring supplier credit, it is possible to identify when remedial action is necessary. If ACTOP dropped from three weeks to two weeks, the business in the above example would need to borrow a further £2 000 from the bank. However, it may be possible to regain this credit by systematically reviewing each supplier account and establishing how long payment can be deferred. In many cases, regular payment is more important than paying on time.

Returning to our frozen peas, the question of how much to buy at one time has obvious effects on cash flow. The advantages and disadvantages of buying in bulk may be outlined as follows:

Advantages of buying in bulk
- cheaper because of bulk discount.
- protection against sudden increase in demand.
- protection against sudden shortage in supply.
- protection against inflation.

Disadvantages of buying in bulk
- cash flow position worsens.
- stock-holding costs increase.
- deterioration or pilferage may occur.
- future demand may decrease.

As far far as fresh food is concerned the disadvantages obviously outweigh the advantages. With other products the reverse holds true. With wine, for example, the product may appreciate in value considerably during the storage period.

All businesses need to hold stocks and the ideal stock level for a specific commodity depends on the nature of the business and the characteristics of the commodity, in particular:

the level of sales.

the stability of demand.

the terms of supply

the costs of stock-holding.

cash flow limitations.

the shelf-life of the commodity.

the storage space available.

market trends in price and availability.

In general, unless there is a sound reason to the contrary, stock levels should be kept as low as possible. However, with high cost, high usage items it is often useful to plan the stock levels in more detail. The starting point for planning stock levels is an analysis of the usage rate. Using the example of frozen peas, imagine that the *usage rate* is 28 cases per week, and the time between placing the order and receiving the delivery (the *procurement time*) is five days. As a matter of policy, it is not wise to plan to run stocks down to zero before a delivery is received as an unexpected delay or increase in demand may cause problems. Normal practice is to decide on a minimum safety level or *buffer stock*. The size of this buffer stock is a question of choice, but aim to keep at least seven days' usage in stock. Using this example, an order should be placed five days before the buffer stock is reached – in other words when 48 cases remain.

One question remains. How much should be ordered at one time? The total cost associated with a purchase is a combination of the invoice cost, plus the administration cost (postage, clerical time, etc.) plus the storage cost (running the freezer, etc.). These costs will vary as shown in figure 8.1.

	Invoice cost	Administration cost	Storage cost
Many small orders	high	high	low
Few large orders	low	high	high

Figure 8.1   *Comparison of purchase costs.*

Somewhere between the extremes of one large order and very many small orders lies the point where the total cost will be lowest. This is called the *economic order quantity*. EOQs can be calculated using mathematical formulae or by preparing cost tables. Either method is laborious and time consuming and the useful application of EOQs is limited to very large-scale purchasing. It should be remembered, however, that there is such a thing as an ideal purchase quantity.

There is a wide range of alternative sources of supply for every commodity a catering manager may wish to purchase. The order quantity is one of the main factors determining a caterer's choice of sources of supply. The size and scale of a catering business determines the quantities purchased and the larger these are, the greater is the opportunity to purchase from prime sources such as growers and manufacturers. The geographical location of catering units will also determine the viability of purchase from cash and carry outlets or wholesalers. The menu itself dictates the range of commodities required and hence the number and type of different suppliers. Quality assurance will determine the grade of commodities required, and hence the nature of supply; whilst, finally, the amount of available storage space will have implications for the order size and frequency of restocking.

Higher fuel and labour costs and scale economies of distribution are making it less likely that single catering operations will be able to purchase directly from growers and manufacturers in future. For instance, Proctor & Gamble increased their minimum delivery from 40 to 80 cases in 1985. Thus only very large catering chains are likely to purchase direct, other operations will use a middleman.

Large chain operations have two main options with regard to supply. They can either own and operate their own distribution system such as Trusthouse Forte, or they can contract a distributor to make deliveries from the manufacturers to their units on their behalf. Kentucky Fried Chicken, for example, negotiates a bulk price with the manufacturers and then makes delivery arrangements with a distributor. Kentucky Fried Chicken pays the manufacturers directly for the contracted goods. The distributor orders enough goods from the manufacturer to meet the supply requirements of local franchises and is invoiced by Kentucky Fried Chicken at the rates charged to franchisees less a fixed percentage as a distribution allowance. Finally, the franchisees pay the distributor. This has several advantages in that the manufacturer only supplies a limited number of locations in bulk and Kentucky Fried Chicken franchisees are assured of weekly deliveries of all commodities in any order size.

For operators who are not part of a chain commodities must be purchased either from wholesale markets, from wholesale suppliers, from cash and carry outlets or from retail outlets such as supermarkets. The tradition of chefs getting up at five am to go to the local market to select fresh meat, fish, fruit and vegetables has become the exception rather than the rule. The growth in availability and use of frozen and irradiated food has resulted in less reliance on truly fresh commodities, and consequently the number, scale and frequency of markets are declining. As markets decline changes in catering operations, such as the shift from skilled to semi-skilled kitchen personnel, smaller kitchen and store areas and lower profit margins a consequent move is made towards what has been called 'one stop shopping'. This refers to the use of *total supply distributors* who can provide the caterers with all their commodity requirements including foodstuffs, disposables and alcoholic beverages. When using total supply only one delivery is made which cuts down on paperwork, opportunities for pilferage and time spent on receiving goods.

Increased distribution costs now cause many catering suppliers to rethink their delivery policy and, especially where order quantities are small, caterers often have to go to the warehouse or cash and carry themselves. It is estimated that in the UK 131 000 caterers purchase about £750 million of goods from cash and carry outlets and that the cash and carry share of the market will increase rapidly during the late 1980s. The main advantage of cash and carry to independent operators is that there is no minimum order size. There are, however, significant disadvantages, in particular the lack of credit facilities. Caterers who use cash and carry outlets also have to pay for their own distribution costs, which are often comparatively higher than those of a wholesaler.

There is every reason to suppose that there will be further changes in distribution towards the end of the 1980s. In central London, grocery retailers operate an order and delivery service based around Prestel. It will soon be possible for caterers to call up an on-screen list of suppliers' products and prices and, using a keyboard, order items from the warehouse. Such orders will automatically process the wholesaler's own restocking requirements, produce invoices and establish daily delivery routes. Upon delivery of the goods, the caterer will acknowledge receipt of the goods via their terminal and their bank account will be automatically debited for the amount due.

The selection of sources of supply is critical to effective materials management, as this determines both invoice and administration costs. The choice of sources of supply also constrains the order quantity and has a considerable impact on stock levels. Careful planning and control of stock levels for individual commodities is not in itself completely satisfactory as the only method of stock monitoring. It is useful to have an easily monitored measure of total stock value – the use of *number of days' stock* is to be recommended as a system, it is calculated as follows:

$$\frac{\text{value of current stock}}{\text{value of annual consumption}} \times 365$$

If the current value of the stock of food commodities is £2 310 and the value of food consumed during the last 12 months amounted to £38 325, the number of days' stock would be:

$$\frac{2310}{38325} \times 365$$

$$= 22 \text{ days}$$

Trends in number of days' stock give useful control data on a four-weekly basis – but evaluation of the raw data is more difficult. Is 22 days' food stock acceptable? The answer depends on the type of food – fresh or convenience – and the terms of supply, but the norm for catering businesses is about 15 days of food stock. In addition to being useful for assessing total stock, this measure is helpful for highlighting slow-moving stock items.

One of management's most important tasks is to ensure that the assets of the business are adequately protected from theft, loss or misappropriation. The purchase of food, alcohol and other catering materials presents a particular problem as they are attractive to the petty thief and, because of the large number of small suppliers involved, control is difficult. There are two areas which need attention – security of the premises and purchasing control procedures. If managers are successful in this respect then:
- only materials which are required by the business will be ordered.
- only materials received by the business will be paid for – at the agreed price.
- all materials received by the business will be stored securely and, finally, correctly used to generate sales.

This sounds simple but when one considers the hundreds of different materials which are used, the dozens of different suppliers, the problems of incomplete orders and returned substandard goods and the opportunities for dishonesty by employees, suppliers and others, then the problem becomes very complex.

Purchasing control procedures should be designed to ensure that employees take the proper steps to ensure that assets are properly protected and to ensure that loss will quickly be identified when it has occurred. However, physical security is equally important. The design of the goods reception area, the control of keys and the organisation of stores is also essential to effective control.

PEOPLE AS ASSETS

The catering industry has been described as a people industry; the skills of its service staff and the competence of its specialists are factors which determine business success or failure. A decade ago, there was considerable debate in management circles concerning the question of whether the value of an organisation's employees should be reflected in its accounts. Most people agree that this is neither feasible nor particularly useful in respect of the published accounts, as employees are not assets: the employer neither owns them nor leases them – they are free to leave at any time.[3] Some of the discussion of 'human asset accounting' has implications for our considerations of a catering manager's role in protecting assets. The most useful idea to come from human asset accounting was the *initial cost of employment* concept.

Labour turnover has long been recognised as a feature of catering businesses, and turnover rates of 150 or 200 per cent are not uncommon. The initial costs associated with employment are:

Recruitment and selection
Initial job training
Efficiency attainment
Extra supervision

In many respects these costs can be regarded as the investment costs associated with employment and they should be spread over the life of the asset. As an example consider the employment of a chef at a weekly total employment cost of £180. The initial cost of employment is £200 and the cost of termination is £100. The total average costs of employment will vary depending on whether the person is employed for three months, six months or one year, as shown in table 8.4.

Table 8.4 *Total average employment costs*

	3 Months	6 Months	12 Months
Initial Costs	200	200	200
Termination Costs	100	100	100
Continuing Costs	2340	4680	9360
Total Cost	2640	4980	9660
Average weekly cost	203.08	191.54	185.77

Of course, these costs are not highlighted in most operating statements – they hidden away in many account categories: recruitment costs, uniforms, administration and labour costs. Given the effects of labour turnover on total average employment costs, it is clear that catering managers must take effective action to protect one of the business's most valuable assets – its employees.

Managers faced with the problem of reducing their employee turnover are well advised to adopt the same approach as has been advocated throughout this book. Define a measurement criterion, set a target and record a quantified and qualified plan. There are several methods of measuring employee wastage. The most useful of these is to measure the *labour stability index* which assesses the proportion of the workforce which has more than one year's employment and is calculated as follows:

$$\text{Labour stability index} = \frac{\text{no. of employees with} \geq 12 \text{ months' service}}{\text{total number of jobs}}$$

$$= \frac{30}{200} = 0.15$$

In this example, 30 employees out of 200 have more than one year's continuous employment, giving a stability index of 0.15. An improvement is obviously needed, but what target for improvement should be adopted? There is a strong argument which says that a certain degree of labour turnover is desirable, particularly where employees have to maintain a fresh and interested approach to selling and customer service. Generally catering managers should aim for a stability index of no less than 0.6, and that would be a suitable target to adopt in this case.

Managers can influence an employee's stability in a number of ways. The most important of these is to ensure that each employee survives the induction crisis. This is the point at which many employees leave a job and it generally occurs between about 12 to 16 weeks after initial employment. Often the reasons for wastage at this point are concerned either with a failure to fit in with the working group or a dislike for the job content itself; those employees who survive this crisis are those who not only adapt and fit in with the group but also those who find that the job meets their expectations. Much expense can be avoided by simply painting a very accurate picture of the job at the interview. It is a trap to over-glamorise a job to lure employees only to find that they leave as soon as they can – it is better to find someone who realises the full implications of hard, dirty work, with unsocial hours and little pay (if that is what it is!) and still wants the job. Fitting in with the team is partly a question of effective selection. It is also partly a question of time, in allowing new employees time to become accustomed to the other team members. It is, however, easy to overlook the responsibility that each workgroup has for its new members. Briefing the group on what it is expected to do to welcome, train and encourage new members can yield substantial results, especially if this is linked with a sharing of objectives for improving labour stability. Appointing a mentor within a group is the established method of fitting in new employees, and this is very effective in minimising the effects of the induction crisis.

PROPERTY MANAGEMENT

Most of the investment injected into catering businesses is transformed into premises, furnishings and equipment. With the refurbishment costs for a pub to theme-restaurant conversion running at up to £1 million,[4] the cost effective management of the premises is a prime area of concern for catering managers. There are three major themes which should be given attention:

- what standards of cleaning and maintenance should be aimed at and how should these standards be achieved?
- how can the total cost in use of the premises, furnishings and equipment be kept to a minimum?
- what should be done to protect the premises and its contents from malicious damage, fire or theft?

These three themes are central to both the planning and day-to-day management of catering businesses. In this book focus will be on the latter area, but discussion will by necessity cover certain aspects of planning catering businesses.

The cleanliness and effective operation of premises and equipment have several implications for the management of catering operations. Firstly, these aspects directly affect the quality of the product. The breakdown of a key piece of equipment (for example a slow roasting oven in a carvery-style restaurant) can prejudice all the quality characteristics discussed in chapter 5 – availability, grade and conformity. Similarly, the cleanliness of key parts of the customer environment (for example, the toilets) can have a major impact on quality perception as discussed in chapter 3. From this viewpoint, it can be seen that cleaning and maintenance have major implications for product quality and hence sales volume.

Cleaning and maintenance also feature largely in the costs of the business. There are obvious direct costs associated with cleaning and maintenance activities themselves – labour, materials and replacement parts. These costs can easily be quantified for maintenance, but cleaning activities are often undertaken by many different operative staff and these costs are more difficult to measure and control. Equipment breakdown often has consequential costs of spoiled food and beverages, lost sales and wasted employee time and these costs can be considerable.

It is very difficult to achieve the right balance in cleaning and maintenance expenditure – neither to overspend on unnecessary maintenance, with resultant high maintenance costs, nor to underspend, with resultant high breakdown costs. For a given piece of equipment there is an ideal level of maintenance where the total costs of maintenance and the costs of breakdown are at a minimum.[5]

It can be seen from figure 8.2 that as the frequency of maintenance increases, the cost of breakdown reduces. The optimum level is found where the total cost is at a minimum (point C). This is a useful concept for planning maintenance and cleaning, although actual measurement is often limited to use in larger chain restaurant businesses.

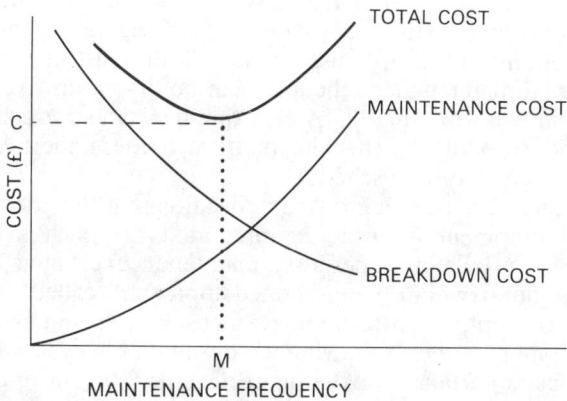

Figure 8.2 *Optimum maintenance frequency.* Adapted from *Production and Operations Management,* Hughes, C.[5]

Poorly maintained equipment and dirty premises have an adverse effect on the morale of employees. However, cleaning tasks are usually thought of as low status activities which makes it difficult to encourage employees to 'clean as they go'. A survey of the problems experienced by newly appointed supervisors[6] showed that maintaining good housekeeping standards was one of the most taxing and persistent problems. This seems to be the case particularly in small catering businesses with peaked demand and low staffing levels: here the premises are often kept clean when they are comparatively empty, but at peak times, when the premises are used by the majority of customers, it proves difficult to maintain a satisfactory customer environment.

Ineffective cleaning and maintenance can also have legislative repercussions. Requirements are defined in different ways, varying from the general requirements of the Health and Safety at Work etc. Act 1974, through to the very specific requirements of The Notification of Accidents and Dangerous Occurrences Regulations 1980.[7] Legislative standards are more clearly defined in the form of *Codes of Practice* and by guidance notes which are issued by Local Authority Environmental Health Departments. Of course, it is not only the risk of fines that necessitates care in this respect – far more damaging is the prospect of the adverse publicity which follows prosecutions for neglect of hygiene standards in catering premises.

Whatever standards are chosen, cleaning and maintenance should be planned and controlled in the same way as any other essential business activity. A clear policy should be written expressing who is responsible for ensuring that the required standards are achieved. Policy statements are in any case required under the Health and Safety at Work etc. Act, and it is suggested that these are extended to cover all cleaning and maintenance activities. There are two approaches to undertaking cleaning and maintenance activities:

Preventive Action is planned to take place on a cyclic basis (for example daily cleaning or annual maintenance).

Corrective Action only takes place when deemed necessary, usually following an inspection, but occasionally as a response to a breakdown, customer complaint or other pressure.

The choice of corrective or preventive action is largely governed by the risks to product quality, cost, employee performance and legislative compliance associated with the failure of cleaning or maintenance of a particular facility. Analysis of the importance of activities into *critical* (for instance, the maintenance of a computer point-of-sales system), *major* (internal cleaning of a refrigerator) and *minor* (cleaning behind the radiators in a back-of-house corridor) will assist in planning. From this analysis cleaning and maintenance schedules can be drawn up. Actual performance can be monitored in two ways: firstly, by checking the standards achieved (is the end result correct?) and, secondly, by checking on the activities undertaken (has the work been completed as shown on the schedule?)

In recent years there has been a growing realisation that the effective management of premises and equipment requires an integrated approach to the activities of specification, design, installation, operation, maintenance, cleaning and replacement. These activities are not new, but the integrated approach – called *Terotechnology* – is a relatively new concept.[8] Terotechnology focuses on planning the life-cycle of premises and equipment and on achieving the optimum life-cycle cost for each asset. This has an obvious importance for the planned refurbishment of catering facilities, where the asset life-cycle has to be meshed with the product life-cycle. Terotechnology draws heavily on the concept of *cost-in-use*. For a given piece of equipment, the cost-in-use consists of the acquisition costs (such as purchase price and installation costs) which need to be spread over the life of the asset, and the running costs (such as cleaning, maintenance, energy, labour and materials). The cost in use concept provides a useful basis for comparing alternative courses of action – such as the purchase of machine A compared with the rental of machine B.

A catering manager has a clear responsibility to protect the premises and its contents from malicious damage, fire and theft. Success in this area depends on the design of the premises, the attitude and performance of the employees and the effective implementation of security systems. The number and location of exits and the security of windows and emergency doors have an obvious influence on the security of a building. Less obvious is the influence of external features such as balconies, ledges, pipes and nearby trees. Advice is essential here from police crime prevention officers, insurance companies, specialist security firms and the local fire prevention officer. The result should be not only effectively designed premises, but also security procedures which enable staff to deal effectively with emergencies such as fires, robberies or bomb-scares.

Twenty-four hour operations are often prime targets for robbery, especially when there are large quantities of cash kept on the premises. Frequent banking of cash will assist in limiting this risk, but it is also important to avoid a predictable routine as this will encourage robbery. The use of direct alarms and closed circuit television is advisable where only one or two employees are left on duty with large amounts of cash. Finally, a wise choice of safe (a drop safe is useful when few employees are on the premises) and good cash handling procedures are essential.

Table 8.5 *Main forms of insurance*

Fire insurance	
Consequential Loss Insurance	may cover loss of profits arising from closure following fire flood or explosion.
Fidelity Guarantee Insurance	covers possible loss caused by employee theft.
Cash in Transit Insurance	covers cash robbery between the catering premises and the bank.
Employer's Liability Insurance	covers injuries to employees that may occur due to employer's negligence.
Public Liability Insurance	covers injuries to the public caused by employer or employee negligence. This usually includes food poisoning.
Burglary Insurance	
Engineering Insurance	covers damage to plant.
Credit Insurance	covers bad debts, usually to 75% of the full amount.

Adapted from *Management Accounting*, Batty, J.[9]

Much of cost-effective premises management is concerned with assessing risks and judging what action should be taken to protect the building and its contents from these risks. Many of these risks will be offset by insurance. Managers have to decide the risks to be covered, a premium is then payable to the insurance company, and if the eventuality covered by the policy occurs then a claim may be made.

SUMMARY

This chapter discussed the manager's role as a custodian of the firm's assets. If no action is taken, erosion, decay, theft and wastage will destroy physical assets. Cash needs to be carefully controlled to gain maximum benefit from possible interest and to ensure that sufficient funds are available for business needs. People have been compared in some respects to assets, and here too the manager needs to take particular care to avoid unnecessary wastage of skills and experience.

REFERENCES

1. *Restaurant and Bar Security*, Security World, 1974.
2. Pannett, A., *Principles of Hotel and Catering Law*, Holt, Rinehart and Winston 1984.
3. Whiting, E., *How to Get Your Employment Costs Right*, ICAEW, 1985.
4. Brady, J., 'The fast food feast', *Management Today*, pp. 58–65, April 1985.
5. Hughes, C., *Production and Operations Management*, Pan, 1985.

6. Bittel, L.R., *Essentials of Supervisory Management,* McGraw-Hill, 1981.
7. Pannett, A., *op. cit.*
8. Department of Industry, *Terotechnology: An Introduction to the Management of Physical Resources*, HMSO, 1975.
9. Batty, J., *Management Accounting*, Macdonald & Evans, 1970.

9

Increasing Productivity

OBJECTIVES

Analyse problems of measuring catering productivity . . . compare and contrast approaches to reducing material costs . . . evaluate labour productivity improvement techniques . . . examine overhead cost reduction methods.

INTRODUCTION

Productivity is the term relating to cost reduction. It is most commonly used in conjunction with labour costs, but it actually describes all activities that result in a lower unit cost of the product or service. The simplest way to define productivity is:

$$\text{Productivity} = \frac{\text{Output}}{\text{Input}}$$

Input refers to the cost of resources employed in making the product or providing the service, such as in catering foodstuffs, staff, energy and other overhead costs. Output is the value of the product or service, in this case meals and drinks.

The reduction of cost and increased productivity are major issues facing British industry in the 1980s. All catering operations have costs and sound business practice dictates that these should be as low as possible with respect to the supply of the established quality of product or service. In the catering industry there has always been an emphasis on controlling costs, particularly in those sectors that traditionally are cost-oriented, rather than market focused. As we have seen with trends in regard to privatisation of the public sector, lower subsidies of industrial catering operations, and a narrowing of the price differential between the cheapest and most expensive restaurants the difference between cost and market oriented businesses is increasingly less apparent.

The financial environment was discussed in chapter 1 along with the idea that sectors of the catering industry have different cost structures. Hotels and restaurants have high fixed costs relative to their variable costs, and industrial and welfare catering have relatively low fixed costs as a proportion of total cost. These two types of cost structure have implications for a number of operational key result areas, but in particular productivity. Kotas[1] has argued that high fixed cost operations must adopt a 'market orientation' as they operate close to their breakeven point, and hence must be

Table 9.1   *Comparison of market and cost orientation in the catering industry.*

	Market orientation	Cost orientation
Cost structure	High proportion fixed cost & low proportion variable cost	Low proportion fixed cost & high proportion variable cost
Investment	High level of capital investment	Low level of capital investment
Product design	Emphasis on service aspects & atmosphere	Emphasis on food & beverage product
Average spend	Relatively high	Relatively low
Gross profit	Relatively high	Relatively low
Sales volume per employee	Low number of transactions	High number of transactions
Number of staff	High in proportion to number of customers	Low in proportion to number of customers
Rates of pay	Relatively high	Relatively low

Adapted from *Marketing Orientation in the Hotel and Catering Industry*, Kotas, R.

highly responsive to market needs. High variable cost units will have a 'cost orientation' and focus a great deal on reducing or minimising such costs. Such orientation and structure results in fundamental differences between operations with regard to their turnover, profitability and labour costs. This is illustrated in table 9.1.

ALTERNATIVE WAYS OF INCREASING PRODUCTIVITY

Since productivity is the relationship between inputs (or costs) and outputs (or products/services) it can be increased by:
Lower costs and greater services.
Lower costs and constant services.
Constant costs and greater services.
Higher costs and greater relative increase in services.
Lower costs and smaller relative decrease in services.
These are illustrated in figure 9.1.

By expressing productivity in this way it is apparent that no decision or action can be taken about it without implications for quality and standards. It is also apparent that the first three models of productivity improvement are less problematic than the last two. It can be argued that any manager who could improve or maintain services at the same or lower costs has not been managing his business effectively. Of course, the opportunities for such improvement may be due to the dynamic circumstances of the business or the intrinsic nature of the operational activity. Typical changes that have taken place in the catering industry relate to technology, so that more sophisticated plant and machinery may become available which, even allowing for capital investment, result in lower operating costs. It may also be the case that inputs cannot vary directly with output, for instance, in a restaurant once a waitress is on duty she could serve one person or thirty people.

Often, however, a manager is required to evaluate whether or not a change in productivity will have a greater or lesser relative impact on services. For example, a banqueting manager may decide that instead of having one waiter for every ten dining

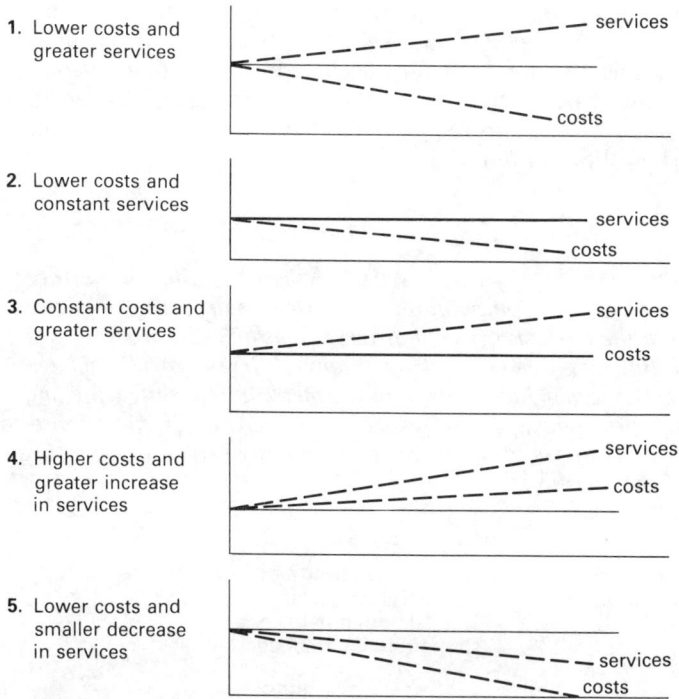

1. Lower costs and greater services
   — services
   — costs

2. Lower costs and constant services
   — services
   — costs

3. Constant costs and greater services
   — services
   — costs

4. Higher costs and greater increase in services
   — services
   — costs

5. Lower costs and smaller decrease in services
   — services
   — costs

Figure 9.1 *Models of increasing productivity.* – – – indicates change in costs or services.

customers, each waiter will serve twelve customers. Clearly this will lead to lower costs, but inevitably there will be consequences for the level of service provided. The manager must be sure that the savings achieved will be greater than the potential fall in sales such a policy could cause.

In addition to the complexity of the alternative approaches, there is a tendency for cost-oriented operations to concentrate on approaches 1, 2, and 5 (figure 9.1), whilst market-oriented operations will be concerned with approaches 3 and 4. Just as the distinction between these two orientations is slowly being broken down, so is the appropriateness of a particular approach to productivity. For instance, many local education authority catering departments are examining ways of attracting higher take-up and increasing average spends.

PROBLEMS WITH CATERING PRODUCTIVITY

The major problem facing catering managers in their attempt to improve productivity is the inexact and diverse nature of the product/service being sold. Productivity improvement techniques in other industries are inapplicable because there is usually a mass produced standard output of a clearly definable product. In the catering industry, as well as the intangibilities of service and ambiance examined in chapter 6, even the tangible product itself is almost infinitely variable. This is because the total product is made up of components selected by the customers in any combination they desire in order to arrive at a meal package they want. It is rather like a customer walking into a factory manufacturing transistor radios, selecting from the list of components those which he or she wants and asking the factory manager to assemble them in the order that the customer requests! It is hard to imagine manufacturing industry being able to cope with this, so it is fortunate that customers leave radio design and manufacture to the experts. But, since all customers eat, they are all their own experts when it comes to food, hence they expect to and are allowed to design their meals when they eat out.

Case example 9.1   Brown's Restaurant Menu

(a) Look at the menu in figure 9.2. Assume every customer has a three course meal. How many different dish combinations of starter, main course and sweet are there?
(b) Assume that the bar can offer 30 different aperitifs, the wine list has 20 wines, and there are ten liqueurs available. How many different meal packages are possible assuming every customer has a three course meal, an aperitif, wine and a liqueur?
(c) How many meal packages are possible if the customer can choose to have a two course meal, i.e., starter and main course or main course and sweet, instead of a three course meal if they wish?

STARTERS
Chicken liver paté
Niçoise salad
Beef and tomato soup
Grapefruit and mint cocktail

MAIN COURSES
Trout with almonds
Turkey breast in mushroom sauce
Honey roast gammon with rosemary
Steak and kidney pudding
Fricassee of lamb
Vegetarian nut cutlet with piquant sauce

SWEETS
Pear in red wine sauce
Chilled hazelnut soufflé
Blackberry and apple pie
Pistachio ice cream
Treacle tart

Figure 9.2   *Typical table d'hôte menu.*

(a) To find the total number of possible dish combinations multiply the number of dishes in each course – $4 \times 6 \times 5 = 120$ different dish combinations or meals.
(b) The number of meal packages is $120 \times 30 \times 20 \times 10 = 720\ 000$
(c) When it is possible to have two or three course meals the total number of possible meals (output) is 1·044 million!

This case illustrates that, even in a relatively small catering operation, the output is extremely varied and difficult to define. It follows that if the output is diverse, then the inputs are likely to be even more highly variable since each dish will be made up of a wide range of ingredients making the multiplicity and possible combinations of inputs almost incalculable. The main implications of this are that there are very few instances where higher productivity can be achieved by one simple change in the production process or working practices and that trying to examine possible productivity improvements is extremely complex and difficult.

The industry has traditionally ignored or overcome this problem by adding together the total inputs and outputs and comparing the two aggregates. In the case of raw materials the food cost percentage is used as the productivity measure, and for labour the labour cost percentage. As chapter 4 illustrated there are implications for using gross profit contribution as a measure of business effectiveness and these were examined in some detail. Similar problems arise when staffing costs are aggregated as a means of measuring productivity in the labour cost percentage.

The major problem with labour cost percentage is its variation with sales revenue. Thus it will change if the number of sales transactions rises or falls and no change is made to staffing; or if sales per cover increase or decrease and staffing levels are static; if sales are static but more or fewer staff are scheduled or if wage rates are changed and no change in sales is achieved. But with the simple labour cost percentage it is impossible to differentiate between these four reasons for the apparent change in productivity. This weakness is further compounded by the aggregation of data, often over a period of a month, so that it is not possible to specify whether the variations from standard cost expectations are caused at specific meal times, on certain days or by the inadequacies of scheduling different grades of staff. This is illustrated in table 9.2.

Table 9.2 *A Comparison of Labour Costs*

	Unit A	Unit B
Sales	£25 000	£28 000
Wages	£7 500	£7 500
Labour cost percentage	30	26.8
Total work hours	3 850	3 850
Average hourly rate	£1.95	£1.95
Sales per work hour	£6.50	£7.27
Average spend	£5.21	£6.80
Number of covers	4 800	4 120
Covers per work hour	1.25	1.07
Labour cost per cover	£1.56	£1.82

Adapted from *The Myth of Labour Cost Percentages*, Pavesic, D.V.[2]

As table 9.2 illustrates, using labour cost percentage as a measure suggests that Unit B is more productive, since it has higher sales revenue for the same labour cost as Unit A. Closer analysis reveals that it has achieved this by having a higher average spend than Unit A, and it has actually served fewer customers. In fact, the staff in Unit A have served more people and therefore it is using its labour more productively. Thus the manager in Unit A needs to maximise gross profit, whilst Unit B's manager needs to consider how to improve productivity.

From this it can be seen that there are six measures needed to analyse productivity effectively, the data for which is usually available already. These six measures are:
- labour cost percentage.
- total man hours.
- sales per man hour.
- covers per man hour.
- labour cost per man hour.
- labour cost per cover.

The three main cost areas over which productivity improvements can be made are raw material costs, labour costs and overhead costs. In this chapter each will be examined in turn, with a consideration of the appropriateness of three specific approaches – in looking at material costs 'value analysis' is considered; when reviewing labour costs different ideas about work improvement will be examined; finally, the role of zero-based budgeting in reducing overhead costs will be explored.

REDUCING RAW MATERIAL COSTS

As chapter 10 will show, raw material costs represent the largest cost element of most catering operations – somewhere between 35 per cent and 43 per cent of sales volume. It is therefore evident that any measures that are taken to reduce raw material costs will potentially reap the largest reward in terms of productivity gains. As chapter 5 noted there are four main ways of reducing the dish or portion cost of food or drink. These were:

- substituting a cheaper commodity.
- reducing the actual quantity of raw materials used.
- renegotiating raw material costs with suppliers.
- reducing variances due to wastage, pilferage and overproduction.

This section is primarily concerned with the first two of these options. Chapter 8 looked at supplier evaluation and variance control will be considered in chapter 10.

In most cases, raw material costs are variable, that is to say they should have a direct relationship with the volume of sales. This is another reason why productivity gains can potentially be made in this area, since theoretically the nature of these costs is such that management should have a great deal of control over them. One particular technique that achieves this is 'value analysis'.

In determining product quality, it has been shown that great care is taken over controlling each stage of the production and service process to ensure that quality is maintained throughout. Chapter 5 considered aspects of quality without considering the cost trade-off that has to be made. In reality the costs of devising a catering product, implementing a purchasing policy and operating with purchase specifications, standard recipes and other quality control procedures have to be a major consideration. But there is a tendency, once product development is completed and supported by a quality control programme, to assume that no futher cost savings can be made. In fact there are several reasons why, after a period of time, it may be possible to review material costs and eliminate unnecessary costs. Firstly, procedures and material inputs may have been based on a sales mix that has changed as consumer tastes change. Secondly, new equipment or a new range of commodities may have become available that were unavailable or too expensive when the original concept was devised. Thirdly, there may have been a mismatch with regard to the detailed aspects of the product package and the market for which it was devised.

A reappraisal of each aspect of the concept, in this case each dish on the menu, may not result in any fall in quality, even when cost savings are made. There are basically two ways of examining potential cost savings, by recipe development and by yield testing. Recipe development refers to experimentation with dishes to produce a dish of the appropriate quality but at lower cost. Each of the ingredients is costed very accurately and their contribution in 'value' terms is assessed. An example of this has been the substitution of lumpfish roe for caviar as a garnish or on canapés. Chefs are of the opinion that the public cannot discriminate between the two commodities when used in this way, so that their quality perception remains high, even though a much lower cost item is being used. To test out ideas, some catering organisations use tasting panels to evaluate their dishes, with specialists who are expert in this role, just as there are wine tasters. For smaller operators, however, the traditional approach of the chef and manager sitting down to eat and appraise a dish is still common.

Yield testing does not redesign the recipe, but tests to see that waste during the preparation and cooking stages is kept within acceptable limits, and from this is taken the yield specification. The theoretical approach to yield control is a series of scientifically carried out experiments designed to identify the characteristics and behaviour of foodstuffs during the production process. Such experimentation is highly detailed and ensures that a large number of different variables that may affect yield are systematically examined. The results are analysed to arrive at the yield specification which meets the quality standards required at the lowest cost. In practice, this methodology requires a food production laboratory and hence is not widely practised in the catering industry. It is more frequently utilised by frozen food manufacturers, although some large chain operators have carried out such experimentation. For instance, during the 1970s, the Carlton Tower hotel carried out extensive testing to establish the best method of producing roast beef for its then newly conceived 'Rib Room' restaurant. On the basis of their findings they identified and installed one specific type of oven solely for the roasting of ribs of beef.

Whilst such detailed and scientific yield testing is rare, throughout the industry experimentation is continually being carried out. A typical example might be the hotel which is producing large quantities of apple pie. Rather than use a standard recipe without question, it could purchase different brands of A10 solid pack apple and over a period of time decide which brand it wished to use, based on the opinion of the manager, chef and customer reaction.

As well as examining each individual dish, both its ingredient cost and manufacture cost, it is also worth examining the total product cost by evaluating the menu. Effective menu design can improve productivity in a synergic creation of reduced costs and optimised product usage. Savings can be made in a number of ways:
- fewer commodities held thereby reducing order costs and control costs.
- commodities used in several ways so that usage rates are high thereby reducing the likelihood of wastage because of over-long stock-holding.
- previously non-saleable parts of a raw material, for instance chicken livers, may become a revenue earning item.

A feature of fast food stores has been that menu choice is provided by minor variations of basic recipes which use only a very few commodity items, e.g. french fries, bun, burger, garnish and relish. On the other hand, traditional à la carte restaurants have a very large number of dish items. To overcome the potentially high level of wastage, such restaurants also have table d'hôte menus, devised on a daily basis. Each day the chef examines the raw materials and partly processed items available in the kitchen and determines their future shelf-life. From this, the table d'hôte menu is planned using up as much as possible of those items that would soon need to be sold or thrown away. Typical examples of this economy would be to use prepared or partly cooked vegetables as a garnish in casseroles or soup; utilise cooked meats in dishes requiring minced meat, such as moussaka or lasagne and so on.

LABOUR PRODUCTIVITY IMPROVEMENT TECHNIQUES

In broad terms labour productivity can be achieved by firstly increasing the level of possible performance by individual members of staff after work study and related techniques, and secondly by combining staff into teams more efficiently through scheduling. An essential feature of either approach is the need to ensure high levels of staff motivation, without which it is extremely unlikely that any improvement in productivity can be made (see chapter 7). In very modern, highly technocratic operations the operational manager's opportunities and need for improved productivity are considerably reduced, due to the highly researched analysis of unit layout, work procedures and scheduling that are incorporated into chain restaurant design. None the less it is likely that a catering manager will need at some time to implement ideas about how to improve labour productivity.

Work measurement is inherent in every catering operation. Whilst in most cases it is unlikely that formal work evaluation programmes will have been undertaken, staffing levels in kitchens, cafeterias and restaurants are all based on some assumptions about the amount of work a member of staff can do and hence how many staff are needed to perform the task or tasks required. Work measurement in itself is not a means of improving productivity, instead it forms the basis on which improvements can be made. It does this by establishing standards of performance against which existing staff and new staff can be judged, staffing levels can be determined, rates of pay agreed, and so on. Work measurement is defined as 'the application of techniques designed to establish the time for a qualified worker to carry out a specific job at a defined level of performance' (British Standards Institute).

There are a variety of techniques used in manufacturing industry, most of which are rarely applied to catering because of the complexity of the delivery systems just described. The most common technique that is used in the catering industry is *estimating*. This technique is based on past experience, previous knowledge and assessment of similar operations. A simple example of this is the way in which function catering staffing levels are commonly established. Staff are employed using a ratio of customers to staff, such as 10:1 for waiting staff and 30:1 for wine service staff. Other sectors use more sophisticated ratios, although still based on the estimating technique. For instance, staffing levels in the school meals sector may be based on each school's take-up of meals. One authority measures this take-up over a two-week period in February in each of its primary schools to establish the average daily take-up for each school. This is used to calculate the total number of allocated staff hours per week for each school. Typically a school with a take-up per day of 200 meals might have 113 staff hours per week allocated. From this, the total is broken down into grades of staff, such as cook supervisor (30 hours), assistant cook (30 hours) and general kitchen assistants to make up the total of allocated hours.[4]

There are two other main types of work measurement techniques that may be of some relevance and value in evaluating performance in the catering industry and provide a guide for potential productivity gains. *Time study* analyses in detail every aspect of an operator performing a certain task. This is mainly suitable for establishing performance where relatively simple, repetitive tasks are undertaken. As an earlier chapter pointed out these are rare in the restaurant business, but with the move towards technocratic approaches to catering the opportunities may increase. Indeed, this technique may be appropriate for some sectors such as large-scale production kitchens, cook–chill or cook–freeze catering, or fast food operations.

Activity sampling is the third technique. This studies the activities of a team of people operating over a relatively long period of time. Depending upon the degree of accuracy required, a number of random visits are made during the work period and either or both the staff and equipment activities are noted according to a previously determined classification. Examples of such a classification are shown in figure 9.3. Such techniques however are only of value if work is being performed correctly. If not, it may be necessary to establish correct work practices by carrying out method study.

(a) Classification of chef's work activity

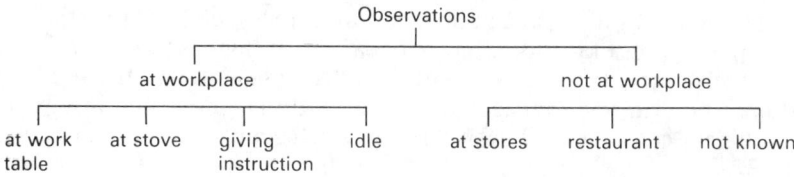

```
                              Observations
          ┌───────────────────────┴───────────────────────┐
      at workplace                                  not at workplace
  ┌──────┬──────┬──────┐                      ┌──────────┬──────────┬──────────┐
at work  at stove  giving  idle            at stores  restaurant  not known
table              instruction
```

(b) Classification of deep fryer usage

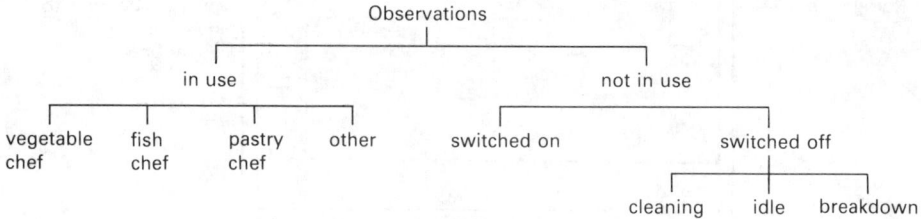

```
                              Observations
          ┌───────────────────────┴───────────────────────┐
        in use                                         not in use
  ┌──────┬──────┬──────┐                      ┌──────────┬──────────────────┐
vegetable  fish  pastry  other            switched on           switched off
chef       chef  chef                                      ┌──────────┬──────────┐
                                                        cleaning   idle   breakdown
```

Figure 9.3 *Examples of activity sampling.*

Method study is a simple, systematic problem-solving technique which makes possible productivity improvements. It is defined as 'the systematic recording and critical examination of existing and proposed ways of doing work, as a means of developing and applying easier and more effective methods and reducing costs' (British Standards Institute). It is most commonly used when new equipment is installed, a new product is being introduced or training needs to be reviewed or developed. It may also be an appropriate technique to apply when absenteeism and staff turnover indicate that poor working conditions are perceived by staff. It is not an approach that can be applied to the total process of catering, because of the complexities of food production and service, so that one particular activity or process must be selected for detailed examination. It is therefore important to select an area that will benefit from such a study and hence recoup the cost of undertaking the study, through improved productivity or lower absenteeism.

Once selected, the process is recorded, either in writing or on film, and broken down into its component stages. These stages are typically categorised and symbolised as follows:

Category	Symbol	Explanation
Operation	○	operative activity or processing of product.
Inspection	☐	quality check.
Transport	⇨	movement of operative or product.
Delay	D	no change or movement of product or operative unable to proceed.
Storage	▽	intentional storage before, during or after process.

As this categorisation suggests the charting activity, using the symbols shown, can examine an operative's activity and either or both the materials or equipment in use.

The recording and charting of the existing procedure then allows analysis with a view to eliminating unnecessary activities and excessive waste, combining activities or rearranging the sequence of activities to speed up the process or employ fewer operatives.

Case Example 9.2   Still Room at Whites Hotel

This case illustrates a hotel still room and the operative process chart of the still room person whilst preparing pots of tea for afternoon tea service (figures 9.4 and 9.5). The problem was that customers (and service staff) were complaining that the service of tea was too slow. The Catering Manager was concerned that she would lose repeat custom if the problem continued. However she was reluctant to employ extra staff

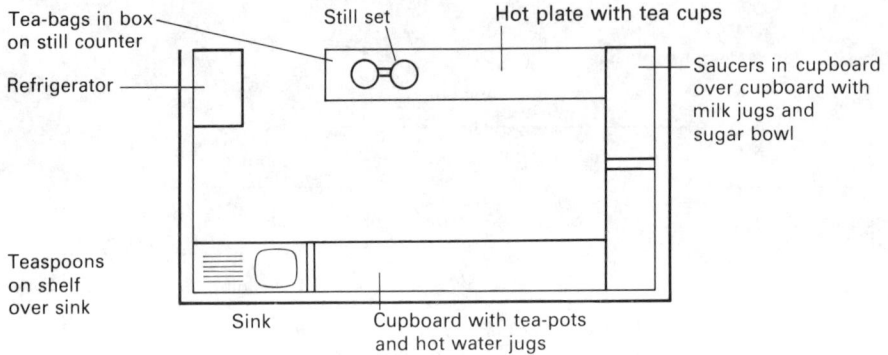

Figure 9.4 *Plan of hotel still room.*

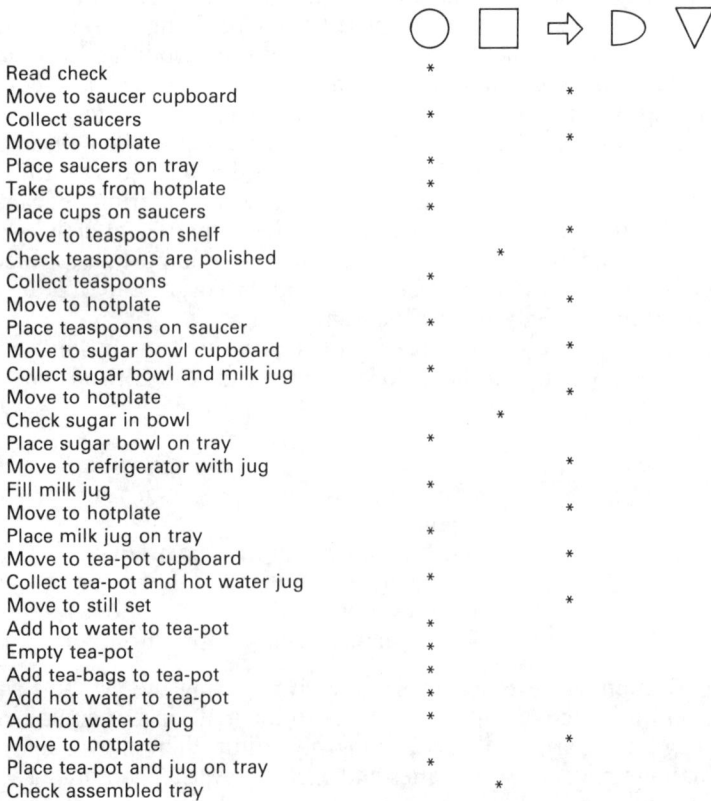

	○	□	⇨	D	▽
Read check	*				
Move to saucer cupboard			*		
Collect saucers	*				
Move to hotplate			*		
Place saucers on tray	*				
Take cups from hotplate	*				
Place cups on saucers	*				
Move to teaspoon shelf			*		
Check teaspoons are polished		*			
Collect teaspoons	*				
Move to hotplate			*		
Place teaspoons on saucer	*				
Move to sugar bowl cupboard			*		
Collect sugar bowl and milk jug	*				
Move to hotplate			*		
Check sugar in bowl		*			
Place sugar bowl on tray	*				
Move to refrigerator with jug			*		
Fill milk jug	*				
Move to hotplate			*		
Place milk jug on tray	*				
Move to tea-pot cupboard			*		
Collect tea-pot and hot water jug	*				
Move to still set			*		
Add hot water to tea-pot	*				
Empty tea-pot	*				
Add tea-bags to tea-pot	*				
Add hot water to tea-pot	*				
Add hot water to jug	*				
Move to hotplate			*		
Place tea-pot and jug on tray	*				
Check assembled tray		*			

Figure 9.5 *Process chart for tea making.*

since the margin of profit on afternoon teas was not great. None the less it provided an opportunity to create revenue at an off-peak time of day, as well as rota some staff on full shifts as opposed to split shifts.

An initial investigation of the problem indicated that orders were taken quickly, but that the still room attendant appeared to take a long time to serve each waitress.

There were several possible solutions. The one shown here relies on some simple mise-en-place prior to service by placing tea-pots and hot water jugs on the hotplate counter (so they do not need pre-warming), pouring the milk into jugs and storing them in the refrigerator, and storing polished teaspoons with the saucers. This is illustrated in figure 9.6.

In a simple case such as this, the manager may not need to resort to recording the work flow in this precise form. It is much more likely that observation of the still room attendant at work would be sufficient to identify how to improve the situation. But it is important to understand the analytical framework of method study, when faced with more complex problems. These often arise with the introduction of new equipment or a redesign of kitchens, cafeterias or restaurants.

It is important to note that method study does not result in an automatic improvement in productivity. In this still room example although the still person is now much better organised, no productivity gains have been made since the cost of inputs, in this case the still person's wages, have remained the same. It is not until ouput increases at no extra cost, or input costs are reduced that productivity improves. In this case, the new working methods may mean that more customers can be served afternoon tea because service has been speeded up, so that output increases at no extra labour cost, or that the still person can be employed in additional activities, using the spare time created productively in some other activities, thereby reducing costs.

Neither work measurement nor method study will necessarily produce immediate results. Both are concerned with how people work and interact with the plant and

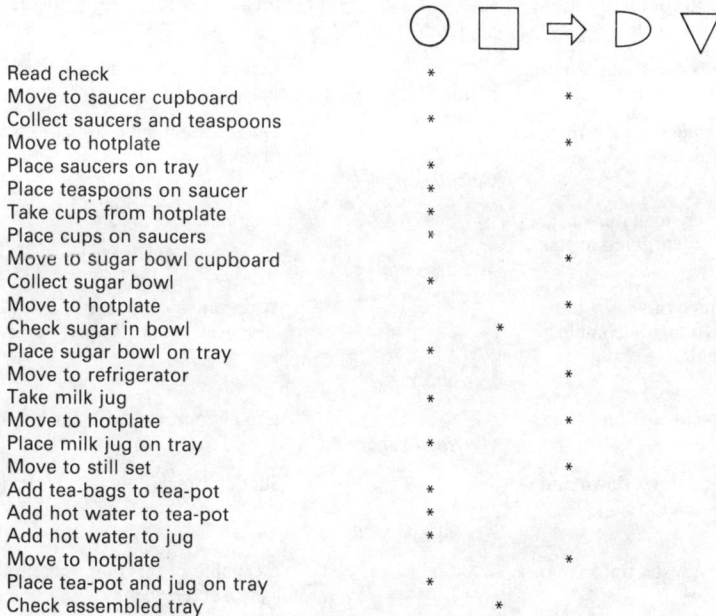

	○	□	⇨	◗	▽
Read check	*				
Move to saucer cupboard			*		
Collect saucers and teaspoons	*				
Move to hotplate			*		
Place saucers on tray	*				
Place teaspoons on saucer	*				
Take cups from hotplate	*				
Place cups on saucers	*				
Move to sugar bowl cupboard			*		
Collect sugar bowl	*				
Move to hotplate			*		
Check sugar in bowl		*			
Place sugar bowl on tray	*				
Move to refrigerator			*		
Take milk jug	*				
Move to hotplate			*		
Place milk jug on tray	*				
Move to still set			*		
Add tea-bags to tea-pot	*				
Add hot water to tea-pot	*				
Add hot water to jug	*				
Move to hotplate			*		
Place tea-pot and jug on tray	*				
Check assembled tray		*			

Figure 9.6   *Revised process chart for tea making.*

equipment around them. Unlike machines, however, people have minds of their own and are subject to human frailties. Training an operative to do work in a certain way will not ensure that he or she will operate at the highest level of output. Unless working conditions for the employee are designed to facilitate output, there is the likelihood that operatives will perform at below their best, make mistakes and, as was said earlier, under very poor working conditions, there can be high levels of absenteeism and staff turnover. The design of optimal working conditions is 'ergonomics'.

Ergonomics was first brought to the attention of the majority of the catering industry in 1971 by the publication of a booklet by Strank.[5] Strank identified the fact that for many of the activities undertaken in the industry, there is the choice between people or machines. The trend is very much towards systematising catering operations and using technology, so it is useful to here compare the characteristics and abilities of men and machines.

Table 9.3 provides a framework for analysing tasks in order to decide whether a particular function should be mechanised in some way. The cashiering function is a good example of the value of both a person and a machine. The point-of-sale

Table 9.3   *Comparison of characteristics and abilities of men and machines.*

MEN		MACHINES
	Speed	
Relatively slow		Capable of very high speeds
Reaction speed of 1 second		Reaction speed almost instantaneous
	Power	
Highly variable		Constant and consistent
	Consistency	
Not suited to routine tasks		Ideal for precise, repetitive tasks
	Complexity of task	
Can only do one thing at a time		Can perform several tasks simultaneously
	Memory	
Good at remembering principles and strategies		Good at remembering large amounts of data
	Calculation	
Slow and may make errors Capable of identifying mistakes		Fast and error free
	Sensory abilities	
Limited range of senses but capable of highly complex interpretation		Wide range of sensory data, e.g. electrical signals, sound waves, etc.
	Versatility	
Highly versatile		Usually purpose built for one function
	Overload capacity	
Performance slows down and becomes selective		Sudden break down
	Reactive capabilities	
Can cope with the unforeseen		Incapable of reacting, must follow logical sequence

Adapted from *Ergonomics: Functional Design for the Catering Industry*, Strank, H.

equipment can calculate more accurately and faster, store much more data, and is extremely reliable; but the cashier can respond to customer enquiries, handle a wide range of proffered means of payment, and cope with any problems.

Since catering is usually reliant on effective teamwork, it is important to ensure that teams as well as individuals work productively. Quite simply, staffing levels must reflect the level of activity. A good example is the fast food sector where point-of-sale equipment can provide a detailed analysis of demand on an hourly basis. Using this historic data and estimates of past performance, fast food managers staff their units to ensure the optimal level of staff throughout the day. To do this a large number of part-time staff are recruited. These staff are then rostered to start and finish their shifts either on the hour, half hour or quarter hour, with shifts varying in length from two up to seven hours. This is illustrated in figure 9.7.

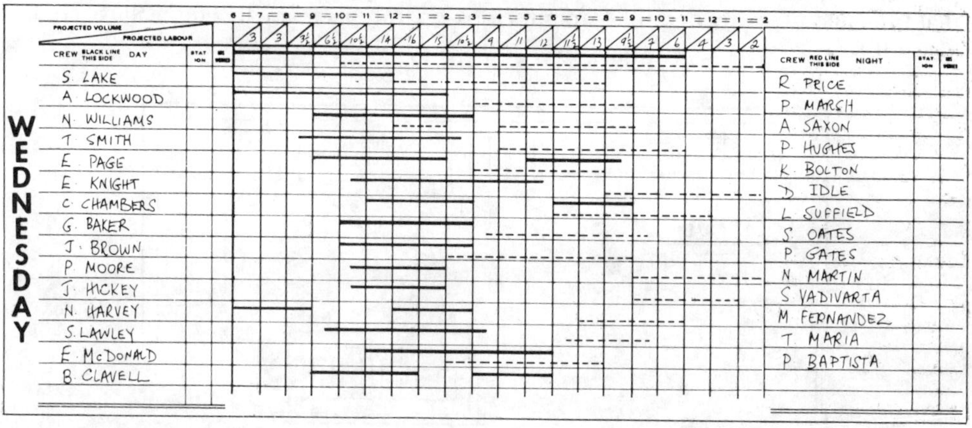

Figure 9.7 *Fast food restaurant staff rota.* Reproduced with permission.

The range of techniques available for determining the optimal level of staffing range from the intuitive estimate, prevalent in the industry, up to highly complex algorithms, usually as a computer model of the operation.[6] In those businesses with a predictable and fairly stable level of demand, scheduling of staff is not really a problem. Effective work study can determine that every member of the team is working at the optimal level and the number of workers required is more or less the same from day to day. This approach is exemplified by the staffing of school meals described earlier. Typically in such a business most staff members will be specialists with specific duties to perform, so that the cashiering function, for example, would be performed by a cashier. This has the usual advantages associated with specialisation, namely increased speed and accuracy of performance.

Where there is a wide fluctuation in demand, however, much greater flexibility is required in order to respond quickly to that demand. Scheduling therefore becomes much more of a problem, and the fast food industry exemplifies the approach that can be adopted to cope with this. Again, using the cashiering function as an example, it is possible to see that this is not carried out by one person, but performed by all those operatives in contact with the customer. Staff are not specialists in one area but are multi-skilled and can perform a variety of different roles during the course of their working shift. This allows much greater flexibility in terms of staff work activity and scheduling need only ensure that the total number of staff on duty is appropriate, as opposed to ensuring the specific types of staff are present. In the case of the cashiering function in fast food it becomes a variabie cost related to the number of counter staff on duty (which should reflect demand in any case), as opposed to the fixed cost of employing a cashier irrespective of demand.

Case Example 9.3   *Captain Hook's Grill Room*

Since reasonably accurate predictions of hourly sales can be made from point-of-sale equipment, staffing levels required for a given time period can be planned. As in most fast food outlets, the Captain Hook staff are multi-skilled, so for each hour of the day only the total staffing requirement need be established. At busy periods, over lunchtime for instance, perhaps 20 staff are needed, whilst at quieter periods, particularly at start-up and close-down, only five staff may need to be on duty. The actual role and position of each staff member is then determined by the number of staff on duty at that time and prescribed in the Captain Hook operations manual. This is illustrated in figure 9.8.

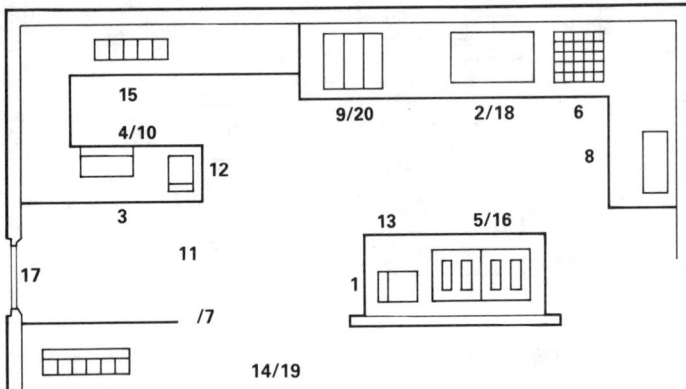

1. Restaurant register	11. Take-away service co-ordinator
2. Restaurant grill	12. Take-away change operator
3. Take-away service point	13. Restaurant counter co-ordinator
4. Take-away sandwich position	14. Order taker
5. Restaurant sandwich position	15. 2nd take-away sandwich maker
6. Fry position	16. 2nd restaurant sandwich maker
7. Take-away drink position	17. Take-away order taker
8. Restaurant drink position	18. Back-up grill position
9. Take-away grill position	19. Back-up dining area person
10. 2nd take-away sandwich maker	20. Back-up take-away grill person

Figure 9.8 *Work stations for Captain Hook's grill room.*

As the change in demand from quiet to busy periods will be incremental, rather than sudden, the manager can rota staff to come on duty and assume responsibilities according to the specifications outlined above. Thus, when there are only five staff on duty they cover all the positions between them. Operative 5 would then have responsibility not only for 'restaurant sandwiches', but also for assisting with restaurant drinks, bagging orders to go out and assisting with fries. But when 20 staff are on duty, Operative 5 will only be concerned with preparing restaurant sandwiches, being assisted by Operative 16.

Quite clearly, the more responsive to demand the scheduling is, the greater the need for staff to work flexible shift patterns and the greater the number of part-time staff. The study by Smith and Giglio[7] suggested four possible categories of schedule:

Full-time shift – all employees work an eight-hour day.

Split shift – all employees work an eight-hour day with a break in the middle of the working day.

Part-time shift – all employees work less than an eight-hour day.

Combination – a combination of any of the other three.

From previous study it is clear that all these categories are in use in the catering industry, reflecting the nature of particular operations. Each approach has its advantages. The full-time shift schedule is simple to plan, treats labour cost as fixed, hence facilitating break-even analysis and provides stable conditions of service for employees. Split shifts are appropriate for operations that peak more than once during the daily operational period, i.e. at lunch and dinner. Part-time schedules are flexible and responsive, have a greater pool of manpower from which to cover holiday periods or absenteeism and provide conditions of service that reflect the needs of employees, such as working parents who can only work during school hours or students who do not wish to work for too many hours for tax reasons. Finally, the combination schedule is the approach that is likely to achieve the highest levels of productivity, although it is the most complex to plan and operate.

REDUCING OVERHEAD COSTS

Until recently, there has been a preoccupation in the catering industry with reducing food cost and labour cost, almost to the point of completely ignoring overhead cost. This is primarily because of the belief that overhead costs are fixed, and hence uncontrollable. This perception usually results in budgets being based on previous years' targets or performance, plus something for inflation. Recently, a new approach – zero-based budgeting – has been applied in the industry to change this perception and attempt to keep overhead costs as low as possible. Each item of overhead is analysed in terms of its cost, purpose, possible alternatives, performance measures and the benefits to be derived from it. Underlying this is the assumption that the need for any item of overhead may at least be queried and that the current activity is not necessarily the most appropriate way of achieving strategic goals.

In order to undertake this analysis, each item of overhead needs to be broken down into its components. For instance, the energy costs of a catering operation might be sub-divided into lighting costs, heating costs and production costs. Working from a zero-base the manager must justify expenditure in each of these areas. For each area potential alternatives should be identified for cost comparison purposes. Thus in the kitchen production costs might be reduced by spreading the start-up energy loading of equipment, optimising batch cooking techniques and so on. With regards to lighting savings may be made by using lower wattage bulbs, having fewer lights or using long-life, low energy bulbs. The heating overhead can be affected by thermostat control, draught excluders and double glazing, or just by changing the perception of heat by installing a fake open coal fire.[8]

Zero-based budgeting has several beneficial advantages. Firstly, managers are made to think about every item of expenditure, and in this way are being developed for more senior positions since they must analyse, decide and make out a case. Secondly, changes in expenditure are responses to need rather than conventionalised percentage increases from year to year. Thirdly, creative responses and original ideas are encouraged from managers which may show savings applicable in other units.

Finally, top managers have a much clearer idea of future cash flow than traditional approaches to budgeting may provide.

THE PRODUCTIVITY TRAP

In the economic climate of the 1980s, cost reduction and productivity improvements have become something of a sacred cow. British industry, we are told, is uncompetitive, overmanned and in need of sweeping changes. The shake-out, i.e. shedding of staff, has become as common in the 1980s in Britain as was the shoot-out in Dodge City in the 1880s. But there is a danger in seeking higher and higher levels of productivity. The manager can easily fall into this 'productivity trap'. The pressure to improve productivity is started by a fall in demand and hence a fall in profitability. The reaction of management is to introduce traditional cost cutting measures to maintain the level of profit, but these measures often lead to a fall in quality of the product and thence to the perception of the consumer of less value for money. This in turn leads to a fall in demand, and so the cycle is begun again.

Another factor that needs to be considered is the impact on staff morale that pressure to improve productivity may have. The catering industry places demands on personnel that are almost unique and potentially very stressful. These demands include the need to co-operate and co-ordinate activity within a team of people, to produce a unique product/service package for each consumer, to respond to nuances of consumer behaviour to provide satisfaction, to carry out this subtle exchange with customers and complex interaction with colleagues in full view of both parties at a time of heightened tension and to maintain a high level of technical and social skills.

SUMMARY

Productivity is the ratio of output to input in a business. Productivity improvements are achieved in five ways. The most problematic of these for the catering manager is when a proportional change to inputs will result in a proportional change in outputs, from which productivity gains are achieved. This chapter identified the market and cost orientation of different types of catering business and the tendency for them to utilise specific approaches to productivity improvement.

The major problem with measuring productivity in the catering industry is the complexity of possible outputs from a typical operation. This is usually overcome by aggregating both inputs and outputs. However, aggregates, such as gross profit percentage and labour cost percentage, can provide misleading signals with regards to performance. A critical examination of gross profit was made in chapter 4 and labour cost percentage in this chapter.

Several productivity improvement techniques can be used to reduce raw material costs. These include value analysis, which in the catering industry involves recipe development, yield testing and menu rationalisation. The two main methods of reducing labour costs are work study and scheduling. The former is predominantly concerned with improving individuals' performance, whilst the latter ensures the most efficient use of team members. The particular approach to overhead costs advocated in this chapter was zero-based budgeting. Finally, the productivity trap was considered and with it the need to ensure that the trade-off between productivity and quality was managed effectively.

In summary, a unit manager should constantly be reviewing performance. In particular, he or she should analyse key indicators with regard to materials and labour costs such as cost percentage, average spend, sales turnover, seat turnover, meals served per employee and so on. The frequency and complexity of this continual analysis will vary from sector to sector. For instance, popular catering units would look at daily figures, whereas a monthly check might be adequate for school meals catering. The manager should be able to identify opportunities for productivity improvement if the information generated shows an inconsistent level of productivity over time, or between one unit and another. A careful analysis of how high are the levels of productivity achieved should enable the manager to institute changes that will eliminate the periods or operations with poor productivity.

REFERENCES

1. Kotas, R., *Marketing Orientation in the Hotel and Catering Industry*, Surrey University Press.
2. Pavesic, D.V., 'The myth of labour cost percentages', *Cornell HRA Quarterly*, pp. 27–31, November 1983.
3. Hughes, C., *Production and Operations Management*, Holt, Rinehart and Winston, 1985.
4. Jones, P.L.M., *Food Service Operations*, Holt, Rinehart and Winston, 1983.
5. Strank, H., *Ergonomics: Functional Design for the Catering Industry*, Edward Arnold, 1973.
6. Smith, R.S. and Giglio, R.J., 'Reducing labour costs in food service operations by scheduling', in (Eds.) Livingstone, G.E. and Chong, C.M., *Food Service Systems*, Academic Press, 1979.
7. Smith, R.S. and Giglio, R.J., *op. cit.*
8. Jones, P.L.M., *op. cit.*

10

Controlling Costs

OBJECTIVES

Understand the principles of catering cost control . . . select appropriate techniques for controlling food and beverage costs . . . select appropriate techniques for controlling labour costs . . . discuss the functional requirements of computer based catering cost control systems . . . discuss the behavioural considerations of cost control activities.

INTRODUCTION

Figure 9.1 showed how the cost structures of catering businesses differ considerably depending on the type of business, the market situation and the operating methods. As a general guide, costs for units in the commercial restaurant sector normally fall within the range shown in the following table:

Table 10.1 *Example ranges of restaurant operating costs expressed as a percentage of sales.*

Sales	Percentage range
	100
Cost of sales	34 – 43
Wages and related costs	19 – 38
Advertising & promotion	0 – 4
Other operating expenses	9 – 11
Rent	4 – 15
Depreciation	2 – 5
Insurance	<1

Relatively small fluctuations in one category of cost – such as food or wages – will have a considerable impact on profitability. This point is well illustrated by Richard Kotas using the technique of profit sensitivity analysis.[1]

The ranges for each cost category show that there is no ideal 'template' for business success. Different restaurants have different cost structures. Cost behaviour will also vary from business to business. Wages may be a largely fixed cost in one restaurant and a largely variable cost in another. The cost structures within the commercial restaurant sector vary considerably – but in the institutional sector, particularly where a catering operation is performed on a subsidised basis, the cost structure and cost behaviour will be dramatically different. The catering industry is a diverse industry, and each business will have its own particular cost problems and its own most appropriate system of control.

One of the themes of this book is the necessity of adopting a contingent approach to management. Success in any business comes not from doing things right but from doing the right things. This is particularly true in the area of cost control, because managers with a limited amount of time and resources have to decide where to concentrate the control effort. The control of the costs of paperclips, for example, need not be as rigorous as the control of the costs of whisky. Also, different costs should be controlled in different ways: the costs of rent and energy might be the same for a year, but the method of control should obviously be different. Managers have choices in the emphasis placed on the control of different costs and the control methods which should be used. There is no perfect control system which will meet the needs of all catering businesses. Each business will have a preferred control system depending on its business environment and operational process. The intention here is to help the reader decide the best fit for a particular business.

CONTROL AS PART OF THE MANAGEMENT PROCESS

Before discussing control systems, a restatement of the definition of cost control will be useful, as this is a phrase that is frequently misunderstood. Cost control is the management function which is concerned with keeping costs in line with standards. Cost control is not concerned with finding more efficient and less expensive ways of providing the same quality – that is cost reduction and is dealt with in the preceding chapter of this book.

Control is part of the management process and is concerned with keeping performance in line with plans, as represented in figure 10.1. The model of the management process starts with setting objectives. Business objectives were discussed in the earlier chapters of this book. Most catering businesses will have a profit objective; all will certainly have some form of financial objective; many will have other business objectives. An example of a specific financial objective might be: to produce pre-tax profits of £90 000 in 1986. This will enable the company to pay a dividend of 9.8p on each ordinary share, and retain profits of £11 000.

All employees' activities should be directed towards achieving the objectives of the business. To do this, objectives are translated into detailed plans in the areas of finance, marketing and operations. These plans will cover the target market and the marketing mix, the specifications for the product itself and the operational methods. Central to these plans is the primary tool of financial control – the budget – covering how money will be earned and spent. At corporate level, the responsibilities for these three activities – finance, marketing and operations – will probably rest with three different departments. This necessitates the development and co-ordination of three separate plans. Fortunately, at unit level, or in the individual business, this functional division need not occur and managers can get on with planning the business in an integrated way.

The financial control function is concerned with setting a standard (for example, the budgeted wages cost), measuring the actual performance (the wages cost incurred), identifying any variance and if necessary taking corrective action in order to ensure

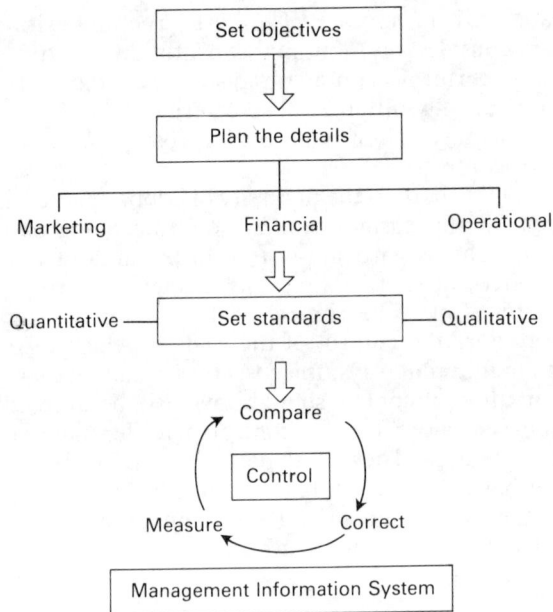

Figure 10.1   *The management process.*

that profit objectives are still achieved. The information needed for planning and control is provided by a Management Information System.

CONSIDERATIONS IN DESIGNING A COST CONTROL SYSTEM

Managers have to decide how to design a control system which is appropriate for the needs of a particular business. In this chapter the key questions of how different cost should best be measured will be examined and what type of yardstick, or comparator, should be adopted as a standard for evaluating the actual performance.

There are two distinct approaches which can be taken to cost control. The first of these is called *pre-operational control*. Here management effort is directed towards limiting the amount available for subordinates to use. For example, Gamble and Kipps[2] describe a hospital catering food costs control system, which, in essence, only releases from stores the necessary issues required to produce the requested dishes for the day according to standard recipes. The manager has exercised control over the costs which will be incurred before the production takes place. Labour costs are often controlled using pre-operational principles, whereby the manager authorises the labour utilisation in advance (using a roster) and any subsequent changes to that plan (such as overtime) need the manager's authorisation. Pre-operational control is most useful in situations where volume and sales mix can be forecast with a high degree of certainty, for example in banqueting, school and hospital meals catering is focused on the control of resources.

The second approach is called *post-operational control*. Here standards are set, staff are trained and the operation is run in accordance with those standards. The costs are measured after the event. If costs show an adverse variance compared with standard, management action is centred on people problems – finding out who did not comply with standards and preventing the same problem occurring in the future. Post-operational control is necessary where managers cannot plan and control the allocation of resources in detail in advance. For example, food costs in an à la carte restaurant could not be controlled on a pre-operational basis because of the difficulty in accurately predicting sales volume and mix. Post-operational controls require managers to focus on corrective action, which usually involves staff performance.

So a major decision area in the design of control systems is the choice between pre-operational and post-operational controls. The former in our opinion are generally preferable from the point of view of effective resources management and positive employee supervision – but pre-operational control is largely limited to situations where demand is predictable. In practice both forms of control are often used together, pre-operational controls to limit the use of resources together with post-operational controls to check that the pre-operational control system is working effectively.

Managers who are involved in designing or reviewing a cost control system have to specify what information will be required – but weigh this against the costs and benefits of having such information. In specifying the control information needed for a business, managers have to decide on three dimensions of information. They have to decide how specific the information will be – for example, will productivity data be prepared for each employee, or for each shift, or for each department? Secondly, managers have to decide how frequently the information will be prepared – will food costs be calculated on a daily, weekly or four-weekly basis? Thirdly, the accuracy of the information has to be determined – is it necessary to measure beverage costs to the nearest pound, or the nearest ten pounds or will an estimate to the nearest hundred pounds suffice? The required accuracy, specificity and frequency of control information will depend on the scope that exists for remedial management action.

Sometimes control information which was needed some time ago for the improvement of a certain aspect of business performance, is still being produced unnecessarily. There are obvious costs associated with the production of control information, but there are significant hidden costs in management time which is taken up with examining, interpreting, and discussing inappropriate information. Control information should be regularly reviewed, with a critical examination of its costs and benefits. It is advisable to take a zero-base approach, starting with an assumption of no control information, and justifying the production of each item of data (accuracy, specificity and frequency) in terms of its impact on profit improvement.

THE BUDGET AS A CONTROL TOOL

The primary tool of financial planning and control is the budget – which is simply a statement of intention in financial terms. The budget is primarily a device to control the overall profit performance of the business. This is done in order to ensure that sufficient profit is made to satisfy the requirements of financial backers, and in order to ensure that cash flow is managed effectively.

Budgets are designed to control overall profit performance. They are not primarily designed to ensure the most effective control of specific cost categories. In certain cases over-reliant or indiscriminate use of the budget as a cost control tool can lead to inappropriate corrective action being taken by management. For example, a restaurant budget may include a kitchen wage cost of £560 per week. A policy change concerning, for example, the number of hours in the working week, may result in an actual wage bill of £610 per week. The budget will tell management that an adverse variance has occurred and that some corrective action is needed if the profit target is to be achieved, but the corrective action may not necessarily be a reduction in the hours worked in the kitchen. In fact, that action might have an adverse effect on profit in the longer run, as reduction in staffing levels may bring about a fall in quality standards and consequently volume. Consider the alternative case that an actual wage bill of £610 had resulted from careless rostering and unnecessary overtime. This would be a cost control problem and corrective action of reducing hours would be appropriate. Simple budgetary control systems often cannot distinguish a policy problem which usually requires creative profit improvement and a cost control problem which usually requires direct action on the cost category concerned.

Reporting systems which compare budget and actual figures in catering businesses, should make a distinction between budgetary variances caused by policy changes and budgetary variances caused by ineffective operational control – sometimes called efficiency variances.[3] The techniques of variance analysis are designed to marry budgetary control and cost control objectives.[4] There is no doubt that it is highly desirable for managers to know how much profit variance has been caused by cost inflation which was not included in the original budget, and how much variance has been caused by failure to recover cost inflation through selling price increases. This information can either be derived from a periodic special exercise or it can be produced regularly as part of the budgetary control system. The former is usually more appropriate to small businesses, because it is costly to maintain the database necessary to provide the information for such variance analysis. This is not to say that variance analysis is not appropriate for small businesses, far from it, but it needs to be considered carefully.

In larger businesses, variance analysis provides a useful way of separating the responsibilities of different senior managers – where, for example, one manager is responsible for deciding on the implementation of selling price reviews and another is responsible for the negotiation of purchasing contracts and yet another is responsible for the efficient use of those materials. In this instance, variance analysis can provide a cost effective way of planning and controlling these activities – but it is done at corporate, rather than unit, level.

Kotas[5] relates the optimum type of budget to business orientation, suggesting that flexible budgets are more appropriate to market-oriented catering businesses, and fixed budgets more suited to cost-oriented businesses. There is some confusion over the purpose and use of flexible budgets. Some people believe that the budget should be adjusted in the light of actual sales volume. This negates the real purpose of budgetary control – to measure the progress of the business towards its profit objective – and it shows the problems of trying to use a simple budget for both profit and cost control. In our opinion, the budget should form a static plan for profit achievement, which may be revised on a rolling basis depending on the business environment. Budgetary variance analysis can be quite useful for explaining why actual performance does not meet the plan – but the cost of obtaining the data necessary to analyse key variances make it more suitable to large operations or corporate departments.

The value of a budget as a means of cost control is often limited by the frequency of reporting and the time lag between the period end and the publishing of the data. In market-oriented businesses, there is a need for a shorter reporting period (weekly, or in certain instances daily, for some expenses and revenue categories). In cost-oriented business however, the reporting period can be less frequent (weekly or four-weekly).

Whatever reporting period is selected, a budget will always be a form of post-operational control. There may well be a time lag of four weeks between the time a cost is incurred and the subsequent time at which it is reported. If this results in an adverse variance against a budget, many managers spend time and effort investigating the reasons for the variance (often to report to Head Office). Meanwhile the day-to-day control of other costs has slipped away and the process repeats itself. It is the classic reactive trap – the manager is caught into a cycle of investigating what has happened, rather than influencing what will happen.

MEASURING FOOD AND BEVERAGE COSTS

Food and beverage commodities usually constitute the largest single cost classifications in a catering business. A variation of one per cent in these material costs will have very significant effects on profit. However, managers are faced with a dilemma: traditional food and beverage control systems can be paper intensive and expensive, but the presentation of management control information may be so late as to preclude effective management action. There are alternatives, and this section discusses what options exist for food and beverage control and draws some conclusions as to which types of system are most appropriate to certain situations.

Food and beverage materials enter the establishment as purchases received, they are stored and issued from the store, they are processed and are either sold or wasted. This is portrayed in figure 10.2.

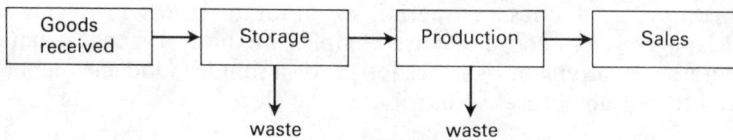

Figure 10.2   *The flow of materials.*

A Catering Manager who is planning a food and beverage control system has to select at which point costs should be measured – at goods inward, on leaving the store, when wastage occurs, after production has taken place, or after service. Any or all of these measurements could be useful in controlling costs. The most widely used approach is the 'opening stock, plus issues, minus closing stock' model used for the purpose of profit measurement. All businesses need to measure the costs of commodities accurately on this basis at least once a year, for the purpose of preparing annual accounts. Physical stocktaking of this type is usually done by a firm of external stocktakers, but this may cost a business up to several hundreds of pounds for the production of one stocktaking result.

Apart from the production of annual accounts, almost all businesses produce a periodic operating statement, usually on a four-weekly basis and this, of course, requires the measurement of food and beverage costs. Production of accurate consumption figures, based on stocktaking results, has a high cost of control particularly when external stocktakers are employed. Frequent external stocktaking is usually only considered necessary in chain operations when turnover is very high and the chance of fraud is considerable, for example, in managed pubs and travel catering. An alternative for chain operations where the possibilities of local fraud are less significant, is to get local management to undertake periodic stocktakes, with an annual or six-monthly validation by external stocktakers. Large single-unit catering operations will often have their own food and beverage control department, which undertakes periodic stocktakes, sometimes with the co-operation of other staff.

The main technique for measuring food and beverage costs is by the valuation of stocks and purchases and the choice of valuation method, particularly in times of rapid inflation, can have significant implications for profit and asset reporting. There are four textbook methods of stock valuation, which are described in detail in Donald Sutton's book:[6]

FIFO – which tends to give the highest value to stocks and to inflate profits.

LIFO – which tends to undervalue stocks, with a more realistic profit valuation.

AVERAGE – which tends to overvalue stocks and consequently overstates profit. This has the advantage of being administratively convenient.

STANDARD – which is a sophisticated technique forming the basis for a comprehensive cost control system.

These stock valuation methods can all be used for the valuation of issues from stores. The use of any one of these methods facilitates the preparation of a stores reconciliation which will accurately identify any loss (possibly through pilferage) from the stores. Computer based stock control systems may utilise one or another of these methods. However, if utilised in manual stores issue systems, they present a burdensome administrative task.

There is an alternative method of stock valuation which is administratively far simpler – and is commonly used in many catering businesses. This is to value stock using the most recent price paid for a commodity – also known as the current price. There is a significant disadvantage associated with the use of this current stock valuation method, as it does not permit an accurate stores reconciliation to be prepared. Managers can choose a more complex method of stock valuation which permits accurate measurement of stores losses, or a simpler (and cheaper) method of valuation and forfeit an accurate control over the stores.

EVALUATING FOOD AND BEVERAGE COST PERFORMANCE

Thus there are a number of options open to management in measuring food and beverage costs. In order for effective control to take place, a standard is needed for comparison purposes. Managers have options concerning the choice of comparator and must take that which is the most appropriate to them.

There are four types of comparator which can be used for the control of food and beverage costs. The first of these is by using a *target cost percentage* – usually known as a target kitchen percentage or a target food cost percentage. This is widely used in commercial catering operations. The actual food cost percentage is easy to calculate. In small businesses, where one person can keep personal control over profits, volume, quality standards and production techniques, a target food cost percentage is an entirely appropriate way to control costs. In businesses with large turnover and division of responsibility, the choice of an arbitrary and constant target food cost percentage (for example, 35 per cent) may affect the optimum balance between quality and cost. Where sales mix and purchase price variations may bring about an increase in food costs, undue pressure on food production staff to attain an arbitrary food cost percentage may result in loss of quality and drop in volume. Instead of adopting an arbitrary target food cost percentage, larger businesses are well advised to calculate a potential food cost percentage based on sales mix, current portion costs and selling prices. The calculation of potential food cost percentages was explored in chapter 4. Depending on the changes in the sales mix and the movements in food prices, the potential food cost percentage may need to be recalculated on a four-weekly basis. With a large sales mix and complex dishes, this is a daunting task if done by hand. However, the selection of a computerised point-of-sale system which stores sales mix data, and the use of an inventory control and dish costing computer package enable this task to be achieved in a matter of an hour or so.

Nicholas Lepard[7] makes a very useful distinction between the budget food (or beverage) cost, the actual food cost and the potential food cost. The budget is the cost which the business intends to incur. The potential is the cost that should be incurred based on current purchase prices, selling prices, sales mix, standard recipes and portion sizes. The actual cost is derived from the trading account. Lepard distinguishes between control problems and policy problems. A gap between the budget food cost and the potential food cost is a policy problem, which can be rectified by changing prices, portions, recipes, or sales mix. A gap between potential cost and actual cost is a control problem, which can be rectified by control of wastage or attention to operating procedures.

The isolation of control problems and policy problems is paramount in market-oriented businesses, because of the previously discussed dilemma of pressure for costs reduction versus pressure for quality maintenance. A carefully constructed food cost report can focus management and staff attention on the important problem areas, as shown in the following table.

Table 10.2   *Simplified food cost report — with variances.*

Food Cost Report — week ending:				
	%	£	%	£
Food sales	100	4 997		
Budget food cost percentage	36			
Budget food cost		1 800		
Potential food cost percentage	39			
Potential food cost		1 950		
Policy variance			3 A	150 A
Actual food cost (from stocktake)		1 848		
Actual food cost percentage	37			
Control variance			2 F	102 F
Total food cost variance			1 A	48 A

F = favourable variance, A = adverse variance.

In the example in table 10.2, the report highlights that although food costs were one per cent or £48 worse than budget levels, this was attributable to policy problems rather than kitchen inefficiency.

This analysis of food cost variances will only give a realistic division between policy and control variances if standard recipes have been written realistically and waste has been accounted for in a realistic manner. There are two possible methods of treating waste food – either an allowance for waste can be built into the potential food cost percentage or waste can be included in the control variance. Different approaches are taken in industry – but, in the authors' opinion, it is more useful to highlight possible waste as part of the control variance. If waste is a significant problem worthy of individual control an alternative is to record waste written off, value this at portion cost and itemise the total as a separate variance. The principle is that variances should be selected to reflect the current control problems.

The second comparator for food or beverage costs is the *per capita cost*. This is appropriate to the institutional sector, where managers have to operate within closely defined subsidy levels. For example, an RAF catering officer will have a set feeding allowance for each airman, each day. This is an ideal situation for the use of pre-operational control, where menus can be pre-costed and only sufficient food requisitioned to meet the requirements of the day's planned production. The army's CATPAC computer catering control system is based on this principle.[8] Paul Gamble's CATSIS inventory and food cost control system for hospital caterers also works on the pre-operational control system – and is focused on the calculation of per capita food costs as the main control comparator.[9]

The third comparator for food or beverage cost control is the production of *potential commodity usage* data. This type of comparator is most appropriate to businesses with limited product range and a high degree of standardisation, as in fast food operations. For example, point-of-sale systems such as the Positran system do much more than analyse a sales mix and control cash. The systems store details of the standard recipes used for each item. Stock levels for each commodity are also stored and updated as deliveries are received. As each item is sold, the system decreases the inventory totals for each ingredient by the amount specified in the standard recipe. On demand, managers can obtain a printout of the potential stock levels of each commodity. A quick check of what is actually in store will reveal exactly where shortages have occurred.

Potential commodity usage is also widely used for the control of wine sales by the bottle – using either the traditional cellar ledger, or a computer based inventory control system. Potential commodity usage is also used selectively to control high cost items – such as steaks – and this usage is well explained by Richard Kotas and Bernard Davis.[10] However, potential commodity usage is not suitable for operations where a wide range of commodities are processed into a wide range of different items for sale.

The fourth comparator for control of food and beverage costs is somewhat different from the previous three, because it focuses on the *potential sales value* of the commodities that have been consumed. It is most useful for ensuring that commodities have been correctly transformed into revenue, and is widely used in bars or retail outlets. The principle is that each commodity (for example, a bottle of Guinness) is valued at its retail value (£0.80). After a stocktake, the sum of the potential sales value of all commodities used is compared with the actual sales revenue. Any shortage suggests that either money or stock has been wasted or misappropriated. This method is suitable for sales outlets where items are resold, for example, a kiosk selling prepacked snacks and portion controlled drinks – but not suitable for sales outlets where commodities are processed, for example, a cocktail bar. Some people suggest that mixed items, like cocktails, should be priced according to the potential sales value of their ingredients. This does not seem a sensible approach for businesses in the commercial sector – it is, in effect, the control tail wagging the pricing dog! This was discussed in chapter 4 where pricing practices were examined.

Managers can select the comparators which suit their business needs. In practice, several comparators may be used within one cost control system. Within a hotel the food from the main kitchen may be controlled by means of a potential gross profit percentage, and, equally, certain high cost items – for example, preportioned meats – may be controlled by commodity usage. The sandwiches issued to the night porter may be controlled by a potential sales value and staff meals may be controlled on a per

Table 10.3   *Comparators for food and beverage control.*

Comparator	Focus	Common applications
Cost percentage	Relationship of cost and revenue	Commercial restaurants
Per capita cost	Relationship of cost and volume	Institutional catering
Commodity usage	Correct usage of each ingredient	Fast food Bottle wine sales Retailing High cost items
Potential sales	Correct sale of each ingredient	Bars Retailing

capita basis. Similarly, a cocktail bar may be controlled by commodity usage based around a sophisticated point-of-sale system, but a doubles bar in the same establishment may be better controlled using potential sales value.

In summary, there are four types of comparator for control of food and beverage costs as shown in table 10.3.

Ascertaining food and beverage costs for the whole business by periodic stocktakes and the preparation of trading accounts is relatively straightforward. However, in a catering business which has more than one sales outlet the management is faced with a difficult problem of cost apportionment. In, for example, a large hotel, the hotel kitchen may serve a restaurant outlet, a coffee shop, banqueting, floor service and the hotel lounge. Two very important questions need to be answered in such a situation. Firstly, if departmental operating statements are to be prepared for each of these sales outlets, how can food costs be apportioned? Secondly, how can the managerial effectiveness of the head chef be assessed when the kitchen percentage will vary depending on the sales mix in each of the sales outlets?

The Standard System of Catering Accounting[11] side steps the first of these problems, by assuming that only two departmental operating statements will be prepared – one for all food operations and one for all beverage operations. Most managers do not accept that this is adequate, as it forgoes any attempt to measure the profitability of individual outlets, which may have a turnover of several hundred thousands of pounds. This is possibly one of the reasons why the Standard System has not been adopted by many operators in the catering industry.

Nicholas Lepard[12] summarises a method which would seem to be the most effective way of dealing with these problems. In its most sophisticated form, this requires the calculation of a potential gross profit percentage for each outlet, for each meal period. These potential gross profit percentages are applied to the actual sales revenue for each outlet, to give the potential food cost for each outlet, and this is used as the basis for food cost allocation. The difference between the total of the potential food cost for all the outlets and the actual food cost, is a measure of the chef's effectiveness.

MEASUREMENT OF LABOUR COSTS

Many people who buy meals or drinks in a restaurant relate the value of their purchase to the cost of the materials. They compare the restaurant price with what it would have cost to prepare the dish at home – and this ignores labour costs and other overheads. In some catering businesses, the largest single item of cost is no longer food but wages, and the control of labour costs is as important as the control of food and beverage costs.

There are two elements of labour costs which need to be controlled – the time taken and rate of pay. The rate is far more than mere basic pay, as is shown:

Factors determining total rate of pay

Basic rate
Employers' National Insurance contributions
Overtime payment rate
Shift allowances
Public and annual holiday pay
Sick pay scheme
Employers' pension scheme contributions
Costs of meals and accommodation, if provided
Costs of commission or other bonuses

These factors are determined by an employee's contract of employment. Many of the factors mentioned above are also fixed either by law, by corporate policy or by agreement with trades unions – so managers' ability to change most of these rate factors is very limited. They can only be controlled when a new employee is recruited or when an existing employee's rates are revised, at, for example, an annual merit review. These rate factors are largely uncontrollable, and therefore there is little merit in reporting them in detail in the short term.

Although the factors determining rate are largely uncontrollable in the short term, there is some discretion for influencing the time which will be incurred. The scope for varying an employee's hours is limited by the contractual base of employment, or mode of employment. Each mode has different conditions associated with it.

Table 10.4 *Modes of employment.*

Permanent full-time: working more than 30 hours per week with more than 52 weeks' continuous employment.

Permanent part-time: either 16 to 30 hours for more than 52 weeks or 8 to 16 hours for more than five years.

Temporary full-time: more than 30 hours for less than 52 weeks.

Temporary part-time: either 16 to 30 hours for less than 52 weeks or 8 or 16 hours for less than five years.

Occasional: less than eight hours per week, usually not on a regular basis.

Self-employed & agency workers: technically not employees at all.

In reality, many elements of labour costs are largely uncontrollable – for example, a salaried manager. Other jobs, depending on the rostering system and the modes of employment adopted, may have a high controllable element – for example, an hourly-paid employee in a fast food store who is rostered for a daily minimum period which may or may not be extended depending on the actual sales volume. Classifying jobs as controllable or uncontrollable is a useful prerequisite to cost control.

In most catering businesses, employment costs are reported for the purpose of costs control as a weekly departmental wage bill, often broken down into job categories. This figure usually represents the actual expenditure on wages during the past week, but may include accrued payments for such items as unsettled public sector pay awards. The accounting treatment of certain items of employment costs varies – and in some cases significant items, such as employers' pension fund contributions, may be either reported as a corporate headquarters cost or as an allocated cost at unit level. It is important for managers to understand the basis used for cost allocation. If costs are allocated on the basis of a controllable factor (for example, hours worked) then the canny manager will know how to reduce the apportioned costs. However, if the costs are allocated on the basis of an uncontrollable factor (for example, flooring area) then the costs are to all intents and purposes largely uncontrollable and as such are not a problem worth worrying about.

With businesses which have high daily fluctuations in demand and, consequently, fluctuating staffing requirements, it is advantageous to measure labour costs on a more frequent basis. It is not usually feasible to produce daily wage costs from a manual wage system, but computerised time card systems, such as those provided by Microtime, can provide the necessary information. A number of catering point-of-sale systems can also provide daily payroll control information. Point-of-sale systems, such as the Positran system, described earlier in this book, allow employees to clock in and out using a card reader. The system can hold a list of all employees, together with details of their rates of pay, and details of hours worked for each of the previous 16 days. On request, the system will produce a comprehensive payroll report showing the hours worked and the costs incurred during the day.

The difficulty in allocating food costs between departments in order to prepare profit centre accounts has already been discussed. This is not a significant problem with employment costs as the apportionment is normally achieved using either a manual timesheet or a time card control system.

However promptly or frequently employment costs are reported, they can rarely give managers all the necessary payroll control information. Most managers prefer to have a regular report of the number of hours worked – often broken down by job category. Four types of manhour data should be separately reported, all of which are easily extracted from either manual or computerised payroll systems. The four categories are: basic hours worked, premium hours worked, sickness or absenteeism hours, and holiday hours. The combination of these items of information permits a manager to evaluate employment costs more usefully. For example, total employment costs may have risen substantially, but the manhours' analysis may show that the actual number of hours worked (basic plus overtime) is as normal, however, sickness has occurred and holidays have been taken – both of which incur additional costs. The combination of monetary value and manhours can provide the answers to such questions as why overtime rates had to be incurred.

There is little cause for optimism concerning any possible future decrease in employment costs. Increased benefits, shorter working weeks and the growth of trade unionism will push up the costs of employing food-service personnel. This will make the utilisation of human resources an area of increasing importance – and managers will need to become more exacting in their systems of planning and control.

The choice of comparators when designing a cost control system will have great influence on what managers think of as problems and if and when they take corrective action. There are five types of comparator which are used for the control of catering labour costs. The first of these which emphasises the relationship of labour costs to revenue is the *target labour cost percentage*. For most businesses, labour is a semi-fixed cost and a short-term increase or decrease in volume should not necessarily result in a corresponding change in labour costs.

As discussed in the preceding paragraphs, most businesses do not have a cost-effective system for measuring daily labour costs, and therefore actual percentages are calculated on a weekly basis (or even less frequently). It is easy to overlook the fact that a weekly labour cost percentage is an average figure, and it is erroneous to assume that if target labour cost percentage has been achieved in two consecutive weeks, then cost control has been equally effective in those two weeks. This average weekly labour cost percentage may hide missed opportunities to increase productivity through better rostering or more effective control of overtime. The actual labour cost percentage will also fluctuate due to changes in holiday pay and sick pay.

Target labour cost percentages are usually derived by adopting inter-unit norms or by the use of a 'percentage template' which is deemed to lead to maximum profitability. Neither of these methods recognises the potential cost savings which may (or may not) be possible in a particular unit. In the light of these inherent weaknesses it would seem that a target labour cost percentage alone is not a suitable comparator for food and beverage businesses.

The second comparator is a *target monetary value* of employment costs. This comparator is most appropriate for businesses where labour is largely a fixed cost and/or volume fluctuations are limited – for example, in the institutional sector. The actual figure will also fluctuate due to changes in sick pay and holiday pay, however, for cost-oriented businesses, this comparator is quite appropriate – but in a situation where the use of labour is relatively fixed.

The third type of comparator is *target manhours*. A static target of, say, 320 manhours per day is appropriate to businesses with no fluctuations in demand or with largely fixed jobs. For businesses where volume fluctuates, targets can be set for different levels of volume dependent on the optimum staffing levels as described in the chapter entitled Increasing Productivity – chapter 9. Weekly manhours' targets may hide possible opportunities for improvement. Planning and measuring manhours on a daily basis is worthwhile in businesses which have fluctuating demand and modes of employment which permit flexible rostering. This, of course, requires a system of volume forecasting.

Rather than set detailed manhours' targets for several ranges of volume, in smaller businesses it may be more appropriate to find a less exact method of comparing the utilisation of manpower and the volume of business. The most commonly used measure is *target covers per manhour* – the fourth comparator. Actual 'Covers per Manhour' performance can be assessed on a daily basis without difficulty from payroll or roster data.

The fifth comparator is used to assess how effectively managers have acquired and utilised their manpower – how they have controlled the use of premium rates of pay, how they have used the correct grade of employee for the correct job and how costs of sickness or absenteeism have been minimised. The best single measure of this is *target average rate per hour*. If measured on a weekly basis, and on a moving annual total basis (to smooth out the effects of seasonal holidays, sickness and absenteeism), this will show the short-term and the long-term trends in manpower utilisation.

The five choices of comparator for labour costs are shown in table 10.5. These comparators may be used alone or in combination. In one business different comparators will be more appropriate for different jobs. Most labour costs control systems work predominantly on pre-operational control principles, by relating staffing levels to forecasted volume. Post-operational control is also necessary to review how effectively the staffing and rostering have been undertaken.

Properly applied variance analysis techniques are useful for highlighting the exact cause of shortfalls in performance, and for directing management's attention to the important problem areas. As a general rule, analysis of the profit effect of rate and

Table 10.5   *Comparators for Labour Cost Control.*

Comparator	Focus	Common applications
Cost percentage	Variable nature of labour costs	Commercial restaurants
Monetary value	Fixed nature of labour costs	Institutional catering
Manhours	Efficient productivity	'Fixed' jobs
Covers per manhour	Efficient productivity	'Variable' jobs
Average hourly rate	Proper selection and rostering	All sectors

manhours' variances are useful to all catering businesses. The Standard System of Catering Accounting makes some specific recommendations concerning the control of kitchen wages. The SSCA suggests that the kitchen labour element of each dish should be calculated and that these standard labour costs should be used as a basis for a cost allocation system for distributing kitchen labour costs to sales outlets. Although the SSCA recommendations are theoretically possible, the authors know of no-one who has adopted these ideas. It seems more appropriate to treat a kitchen as a cost centre, responsible for food cost efficiency variance (as previously described) and for kitchen labour costs, fuel and other direct overheads. Kitchen labour costs should be controlled by setting target manhour levels for different volume ranges, and also by using a covers per manhour measure. Periodic reviews of staffing levels, rostering and work organisation should be undertaken with a general view to improving kitchen productivity.

COMPUTER SYSTEMS FOR COST CONTROL

Until the early 1980s, most information for planning and control in food and beverage businesses came from manual records such as payroll documentation, bin cards, restaurant bill summaries, goods received notes and manual sales mix analyses. Information took a long time to prepare and was often of such dubious reliability that managers' first action was to recheck the data! The advent of cheap computing power has dramatically changed the variety, quantity and quality of information that is available to and expected by food and beverage managers.

The growth in catering computer systems has been such that all but the very largest or most specialised businesses will now buy in a package rather than have a system designed to meet specific criteria. In order to be able to select the best package for their needs, managers have to be able to explain clearly the functional requirements of the intended system – or, in other words, what the system should be able to achieve in order to meet the businesses' control requirements. Many people do not find this an easy task as they have been conditioned to think in terms of processes (costing a menu) rather than in terms of results (achievement of potential dish costs).

Of course, not all of the functional requirements of a control system, as shown in table 10.6 are pertinent to all catering businesses. They are only expressed in general terms, and each business will need to specify their exact information needs before deciding how to best meet those needs.

Table 10.6 *Functional requirements for control systems.*

Ease and speed of operation
Particularly important for recording customer transactions, issues from stores or other activities where queues and time wasting may result.

Security of the system
Restrictions may be necessary on who can operate terminals, update records or access information. This may be covered by a system of passwords or security keys. The equipment may also need to be physically robust if it is used in areas such as bars or stores.

Networking capability
The potential to link and integrate a number of terminals for different types of data capture. The possibility of linking to a corporate headquarters.

Cash control
The production of bills, the analysis of payment methods and the production of cashier reports.

Sales analysis information
The number of classifications for analysis and the frequency, specificity and accuracy of sales mix data should be identified.

Labout cost and productivity data
The use of time cards for data entry. The retention of employee data records and the compilation of payrolls. The production of reports of sales per manhour or other productivity data.

Stock control
The retention of stock commodity records, the provision of information regarding low or slow moving stocks, the recording of goods received, and the allocation of costs to responsibility centres. The calculation of comparators for food and beverage costs.

Management reporting
The retention of comparators and the production of management reports — possibly variance analyses — at regular intervals or on demand.

HUMAN ASPECTS OF COST CONTROL

Managers cannot personally control all of the costs associated with a catering business. In the end it is the actions of the employees, in carefully controlling the use of materials or their own time, that determine the financial success of a business.

In larger operations, the food and beverage manager may decide to devolve profit responsibility to some subordinate managers. For example, the food and beverage manager of a large hotel may have the following department heads reporting to her:

Figure 10.3 *Organisation chart for a large hotel.*

The food and beverage manager in this example needs to decide what responsibility for cost control will be delegated to which manager. In certain cases, it may be appropriate to delegate responsibility for volume and gross profit as well. In the case of the Manager of the Knightsbridge Restaurant and Bar, responsibility for volume, gross profit, employment costs and other direct expenses may be delegated – making the subordinate manager fully profit responsible. Of course, authority should match responsibility and may involve the subordinate manager in authorisation of costs, review of prices and the planning of sales promotion activities.

If it is decided to devolve financial responsibility – either by delegating responsibility for several cost items or by setting up cost or profit centres – it is necessary to provide a financial planning and reporting system that takes account of these responsibilities. In practice this means participation in the budget preparation process, authorisation of expenditure, control of costs and accountability for results.

Introducing responsibility centres involves some difficult decisions for the catering manager. A key question concerns the responsibilities for food costs – how should the responsibility be divided between the Head Chef, the Purchasing and Stores Officer and the other managers? All of them have some influence on food costs but in different ways.

Table 10.7   *Possible causes of food cost variance.*

Manager	Influence on food costs
Purchasing Officer	Unnecessarily high prices paid Incorrect Specification ordered Incorrect quality accepted Goods invoiced, but not received Materials stolen or spoilt from stores
Head Chef	Incorrect material used Incorrect recipe used Materials stolen or spoilt Finished dishes wasted
Restaurant Manager	Finished dishes spoilt or stolen Payment not received for dishes Change in sales mix

If these causes of variance a significant and controllable, they should be isolated and reported in a way that highlights each manager's responsibility for the variance. However, separating these different variances is a difficult task, but without them the value of responsibility accounting in catering is somewhat diminished.

A budget may provide a suitable tool to control the overall profitability of a business or a responsibility centre. However, it is the employees such as cooks or waiters who have considerable discretion over the way costs are incurred, by, for example, their adherence to standard recipes and portion sizes. Managers have to achieve cost control through their staff, by breaking cost standards down into a number of specific and measurable performance standards, and by monitoring and correcting performance – or ensuring that their supervisors do so. Therefore, effective cost control is concerned just as much with supervisory skills, as it is with financial skills.

Managers' attitudes towards cost control have implications for the effectiveness of the system. Edwin Caplan[13] conducted a series of interviews with managers, concerning their views on cost control. About half of the respondents put forward the viewpoint that control was necessary because employees, particularly operatives, were at worst deliberately lazy and wasteful and at best indifferent to cost saving efforts. The other half put forward the view that managers (but not the operatives or supervisors) needed the information from a control system in order to reduce costs.

Caplan's conclusion was that managers believe that control systems are there for them to exert control over other employees, rather than for other employees to exert control over their work.

Caplan's research has also shown that managers' attitudes towards the reliability of the cost control system ranged from mildly cautious to openly distrustful and hostile. The authors have also found this to be the case in catering businesses: where their unit's performance is below standard, some managers will take the opportunity to cast doubt on the reliability of the control system, rather than taking action to investigate and overcome potential problems.

Motivation theory also has some implications for cost control. People establish subjective expectations concerning their own performance. Repeated failure to achieve a goal will cause a person to lower their personal expectations. Conversely, people who have been successful in achieving goals in the past are likely to have higher expectations for future performance. There is untapped potential in the catering industry to harness operatives' enthusiasm for cost control. To take advantage of the motivational potential of cost control data it is necessary to provide feedback for operatives on cost performance compared with standard – ensuring that the goals are neither too low nor too high. Of course, employees' perceptions of what is important at work are largely shaped by the discussions which they have with managers and cost control should be a regular topic of discussion between boss and subordinate.

Some managers let control of costs slip away until a crisis is reached and then they have a purge on cost control. Managers who attempt to control costs by such methods are unlikely to achieve success. Employees tend to regard the 'purge standard' as an exception and after the purge is over, they revert to the normal standard.

SUMMARY

Cost controls are powerful behavioural influences and managers need to plan, implement and revise systems carefully to meet current business needs. Off-the-peg control systems seldom provide exactly the right fit for a particular business. Designing a food and beverage control system involves consideration of the accuracy, frequency and specificity of measurement of actual costs. Decisions need to be made regarding pre- or post-operational control techniques. The best comparator or comparators need to be selected – from the available options of cost percentage, per capita cost, commodity usage or potential sales value. If responsibility for cost control is delegated, particularly if profit centres are implemented, the selection of methods for allocating food or beverage costs comes to be of key importance. These decisions are a necessary precursor to the selection of computer based systems. Unless a clear specification of the functional characteristics of a control system is prepared before selection starts, managers end up with the most sophisticated system available rather than the one which fits their business needs.

Control of labour costs cannot be achieved with the same degree of certainty as control of food or beverage costs. An egg is an egg – but, despite efforts to standardise on the calibre of staff, many establishments are faced with employees with widely differing individual abilities. This lack of standardisation in many parts of the industry is still a major factor limiting the use of effective labour cost control techniques. Even so, it seems likely that most businesses do not exercise the same degree of control over their labour costs as the situation merits and the authors anticipate that most businesses will devote more management attention to this area in the coming decade.

Budgetary and cost control systems are powerful behavioural tools. Used insensitively, they can generate distrust and hostility. In the right hands they can produce constructive attitudes and effective action among supervisors and operatives, and are essential tools for managers in any part of the catering industry.

REFERENCES

1. Kotas, R., *Marketing Orientation*, Intertext, 1975.
2. Gamble, P. and Kipps, M., 'The Conception and implementation of a micro-computer based catering information system', *International Journal of Hospitality Management* vol. 2, no. 3, 1983.
3. Lepard, N. and Cade, H., *Improving Food and Beverage Control*, Northwood, (n.d.).
4. Sutton, D., *Financial Management In Hotel and Catering Operations*, Heinemann, 1983.
5. Kotas, R., *op. cit.*
6. Sutton, D., *op. cit.*
7. Lepard, N. and Cade, H., *op. cit.*
8. Jones, Major P., 'The Restaurant – a place for quality control and product maintenance', *International Journal of Hospitality Management* vol. 2, no. 2, 1983.
9. Gamble, P., *Small Computers and Hospitality Management*, Hutchinson, 1984.
10. Kotas, R. and Davis, B., *Food and Beverage Control*, Intertext, 1981.
11. HMSO, *A Standard System of Catering Accounting*.
12. Lepard, N. and Cade, H., *op. cit.*
13. Caplan, E., *Management Accounting and Behavioural Science*, Addison Wesley, 1971.

11
Making Performance Improvement Possible

OBJECTIVES

Identify the organisational context in which managers operate . . . review alternative approaches to the effective management of people, work and systems . . . evaluate approaches to the management of change.

INTRODUCTION

It is clear that the role of the manager makes him or her responsible for organising people's activities and the work load of the operation. Throughout this book, it has been seen that such organisation usually responds to the needs of particular key result areas. For instance, a highly structured, formal system, based on technology is probably desirable to achieve quality control in high volume, low transaction value catering operations. In other words, the operation must be organised in such a way as to meet those business needs and strategic goals which relate to a particular sector of the catering market. This chapter is therefore slightly different to chapters 3 to 10 since it does not address itself to a key result area, i.e. an output, but to how to create circumstances in which such key results can be improved. It is thus concerned not with ends in themselves, but the means to these ends. Whilst the ability to organise the work and operational system effectively will not necessarily lead to improved performance in any specific key area, such improvements will not be possible without effective organisation.

An organisation is made up of three interrelated aspects which create the context in which the manager operates. These three factors are the organisation's *goals*, *technology* and *culture*. Within an organisation, the manager's options and actions are limited by his position. This position determines the demands placed upon the manager, the extent of responsibility, and the formal and informal boundaries placed around him. Since the major thrust of this book is the argument that 'diagnosis lies at the heart of effective management'[1] it is now in order to examine the nature of organisations, specifically those operating in the catering industry, and the manager's role in them in order to provide a framework for analysis and diagnosis which will enable managers to put into practice appropriate strategies for achieving improved performance.

THE ORGANISATIONAL ENVIRONMENT

Chapter 1 examined the external environment affecting the catering industry. Here the concern is with the internal environment that exists within organisations operating in this industry. The previous chapters of this book have made an indirect exploration of the nature of catering organisations. They have differentiated between organisational climates on the basis of technology (see page 60), identifying organisations which can be termed technocratic or humanistic; on the basis of cost structure, into market-oriented organisations or cost-oriented operations (see page 122); and on the basis of the extent to which firms are tied to a single, strongly-branded concept (see page 12). Within these broad spectrums, there are other factors such as the size of the organisation, the position which it has reached on the product/service life-cycle, and the attitude towards profit maximisation which will also be influential factors.

Handy suggests[2] that all managers operate in the short and medium term in a context of three variables – goals, technology and culture. This concept can be introduced into Schaffer's model considered in chapter 2 (Figure 2.1). It can further be assumed that for successful organisations these three variables 'fit', that is to say, they must support and reinforce each other. The exact nature of these three variables will in part be determined by strategic choice of senior management, and in part by the nature of each particular organisation. The authors would suggest that there are at least five factors that make up this contextual framework: ownership of the organisation, its age and size, the level of competition, and the influence of people.

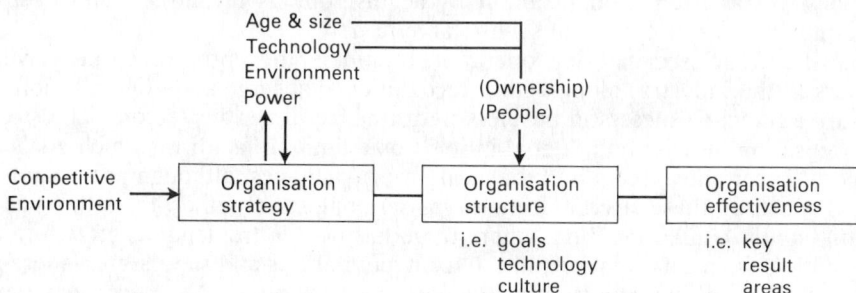

Figure 11.1   *Organisational variables and their contextual framework.* Adapted from *Strategy, Organisation Structure and Success in the Lodging Industry.* Schaffer, J.D.

The impact of these five factors will now be discussed in order, further to explore Handy's variables of goals, technology and culture. Firstly, the *ownership* of the organisation will have implications for the goals set and the culture established. Private organisations can range in size from individually owned and operated units to private companies. The motivations in these organisations are highly personalised and may range from the desire to maximise profit to a wish to achieve fulfilment through running one's own business. The culture will reflect this, and is, therefore, likely to be power based – mirroring the approach and style of the owner or owners. Public companies, on the other hand, will tend to have a large number of shareholders, whose expectations are usually more clearly profit-centred. The companies' goals will in this case tend to concentrate on policies aimed at maximising profit, although growth and market share may also be relevant. In such organisations, unless there is a particularly strong chief executive, the culture tends towards that of a formal hierarchy. Finally, as chapter 1 remarked, catering activity is also carried out in the public sector, where goals will be cost-centred and service-oriented and the organisational climate will tend towards the bureaucratic.

Ownership may also reflect the second factor affecting the three variables, that of *age* or life-cycle. How the priorities of a business may change through the five stages of the life-cycle was discussed in chapter 2. Some companies may indeed have been through a series of several different product life-cycles. As well as influencing the organisations' goals, the nature of the technology is likely to be different for innovative and growing operations than for those in mature or declining markets. Indeed the impetus for the introduction of a new product may well be brought about by technological innovation, such as cook–freeze. For older operations the technology is unlikely to be up to date or 'state of the art' and it is unlikely that any further cost reductions can be made by more efficient use or layout of the plant. The impact of life-cycle on the organisations' culture will also be significant. Young, new organisations will tend to operate in an exciting and dynamic environment where there is likely to be a task-focused culture. Older organisations will have developed more rigidities and a stable environment that is likely to be more resistant to change. On the other hand, their experience may result in a competitive advantage that is derived from their ability to minimise their labour costs, implement product redesigns that lower costs and optimise their resource mix.

A third factor is the *size* and scale of the organisation. There is likely to be a fairly close relationship between this and both ownership and life-cycle, although not necessarily so. Kennedy Brookes is now a large-scale catering organisation, but, since its expansion has been brought about by acquisition, its technology and even its culture may not yet be typical of such a large firm.

Successful franchised catering operations combine the entrepreneurial drive of operators in the industry, along with a recognition that large-scale organisation is a necessary adjunct to successful business performance in certain sectors. The size of the organisation may be both a goal in itself or a limiting factor on which goals are feasible. It is certainly recognised that scale has advantages, although in the catering business most of these accrue from organisational scale rather than the size of operating units. Unlike retailing, where there has been a tremendous growth in the size of outlets from supermarkets into huge hypermarkets and superstores, there are very few advantages in scaling up the individual catering outlet. Most scale economies derive from leverage over suppliers, wider spread of overhead administrative costs, more efficient advertising and so on. None the less, scale can result in such technological economies as the introduction of central kitchens for cook–chill operations have demonstrated. Whereas scale may be seen as beneficial in terms of goals and technology this is not necessarily the case with regards to culture. Hart *et al.* suggest that 'some of the drawbacks of large organisations – slower decision making, less flexibility, management distance from the customer – are self-evident'.[4]

The fourth factor of relevance to the variables is the degree of *competition*. Quite clearly strategic goals will be different in a highly competitive environment to those found in an environment with little or no competition. In the past, the public sector has been uncompetitive, so that its orientation has been cost-centred and decisions about investment based on cost-benefit analysis. But, where competition is high, commercial businesses are likely to be profit-centred and concerned with market share and return on investment. This is also reflected in the culture of the organisation. Resistance to change within the public sector, over plans for privatisation, largely reflects both management and workforce value systems, which are highly critical of the commercialisation of 'welfare' catering. But culture is not a passive factor, organisations can deliberately create an environment to meet their strategic goals.

Fast food chains stress the concept of service, quality and cleanliness to the point that staff totally believe in these concepts, which is important since these factors are fundamental to the business success of the organisation. Equally, a firm's technology has an impact on and relationship with the nature of competition. Indeed, technology can create a competitive advantage for an organisation, through differentiation or lower costs, that is fundamental to its success. For instance, Burger King differentiates its hamburger product on the basis of its charcoal grill technology as opposed to the griddle production methods of its direct competitors.

Finally, goals, technology and culture are all affected by the *people* that make up the organisation. Within any organisation the management and workforce all have their own goals, motivations and attitudes. In many respects, the successful organisation is that which subordinates the individual aims of its employees to the united goals of the organisation. The relative success of the Japanese is often accredited to this particular feature of their industry. As well as providing distinctive goals to which the workforce can relate, the self-image of the workforce will be affected by the role that technology plays within the operation. It has already been seen how the approach to and perception of quality is different in technocratic and humanistic environments. And finally, the nature of the culture, its power and force is derived from the people that make it up. The reasons why the type of people working for one organisation are different to those working for another is highly complex. It stems from the image the organisation presents, the recruitment policy of the organisation, its size and relative standing in the industry, the influence of key personnel, and so on. But there is little doubt that many of the large-scale organisations in the UK catering industry have very distinctive styles of management and types of manager.

For the unit manager attempting to improve performance this model is relatively simple and understandable. Whilst the goals, technology and culture of the organisation may not always be explicit, no manager could work within an organisation for very long without gaining some implicit understanding of these variables. The manager is probably less aware of the factors that modify these variables. However, over a period of time, particularly if he or she works for more than one company, the manager will experience the impact of ownership, age, size, competition and people, and begin to make some sense of how the organisation is changed.

The argument that structure is made of the interlinking of goals, technology and culture has already been put forward. Successful companies create an organisation that successfully moulds these factors into an appropriate means of achieving their strategy for the context in which they operate. They do this by determining the level of formality within the organisation, the degree of complexity and the extent of delegation of responsibility down to unit level. Schaffer, in relating his model to three hotel chains, gives only one example of management effectively creating a structure, namely Hyatt, whilst the other two examples he suggests are instances where the structure was ineffective. Hence, it is important to keep in mind two concerns. Firstly, the extent to which organisations are deliberately planned and structured by senior management is open to question; secondly, even within organisations where such planning is overt and explicit, there is no guarantee that management will 'get it right'.

MANAGING THE ORGANISATION

Managers accepting that catering organisations can vary widely along three dimensions – formality, complexity and centralisation – need to translate the variables of the

organisation into activities for which they have some responsibility. An effective way to do this is to look at the organisation as a set of systems. There are three main systems:
- the operational system, which corresponds to the technology variable.
- the human resource system, which is the formal organisation of the culture.
- the information system, through which goals are communicated and performance assessed.

Organisational performance depends upon modifying components of each of these until an integrated total system is created compatible with organisational goals and performance needs. Each of the three is inextricably linked to the other two. A change in one will have consequences for the other two. But they are not equally important to all key result areas. For instance, the information system is most important in controlling costs, whilst the human resource function is central to successful service quality assurance. Hence the key result areas form a set of appropriate sub-systems that make up the main organisational systems.

The *operational system* is in effect the hardware or technology of the unit. It is made up of the premises, plant, equipment and materials used in the production and service of meals. Every sector tends to have its own distinctive operational system. Some are relatively simple, such as family-style service in Indian and Chinese restaurants, whilst others are very much more complex, such as centralised cook–chill units for school meals or inflight catering. For the unit manager an understanding of the fundamental precepts of the particular system in operation is absolutely essential. Almost certainly the extent to which he can change the system will be very limited. Certainly the switch from one operational system to another is a major strategic decision which will only be made by independent restaurateurs or senior management personnel. But what the manager is and must be capable of doing is implementing the appropriate method for performance improvement in the operational context.

Case example 11.1   Cook–Chill for Barchester Schools

Barchester is a typical English county town. Within a five miles' radius of the town centre there are fourteen primary schools serving, on average, 130 meals daily. The County Catering Officer identified that the new technology of cook–chill might provide opportunities for performance improvement. He therefore commissioned a feasibility study to identify the impact that this operational change would have on the school meals service in the area.

The study recommended that all 1 800 meals should be prepared in the Archbishop Cranmer school which had formerly been producing 500 meals but was currently only serving about 200. This under-utilisation of space and equipment meant that a new central production facility could be installed relatively cheaply and easily. The estimated cost of £90 000 was made up of building alterations, new prime cooking equipment, blast chillers and cold room, and some ancillary costs. As a result of this change, the end-kitchens in all the schools to be serviced – by lorry – would also have to be modified. Such schools would need regeneration equipment and Regithermic ovens were recommended. The cost of the delivery vehicle was £10 000 and of modifications to the end-kitchens £95 000.

The report suggested that the advantages of the new system were a reduction in operating costs and improved quality of service. Major savings would be derived from labour cuts of approximately £35 000, mainly in the end-kitchens, as the grades of cook-supervisors and cooks-in-charge would no longer be required in each location. Further savings in excess of £10 000 were estimated for energy usage and maintenance of plant and equipment. This was offset by the additional operational cost of running the delivery vehicle.

The case illustrates how a major change to a feature of the operational system has implications for many other operational aspects as well as for the human resource system and information system. The decision whether or not to adopt cook–chill was made by a sub-committee of the local council. Whilst it accepted that operationally this production method may provide long-term savings, without any fall in standards, it decided not to go ahead. A major influence on its decision was the impact it would have on the staff of the school meals service.

If the operational system is the hardware of an organisation then the *human resource system* is the software. Without people to use and operate the plant and machinery the business could not be carried out. Chapter 7 in particular showed that there must be a close fit between the two systems, both in terms of the physiological capability and motivational desire of the workforce. Also, as table 9.3 showed, men and machines have different strengths and weaknesses. They are, however, interchangeable to some extent. A catering manager may well be faced with a decision about reducing his workforce due to the introduction of new operational procedures, as the cook–chill case example has illustrated.

Neither the hardware nor software will work, or be able to interact, without being connected up. The *information system* is the means by which both the operational and human resource systems are driven. Throughout the book the text has concentrated on the items of information the manager requires. But of equal importance is the flow of information from one part of the organisation to another. This can be thought of as the wiring of the hardware, through which the information (in the form of electronic pulses) passes. A good information system will respond to the needs of the people who use it, report accurate information, support the goals and culture of the organisation, focus on key result areas, highlight problem areas and respond to changes in the business environment. For example, chapter 10 has shown how different comparators are appropriate for different sectors of the industry.

In general, unit catering managers will rarely be involved in the planning of any of these three systems, unless they become involved in the initiation of a totally new concept. They will however be required to work in the context of these three systems and manage them. All will need to be brought to bear to a greater or lesser extent in order to be effective in improving performance in any of the key result areas.

With regard to the day-to-day operation of the unit, differences in approach can be

Table 11.1 *Percentage of catering managers able to make decisions with little or no reference to others.*

	Contract catering	In-house employee catering	Hotel 3-tiers of manage-ment	Hotel 4-tiers of manage-ment	Licensed trade & chain restaur-ants	Hos-pitals	School meals
Setting service standards	59	77	44	60	36	66	90
Pricing policy	3	14	9	30	18	3	20
Staff selection	84	74	70	80	73	84	80
Wage negotiation	5	3	–	10	9	–	–
Fixing working hours	51	46	57	60	64	58	70
Preparation of budgets	18	26	4	–	18	5	40
Selecting suppliers	5	66	30	30	9	2	20

Reproduced with permission from *A Second Survey of Management Jobs*, HCIMA.

clearly identified from sector to sector. The freedom a catering manager has to make decisions is affected by the extent to which strategic goals are prescribed and formalised, the level of centralisation within the organisation, and the degree of formal control over the organisational climate. The HCIMA Survey of Management Jobs[5] indicates that this varies quite widely throughout the different sectors, as illustrated in table 11.1.

As the sample size of the survey was not high, it is not possible to draw too many conclusions from these figures. But it becomes apparent that in all sectors, catering managers have much less freedom of action concerning financial matters than they do over staffing and operational issues. And yet if organisations were asked to state how they judged their managers, the criteria that would be used would largely be financial, i.e. gross profit percentage, turnover, etc.

UNDERSTANDING THE ADAPTIVE SYSTEM

Handy[6] suggests that in addition to the operational, human and information systems there is a fourth system, which he calls the 'adaptive system'. This adaptive system is the means by which an organisation deals with 'divergencies' from planned performance, either strategic or operational, and initiates change in the organisation. Its role is to ensure that whenever a change occurs, either planned or otherwise, to any of the three other systems then the total system is realigned so that it can continue to interact effectively and efficiently. Thus, in order to make improvements in performance, which by definition suggest change, the manager must be capable of managing the adaptive system. To continue our analogy, if the existing hardware and software are out-of-date, then the user may have to add to or take away some of the peripherals, re-program the software and re-wire or reconnect the system.

Lord Forte of Ripley, in his address 'Training in a Changing World,[7] explored the special problems of change facing the catering industry. In order to care for customers, offer large scale employment and generate enough profit to invest in expansion the industry has to recognise and adapt to the need for change. The industry has to overcome any resistance to change and harness new technology to achieve it. But, as Lord Forte pointed out, this has to be done against a background of personal service. A sensitive use of new technology is required to complement rather than replace personal service.

Often a customer may be unaware that changes have been introduced. For example, Browns Hotel has recently replaced all its traditional boiling tops with induction hobs. This type of change affects the owner through improved efficiency: in the case of Browns, energy costs have been reduced by almost 50 per cent. It also affects the employees – in this example by reducing kitchen temperatures and providing a safer more comfortable working environment. As far as the customers are concerned, Browns remains the epitome of a traditional hotel restaurant. Far from advertising this use of the most modern catering technology to their customers the management have kept it discreetly quiet. This represents one type of change with which management have to cope – technological change which does not directly affect the customer.

Rather different is the type of technological development which improves customer service. An instance of this is given by French[8] of ARA. He mentions the development of a computerised food production system which allows food-service managers 'to spend more time with the customer and less time with the calculator'. In fact, THF's research amongst its own staff has shown conclusively that they appreciated the opportunities technology had given them for increased contact with the customer. Technology can be used to relieve staff of the repetitive and limited skill tasks – thereby allowing them the opportunity to employ their customer skills to the full. This has interesting implications for recruitment and selection: as the technical aspects of customer contact jobs become less demanding, interpersonal skills become relatively more important (compared with say computational skills) for effective performance, and more weight can be given to fewer factors during selection.

Product changes affect staff and customers. Lovelock[9] defines six levels of product change.

Major innovations: are new products for undefined markets, such as the recent launch in the United Kingdom of a home delivery pizza service. These changes involve considerable uncertainty – particularly in respect of customer response.

Start-up businesses: are new products for a market which is already served by existing products that meet the same generic needs. An example here is Granada Motorway Services which adds a takeaway picnic service to its existing range of products for the motorway traveller.

New products for the currently served market: represent an attempt to offer existing customers of the business a product not previously available. For example, a pub which adds bar meal facilities.

Product line extensions: are additions to ranges, such as adding to the range of beers available in a pub, or adding a takeaway service to an Indian Restaurant.

Product improvements: represent the commonest type of product change. Improvements here are not only to food and drink elements of the product but also to service, environment, payment facilities and image.

Style changes: are often highly visible such as a new design of uniform or a different style of exterior signing. The risks involved are minimal.

When catering managers consider product changes it is necessary that they are clear about the level of innovation being considered. The associated risks and the demands placed on management are very different.

MANAGING CHANGE

Changes are usually an adaptive response to variations in the external environment of a business, but for managers to take action it seems to be necessary for them to perceive the existence of a problem which is (a) worth solving and (b) capable of being solved. Many catering managers were painfully aware of the effects that escalating energy costs were having on their business during the 1970s, but few of them put any concerted effort into energy management – probably because they did not believe that the problem could be solved. The advent of cheap, energy saving technology has changed managers' perceptions of this as an area deserving attention and they have subsequently achieved substantial savings. So an important factor influencing the problems on which a manager concentrates, is the manager's belief in his or her ability to solve that problem.

Managers' perceptions of their own ability to change the business will determine the problems which they select to solve. This sees to hold true in catering businesses, as far as subordinate development is concerned. If managers do not believe that they can change behaviour they do not give attention to behavioural problems. Many young managers, particularly in fast food and popular catering, are confident of their ability in influencing sales effectiveness and technical efficiency – so they concentrate on those areas at the expense of 'people problems'. Older managers, in more traditional catering businesses, may be less confident with technological aspects of the business and harder sales techniques – so they will concentrate on problems where they have proven skills in the area of man management.

The first step in problem solving – defining the problem – is often the most difficult. The solution that is found will be limited by the way in which the problem is defined, and incorrect problem definition will lead to a less than satisfactory solution. Take, for example, a problem of declining sales of real ale in a bar. If this problem is defined as decline in popularity, a suitable solution may be to replace the real ale with another product, perhaps an Australian beer. Coverdale suggests that problem solving should make extensive use of the question 'why?' – and if one asks why the beer is declining in popularity, investigation may show that the beer is kept in poor condition. Redefining the problem on this basis as poor product quality might suggest a training solution. However, the product quality may be the symptom of yet another problem. Ask 'why?' again. Further investigation may uncover the fact that whilst the employees may know how to care for the product properly they choose not to clean the pipes correctly. Defining the problem, therefore, as 'knowing how, but choosing not to' may produce a disciplinary solution. Asking 'why?' again may reveal that if the employees clean the pipes regularly, stock shortages occur as there is no satisfactory allowance made in the control procedures for beer lost during pipe cleaning. Asking 'why?' at this stage produces no useful new information – an indication that the root problem has been encountered, rather than any further symptoms. In this example the possible solution might range from changing the product range, to training, to discipline, to changing the control procedures depending on how the problem is defined. Only one of these solutions tackles the root problem.

Managers who are successful problem solvers usually have the ability to generate a wide range of alternative solutions and then select the best. It is easy to fall into the trap of developing just one solution at the expense of other, more creative solutions. Techniques such as brainstorming are useful for generating a wide range of creative solutions.

In addition to developing their skills of problem definition managers need to examine their own attitudes to change. People differ in the readiness to accept change as the following continuum shows:

INITIATORY
ACCEPTIVE
INDIFFERENT
RESISTANT

People who are personally resistant to change will become *risk averters* as managers. They will produce many logical arguments for leaving things exactly as they are. There is some evidence that risk averters can be successful managers in certain types of business – this may be the case in certain parts of the catering industry where the pressures imposed on the business gravitate towards the maintenance of the status quo. Consider a typical London members' club – is this an example of a business which is best managed by a risk averter?

At the other end of the continuum, some managers will have a high need for change and variety – and these people will be *risk seekers*. Risk seekers will look for opportunites to introduce the latest technology, will frequently reorganise working methods and will put considerable effort into product development. This can become change for change's sake! Again there is evidence to suggest that risk seekers can be successful managers in certain types of business – this might be the case where the managers do not have to work within the confines of a centralised chain and where the attitudes of the staff and the needs of the customers facilitate change. Such might be the case in a single unit, owner managed bar and restaurant with a clientele who value variety. The intention here is to demonstrate that a manager's attitude to change has to fit with the requirements of the market, operating systems and employees.

Just as there are two types of manager who can be successful in certain conditions – risk seekers and risk averters – so there are managers whose approach to change is unlikely to make them successful in any circumstances. The first of these, so often to be observed in the catering industry, is the *biased thinker*. This is the manager who will always resort to the same solution whenever a problem presents itself. Often these solutions are those which were learnt during their early career, when they may have been entirely appropriate. This particularly applies to the 'traditional' methods of service, menu construction, staffing and organisation – which may or not fit the current problem. The biased thinker wheels out the same solutions no matter what the situation requires. Often the biased thinker is hampered by value judgements concerning 'proper catering' – so if, for example, they learnt their management systems with British Transport Hotels, they may aspire to reproduce those entirely admirable standards in other completely different businesses, whether the situation requires this or not.

The other type of ineffective manager is the *wishful thinker*. Wishful thinkers want to change; they discuss their ideas and produce grand paper plans. Somehow nothing ever happens. This is not because of their attitude to change or their comprehension of problems and solutions. Wishful thinkers do not have the necessary personal organisation to enable them to achieve the changes they have identified as necessary. Identifying priorities and using time effectively has become a major training need in many businesses. Training organisations such as Time Manager have successfully packaged training in these essential skills. Interested readers are recommended to look at the popular book *The Time of Your Life*.

Change in organisations involves the manager in motivating other people to do things differently. People will often co-operate in change more readily if they feel they have participated in the development of the change. It is not necessary to consult with employees over every problem. The successful solution of some problems will depend on securing employees' acceptance of management's decisions; for example, feeding arrangements for night staff. The successful solution of other problems will depend on making high quality technical decisions, for example, selecting a new supplier for sirloins. Where the employees' *acceptance* of the decision is important and the *quality* of the decision is not crucial to the business managers should consult with staff before formulating any decision. Where the quality of the decision is of key importance, but acceptance is not an issue, then management can take and implement a decision without reference to their staff. Where both quality and acceptance are of great importance, for example, deciding on productivity targets, then managers would be well advised to consult with their staff. Managers should question whether they should spend any time at all on low-quality, low-acceptance decisions.

In addition to deciding if and how they should consult with employees over proposed changes, managers need to decide how they will influence people to adopt the change if necessary. Power to achieve different things from people comes from five main sources:

FORCE
KNOWLEDGE
POSITIONAL AUTHORITY
PERSONAL FRIENDSHIP
DEVELOPMENT INFLUENCE

When the manager of a medium-sized provincial hospital catering department was faced with a change from a traditional kitchen arrangement to a Ganymede system, she realised she might face considerable resistance from her staff. The change would have significant effects on them – job design would change and employees would be required to use new skills, the status of various members of the workgroup would change and the social patterns would be changed because of the change to a production line style technology.

The manager of the hospital catering department thought carefully about implementing the change and decided to use different techniques to influence different employees. For the kitchen assistants she decided to use her personal friendship to assure them that they could trust her to look after their interests and that they would be helping her by co-operating in the change. When dealing with the skilled chefs, she decided to develop an extensive knowledge of the old and new food production systems to overcome any objections they may put forward. Once she had this knowledge (through reading and field visits) she involved the chefs in a series of visits to operational Ganymede systems, equipment manufacturers and specialist training programmes. So, in this example, the manager used different power bases for achieving change with different employee groups: for one group of employees she consciously used personal friendship to achieve change, whereas for other employees she used a combination of knowledge and developmental influence.

Some otherwise well reasoned changes do not work because of a failure to consider the full implications of the change. Consider the decision to replace an existing cashier operated till by a computerised point-of-sale system which is controlled by the waiting staff, each of whom has their own personal key. For senior managers, looking at the costs of the system and the likely savings in wages, the overall benefits are clear and the implementation seems simple enough. However, six months after the implementation it is easy, with the benefit of hindsight, to see why the introduction was less than successful: at breakfast-time the waiters had to queue to complete their bills and whilst they did so their customers became impatient with the long delays in service; the system was not operable for two days because sufficient stocks of stationery were not available – during this period no back-up was available; the waiting staff became very dissatisfied with their additional workload for which there was no extra pay and there was a noticeable change in the atmosphere and there was no procedure for training new waiting staff in the use of the system. All of these factors could and should have been foreseen if the manager had realised that a change in one part of an organisation has repercussions for other parts, as was explained in the discussion of the relationship between the operational system, the human resource system and the information system.

BUSINESS PLANNING AND CHANGE

The culmination of this chapter – and in fact of this book – is an examination of the process of business planning in catering businesses as the framework for planned change. The techniques of strategic planning have long been recognised as being of use to large chain operations, but there seems to be reluctance to apply them to smaller scale operations – at, for example, the level of the individual catering business. The intention here is to demonstrate that the principles of strategic planning can be usefully applied to the single unit.

Strategic planning is a systematic evaluation of the business – where it is now and where it is likely to go. Table 11.2 shows the steps which are usually involved.

Table 11.2 *The strategic planning process.*

---

1. A CRITICAL EVALUATION OF THE PRODUCT

2. A REVIEW OF THE MARKET
    ·to whom is the product sold?
    ·to whom is it not sold?

3. AN ANALYSIS OF THE COMPETITION
    ·how does their product compare?

4. AN INVESTIGATION OF THE BUSINESS ENVIRONMENT
    ·what factors are critical to success?
    ·how are these changing?

5. A FORECAST OF FINANCIAL PERFORMANCE
    ·where are we now?
    ·how will we perform in future if present trends continue?
    ·what gap is there between future forecast performance and the required performance?

6. STRENGTHS, WEAKNESSES, OPPORTUNITIES & THREATS
    ·how can we build on our strengths?
    ·how can we overcome our weaknesses?
    ·how will changes in the competition or business environment create future opportunities for us?
    ·how will changes in the business environment or competition create future threats which we must
        overcome?

7. ALTERNATIVES FOR ACTION
    ·what possible ideas for improvement can we generate in order to ensure future success is assured?
    ·which of those shall we employ to close our profit gap?

8. MAKE AN ACTION PLAN
    ·set down the actions, step by step.
    ·produce a quantified budget.

9. MONITOR THE PLAN AND CONTROL

It is not coincidental that this is the last chapter of the book. The above process is, in the opinion of the authors, the planning framework which links the previous chapter topics of increasing volume, improving gross profit, developing subordinates, protecting assets, increasing productivity, controlling costs, managing product quality, and managing service quality. The chapters on analysing the business environment and introducing change can now be seen as contributors to this process.

CONCLUSION

This is a book about management. We have attempted to deal with the essence of what catering managers have to achieve in order to be successful – and to provide a framework for identifying priorities and setting objectives.

Students of carpentry are not only taught the correct way to use woodworking tools they are also taught which problem requires the use of a certain appropriate tool – for cutting across the grain, a shooting plane is used. In our experience, students of catering management learn a lot about the mechanics of certain management tools but find it more difficult to define problems in a systematic way and to select the appropriate tool to solve a problem. We hope that our book has gone some way to redress this deficiency.

REFERENCES

1. Handy, C., *Understanding Organisations*, Penguin Books, 1981.
2. Handy, C., *op.cit.*
3. Schaffer, J. D., Strategy, organisation structure and success in the lodging industry, *International Journal of Hospitality Management* vol.3 no.4, 1984.
4. Hart, C. W., Spizizen, G. and Wyckoff, D. D., 'Scale economies and the experience curve', *Cornell HRA Quarterly*, May, 1984.
5. HCIMA *A Second Survey of Management Jobs*, 1978.
6. Handy, C., *op.cit.*
7. *Proceedings of the First International Personnel and Training Conference*, HCITB, 1985.
8. French, G. E., 'A president's view of services marketing', in George, W. R., (Ed.) *Developing New Services*, American Marketing Association, 1984.
9. Lovelock, C. H., 'Developing and implementing new services', in George, W. R., *op.cit.*

Index